KIRK S. BOWMAN
and JON R. WILCOX

Reimagining
Global
Philanthropy

The COMMUNITY BANK MODEL
of SOCIAL DEVELOPMENT

Columbia University Press
Publishers Since 1893
New York   Chichester, West Sussex
cup.columbia.edu

Library of Congress Cataloging-in-Publication Data
Names: Bowman, Kirk S., author. | Wilcox, Jon R., author.
Title: Reimagining global philanthropy : the community bank model
of social development / Kirk S. Bowman and Jon R. Wilcox.
Description: New York : Columbia University Press, [2021] |
Includes bibliographical references.
Identifiers: LCCN 2021010820 (print) | LCCN 2021010821 (ebook) |
ISBN 9780231200103 (hardback ; alk. paper) | ISBN 9780231553438 (ebook)
Subjects: LCSH: Economic development projects—Developing countries. |
Humanitarianism—Developing countries.
Classification: LCC HC59.72.E44 B685 2021 (print) |
LCC HC59.72.E44 (ebook) | DDC 361.7/7091724—dc23
LC record available at https://lccn.loc.gov/2021010820
LC ebook record available at https://lccn.loc.gov/2021010821

Columbia University Press books are printed on permanent
and durable acid-free paper.
Printed in the United States of America

Cover design: Noah Arlow
Cover image: NASA

CONTENTS

PREFACE

THE POWER OF DIFFERENT PERSPECTIVES

We come from very different backgrounds and hold different perspectives. Kirk Bowman is a progressive college professor from Atlanta, Georgia, with twenty-five years of development research and practice. Jon Wilcox is a conservative community banker from Orange County, California, with over three decades in banking and finance. Despite our considerable political differences, job experiences, and worldviews, we have been close friends for nearly forty years. We met in Washington, D.C., in 1983 when Jon interned in a suit and tie at the Securities and Exchange Commission and Kirk interned in jeans and a T-shirt at the Council on Hemispheric Affairs. A semester of carpooling into the city from Alexandria, lots of basketball, and regular road trips formed the roots of a lifelong friendship.

In an era of great political division and a lack of empathy, we affirm that there is much to gain by talking and working closely with people who think differently than you do. Indeed, we believe that listening and blending our different perspectives, education, and experience is the driving force for this book. Years of friendship, lively arguments, dozens of trips to South America, a willingness to admit errors, and a few horrifying experiences in the field all contributed to our coalescence on an alternative model for global philanthropy.

Despite our outward differences, we share far more similarities. We both lived for extended periods in the Global South and continue to admire the cultures and peoples. We both encountered and developed enduring relationships with remarkable and creative local community leaders. We are both optimistic about community transformations from the ground up.

As with many epiphanies, ours percolated for several years. We initially discovered Sebastião Oliveira and the Miratus Badminton Association through the serendipity of a random LinkedIn contact in 2011.[1] Meeting Oliveira and watching him train world-class badminton players through samba dancing in a favela in the periphery of Rio de Janeiro was exhilarating. We believed he was singular, a local social entrepreneur unicorn who was famous for his unusual ideas. We were shocked to discover that most people in Rio de Janeiro had no idea who he was. He was invisible outside the favela and network of local activists.

We spoke about Miratus with Julia Michaels, a journalist, author, and activist with decades of experience in Rio de Janeiro. Michaels informed us that while Oliveira is incredible, he is not unique or even rare in the eight hundred favelas of Rio de Janeiro. She knew about dozens of locally led organizations doing innovative and incredible work in the roughest of environments. Michaels then decided to introduce us to Vinicius Daumas and Junior Perim, the founders of the Crescer e Viver social circus, over dinner.[2]

Perim's mind works at an incredible pace, and a conversation with him is both exhausting and exhilarating. He is likely the smartest person in the room, and perhaps he knows it. He is also a tireless activist for human rights, urban development, the arts, and local social entrepreneurs. When we asked him if there were other organizations similar to Miratus and leaders as impressive as Oliveira, Perim looked at us with a sly smile, as if we were naïve children. His answer was to ask if we were free for the next two days. We were, and we drove all over the city with Perim and Daumas in their old SUV, meeting local leader after local leader using innovation and commitment to transform the youth of their neighborhoods. The diversity of activities was as impressive as the energy and long-term commitment of the local social activists. From contemporary dance to filmmaking, and from classical music to boxing, the favelas of Rio de Janeiro are bursting with locally led projects that are critical institutions in their neighborhoods.

When the celebrated economist Albert O. Hirschman was asked how he came to hold the unorthodox views he proposed in *The Strategy of Economic Development*, he would reply, "I went to Colombia early in 1952 without any prior knowledge of . . . development. This turned out to be a real advantage. . . . [I later] discovered I had acquired a point of view of my own that was considerably at odds with current doctrines."[3] This was also our advantage. As a lifelong banker, Jon never studied development. He had never attended a single class. He encountered Rio de Janeiro from a banker's perspective. After meeting Oliveira, Michaels, Perim, and Daumas, and taking the Rio de Janeiro neighborhood activist tour, the community banker remarked that global philanthropy would have a far greater return on investment by providing resources to these impressive and ongoing successful organizations instead of always starting new initiatives. That simple observation represents the theoretical beginnings of this book.

After years of conversation and over a dozen trips to Rio de Janeiro, the conservative banker convinced the left-leaning college professor that good intentions and theoretical rigor are not enough: any successful model must be highly cost-efficient, with the maximum expected rate of return on investment. The college professor convinced the banker that cost-effectiveness was insufficient: a successful model must empower local leaders and subvert existing power relations. These experiences and conversations led us to contemplate, develop, and test a community bank model (CBM) of global philanthropy. We detail this journey in this book.

We are grateful for all the people and institutions that enriched our journey and this book. Sebastião Oliveira, Guti Fraga, Tia Maria, Lazir Sinval, Junior Perim, Vinicius Daumas, Eliana Sousa Silva, Zefa da Guia, Doña D'Ajuda, and Mamae Zezé taught us that real-life superheroes do exist, and they come in all ages, colors, and economic conditions, and with different education levels. You inspired us as you transformed the lives of so many in your communities. We are grateful for you and all that you do.

We also acknowledge and salute all the people who created Rise Up & Care's incredible films and children's books to inspire the world with important stories of these local social champions. They taught us that children of all ages need role models who look like they do and who are from their communities. Special thanks go to Maria Hernandez, Cazé, Luis Lomenha, Eduardo Gripa, Mayara Boaretto, Isa Carneiro, Katia Lund, Lili Fialho, Ana Beraba, Cláudia Belém, and Eric Larson.

We could never thank all the people who shared their dinner tables, advice, contacts, and encouragement along the way. We extend a big *obrigado* to Jimmy Story, Hermano Ribeiro, Julia Michaels, Eduardo Cruxen, Gwen Maitre, Rolando Bossart, and Theresa Williamson.

Alison Bowman, Kole Bowman, Mitch Bowman, Alberto Fuentes, Adam Haggiag, Virginia Webber, Suzanne Wilcox, Leyu Wondwossen, and Brian Woodall all commented on and greatly improved early drafts. Students in three semesters of the Georgia Tech course on Global Philanthropy and Development provided sharp and useful critiques, edits, and suggestions for the manuscript. Kaylin Berinhout, Sam Chappell, Haley McElroy, Hannah Musall, and Mehnaz Ruksana deserve special thanks. Alasdair Young provided helpful advice.

We acknowledge and thank all of our mentors and colleagues who believed in us when many did not. This project would not have been possible without people like Bob Duggan, Ernest Rady, Bob Barth, Ed Carpenter, Adam Stulberg, Felipe Arocena, Mark Hay, and Terry Snell.

The Sam Nunn School of International Affairs and the Georgia Institute of Technology provided generous freedom and time for a long and unconventional endeavor. We applaud the students in our Vertically Integrated Project on Global Social Entrepreneurship for their generous hearts, constant creativity, hard work, and constructive criticism. Edouard Goguillon worked many long nights editing, formatting, and critiquing the manuscript. Chaeeun Park and Jessica Palacios produced many of the figures. The brilliant Rio de Janeiro street artist Cazé produced the illustrations.

Our experience with Columbia University Press could not have been better. We were fortunate to meet Myles Thompson. His embrace of the project, wise guidance, and steady encouragement was invaluable. Brian Smith pushed the project over the finish line. The anonymous reviewers were thorough, thoughtful, and tough yet generous. Thank you.

Finally, we are blessed and fortunate to have the love and support of our families. Thank you to Suzanne, Kole, Leyu, Audrey, James, Mitch, Sadie, and Kai. You are the most important part of this and all future adventures.

REIMAGINING GLOBAL PHILANTHROPY

1

REASSESSING THE
PHILANTHROPIST'S BURDEN

As we look ahead into the next century, leaders will
be those who empower others.

BILL GATES

There is a magical blue door in a small, impoverished community in Rio de Janeiro, Brazil. We entered through that singular portal and will never be the same. We watched dozens of others walk through that door and emerge soon after with a completely different perspective of the world and themselves. That small door is a conduit from one realm to another. Outside are the favela of Chacrinha and a state of chaos. Like many favelas, which are marginalized communities of untitled homes in Brazil, either a drug gang or a militia of former public security forces controls the area. They extort money from the families and businesses in a protection racket. Safety is a constant concern. One hears a barrage of high-caliber weapons far too often. People are weary, stressed, and hypervigilant.

Pass through the blue door that leads into the Miratus Badminton Training Center, and you will discover a whole new world, like walking through the wardrobe in *Narnia*. Instead of the chaos and wariness of the outside, one encounters peace, easy laughter, shelter, determination, and order. Miratus is the life's work of Sebastião Oliviera (figure 1.1), a giant of a man with an infectious smile and enormous hands that cover your entire back with his welcoming embrace. Oliveira is the most unlikely of superheroes. He is an Afro-Brazilian who spent his youth in a detention center, never played

Figure 1.1 Sebastião Oliveira and the 17,000-square-foot Miratus Badminton Center
Source: Photo Marcelo Dias

badminton, has no educational preparation for this endeavor, and has no monetary fortune to sustain his dream. What he possessed was an idea of using sports to transform the youth of a neighborhood, the determination to spend seventeen years constructing the center, a talent for innovation to create a program using samba dancing to train badminton champions, unwavering confidence, and talents that include charisma and leadership. Oliveira's work changes the lives of hundreds of young people of Chacrinha and all who walk through that blue door.[1]

Oliveira inspired us to write this book and to conceptualize, test, and present a more efficient model of global philanthropy and local development. If you ever get the chance to walk through that magical blue door, you should take advantage of the opportunity. Meeting Oliveira will melt away your cynicism and boost your optimism for the world. Until then, we invite you to experience those lessons and perspectives through this book. There is much more of Oliveira and other inspirational local leaders to come.

BIG IDEAS

Do you think your big ideas can change the world? We did too. We were so wrong. Our big epiphany came through a set of development projects in Fiji. We spent a decade working on local development projects in that beautiful country, along with an incredible group of scientists and local partners. We had brilliant ideas for transformative endeavors, along with excellent funding, great local associates, cooperation with stakeholders, and coverage in prestigious magazines.[2] We even sold one product to the planet's largest aquarium. These projects were environmentally sustainable, produced local development for the coastal villages, and were so brilliant that they could not fail. We could easily connect the dots in our imaginations from the idea to the launch, to the philanthropic triumph. We were going to change the world, earn accolades and praise, and help Fiji. We would be philanthropic stars! Most important, we would benefit the environment and the people of the coastal communities. And yet this can't-miss set of projects was a series of failures that ended in local disputes, abandoned infrastructure, a poor return on expended resources, and hurt feelings.

How could we explain this unexpected outcome? At first, we blamed the cultural and other perceived limitations of the Fijians. It must be the inefficient bureaucracy, the laid-back culture, petty leaders, corruption, a tendency to stage military coups, or some other traits of the locals. It could not have been our fault. Our ideas were impeccable.

Taken aback, we began a journey to answer the question: How could such noble intentions, great ideas, hard work, and excellent planning turn out so disastrously? We wanted to discover how global philanthropy could result in greater success. We explored and inquired about other international development projects to try and identify why some succeed and others fail. There are some inspiring projects in the world, many led by selfless and dedicated people. However, we found far fewer successes than failures. The world is littered with abandoned projects, so-called zombie ventures that are barely alive, and projects with low returns on investment.[3]

There is nothing wrong with the local communities and peoples; there is something wrong with the entire paradigm. Is there a better way? Is there a more cost-effective model? Why are people initiating so many doomed projects? This book represents a decade-long journey to find these answers, propose an alternative model with far higher yields, and detail a test of that model through a six-year demonstration project with a total of thirty-two cases.

While we were already familiar with the wide range of social science scholarship on global development, we needed to engage the large body of work on philanthropy. We found helpful works about topics such as planned giving by wealthy donors, how to start a new nonprofit, where to donate money, how the rich philanthrocapitalists are saving the world, how the rich philanthrocapitalists are destroying democracy, how new actors are effectively shaping the financing of global philanthropy, and why philanthropy is a sham that merely maintains the power and privilege of elites.[4] Much of the existing literature focuses on philanthropy in the United States. We realized that these two bodies of scholarship—global development and philanthropy—spoke different languages, used different concepts and jargon, and targeted different audiences. When we began this journey a decade ago, we had no intention of writing a book. We could find no single work that conveyed the concepts and principles that we wanted to share. This book sits directly at the intersection of international philanthropy and global development. It is aimed at a large and important audience of global citizens, activists, adventurers, and students of all ages with a deep affection for the Global South and a yearning to actively participate in improving the human condition.

We consider many widespread practices in this book, and we confess up front that we have been guilty of committing all manner of mistakes and errors. We frequently remind ourselves that when we point a finger, there are three fingers pointing back at us. We misguidedly worked at bringing development and our ideas to people from Honduras to Fiji. We believed that we were sacrificing to help people who needed us, our vision, and our leadership.

We were mistaken.

THE URGE TO HELP

The human urge to help the less fortunate is powerful. Of all the variety of intelligent life on Earth, only humans will sacrifice personal resources such as money or time to assist and uplift people they don't even know on the other side of the world. People travel to Guatemala or The Gambia, witness poverty and children with limited opportunities, and want to help. Thirty new NGOs form each day in Britain alone, and there are more than 1.5 million NGOs in the United States, many with international philanthropic activities.[5] Universities and churches are full of enthusiastic groups traveling abroad to deliver comfort, youth programs, and construction projects. Millions of people in wealthy countries of the Global North[6] voluntarily provide billions of dollars and millions of hours of service to projects intended to improve the living conditions of the less fortunate.[7] Individuals, families, school groups, church members, fraternities and sororities, college professors, celebrities, NGOs, and many others engage, often with the noblest of intentions, in efforts to bring development and to elevate the human condition. Some projects are massive, with budgets in the hundreds of millions of dollars. Most are far smaller. Many merely facilitate short overseas experiences of armies of itinerant volunteers. Others spend years establishing a development project in a far-off land. Global philanthropy launches tens of thousands of projects and tens of thousands of other short-term save-the-world trips each year, often with great fanfare and high expectations from the generous givers and the grateful beneficiaries.

Far too many of these projects fail to reach their objectives. Instead of elevating the status and capacity of local leaders, these international projects often drain and weaken critical local leadership. Most rely on the faulty assumption that the best ideas, the best leadership, and the best solutions originate in wealthy countries of the Global North, and there is honor and obligation to rescue the poor and downtrodden people of the Global South. This thinking has a long and established pedigree.

THE WHITE MAN'S BURDEN

Amid the first great wave of globalization of the late nineteenth century[8], Rudyard Kipling penned his notorious poem "The White Man's Burden." The poem had a very specific policy objective. Kipling hoped to encourage the civilized United States to take on its so-called manifest destiny of colonization and doing "the White Man's work, the business of introducing a sane and orderly administration into the dark places of the earth."[9]

For Kipling, the white Christian world had a profound "responsibility of civilizing—or trying to civilize—all the dark, supposedly backward races of the world."[10] Kipling sent the poem to his friend Theodore Roosevelt in late 1898, who reportedly regarded the poetry as mediocre but the message as excellent: the United States should extend its reach to colonize and civilize the darker and inferior peoples of Cuba, Guam, the Philippines, and Puerto Rico.

"The White Man's Burden" was also published in early 1899 in *The Times* in London and *McClure's Magazine* in the United States and generated an enormous reaction. The poem coincided with the height of the modern eugenics movement, which purported to demonstrate the superiority of the Caucasian race through science conducted at leading universities. Colonization and war with Spain were not acts of aggression but rather acts of kindness and civilizing. Opponents fired back with works such as "The Brown Man's Burden" that openly mocked Kipling and the colonizers.[11]

Colonization and eugenics have lost much of their overt popular appeal since Kipling's time, and most of us would be insulted if we were accused of supporting his vision of the white man's burden.[12] Nonetheless, after more than a century, the core of Kipling's message is subconsciously carried forward by some of the very people who would most vociferously reject it. We refer to some of the people and organizations that travel around the world to bring their American or European know-how and great ideas to advance marginalized people in poor countries with all manner of civilizing and development projects.

Kipling was direct, and his principal points appear in the first twenty-four lines of the short fifty-six-line poem:

> TAKE up the White Man's burden—
> Send forth the best ye breed—
> Go bind your sons to exile
> To serve your captives' need;
> To wait in heavy harness,   5
> On fluttered folk and wild—
> Your new-caught, sullen peoples,
> Half-devil and half-child.
>
> Take up the White Man's Burden—
> In patience to abide,   10
> To veil the threat of terror
> And check the show of pride;
> By open speech and simple,
> An hundred times made plain,
> To seek another's profit,   15
> And work another's gain.
>
> Take up the White Man's burden—
> The savage wars of peace—
> Fill full the mouth of Famine
> And bid the sickness cease;   20
> And when your goal is nearest
> The end for others sought,
> Watch Sloth and heathen Folly
> Bring all your hope to naught.

We know what you are thinking. Kipling's message is about racism and the superiority of Caucasians in the United States or Europe. It has nothing to do with contemporary philanthropy, NGOs, church groups, college students, professors or generous billionaires who genuinely want to help disadvantaged people![13]

If we update Kipling's language, we find precious little has changed. Many international projects follow the pattern of Kipling's twenty-four lines, albeit without the intent to formally colonize. In what ways are today's global philanthropists similar to Kipling's global colonizers?

- We *send forth the best ye breed*, sons and daughters as winners of innovation competitions, grant recipients, elite university clubs and organizations, generous churches, Peace Corps volunteers, and charismatic fundraisers to bring better toilets to Kenya, tilapia farms to Fiji, orphan visitors to India, jewelry cooperatives to Vietnam, water systems to Honduras, newly painted schools to Nicaragua, community farms to Mali, one laptop per child to Uruguay, PlayPumps to Africa, millennium villages to the most impoverished African towns, female soccer NGOs to Cambodia, organic food companies to Bolivia, and more.
- We do this without pride but *to serve your captives' need* because we are generous, fortunate, and superior in technology, innovation, leadership, experience, and can-do culture.
- Our objective is to generate development, *profit* and *gain*, for *sullen peoples* who can't do this on their own.
- We want to improve the human condition, *Fill full the mouth of Famine, And bid the sickness cease.*

The failure rate of these overseas projects is far too high. We believe that our ideas and projects are impeccable and designed to succeed. When they fail, we continue to believe that it is not due to our flaws or our project design but because of the recipients and their corruption, pettiness, inferior culture, and sloth.[14] When we talk to practitioners or supporters of failed international projects, the most common explanation for their failure includes some variation of the phrase "there is something wrong with their culture." We have expressed that sentiment ourselves.

And when your goal is nearest
The end for others sought,
Watch Sloth and heathen Folly
Bring all your hope to naught.

Kipling's explicit racism helped create the patterns, institutions, norms, and media that evolved into the implicit bias that people of the Global South are inferior. We all suffer from implicit bias in categories such as the aged, the disabled, skin tone, obesity, and so on.[15] Implicit bias explains how the practice found in "The White Man's Burden" can manifest today in highly educated and progressive people who categorically reject Kipling's message.

In his book *Latin America in Caricature*, John J. Johnson reproduces 131 newspaper cartoons from the U.S. press that synthesize prevailing stereotypes of Latin Americans and help form symbols and patterns of enduring implicit bias (figure 1.2). Many figures are repeated often: that of Latin Americans as ignorant children requiring adult intervention from the United States, and that of Latin America as a passive woman who must be seduced and fertilized by the virile Anglo-Saxon man. Latin Americans are portrayed as culturally deprived, incapable of competing, dimwitted, childish, and impoverished.

Lars Schoultz, in *Beneath the United States*, convincingly argues that these cartoons are just one of many elements supporting racism and explicit prejudice. These elements metastasized into widespread implicit bias among diplomats and development officials to include unconscious association, beliefs, or attitudes that Latin America is inferior and persistently underdeveloped. Practitioners of global philanthropy and development are neither fans of Kipling nor explicitly biased against Latin America, the Global South, and people of color. Implicit bias, however, continues to shape diplomatic, philanthropic, and development attitudes and practice.

Figure 1.2 Free from the Spanish, John T. McCutcheon, *Chicago Tribune*, April 26, 1914
Source: Wikimedia Commons, Public Domain

A Georgia Tech study abroad program visited the U.S. embassy in Argentina, and five impressive embassy officials spoke to the students. In the question period, one student asked the various attachés and head of the mission: What positive lessons could the United States and the rest of the world learn from Argentina? From the looks of confusion on the faces of the embassy personnel, one would have thought that the student spoke in Martian. The legacy of cartoons, literature, the media, education, and political stereotypes left these highly educated and well-traveled individuals incapable of responding to the question with anything other than confusion or nervous laughter.[16] This concept did not fit their mental patterns. This implicit bias produces the Philanthropist's Burden.

The contemporary Philanthropist's Burden is every bit as problematic as was the White Man's Burden. It is cost-inefficient with too few successes to show for the thousands of projects attempted, the billions of dollars spent, and millions of hours expended. It sets up the philanthropists as superior to the *uncivilized* recipients. It enhances, rather than tears down, existing global and power hierarchies and undermines local leaders. It is time to reconsider our assumptions and strategies.

THE POSTDEVELOPMENT RESPONSE

In recent years, some religious leaders, academics, development practitioners, and others strenuously rejected the entire idea of global philanthropy and even trying to help. The most forceful early statement came from Monsignor Ivan Illich in 1968 to the Conference of InterAmerican Student Projects (CIASP) in Mexico. Illich was a brilliant philosopher, scholar, theologian, and polemicist who identified many of the pillars of modern life, including modern medicine and education, as causing more harm than good. We encourage you to read the entire speech, and we share a few short excerpts here.

> Today, the existence of organizations like yours is offensive to Mexico. I wanted to make this statement in order to explain why I feel sick about it all and in order to make you aware that good intentions have not much to do with what we are discussing here. To hell with good intentions. This is a theological statement. You will not help anybody by your good intentions. There is an Irish saying that the road to hell is paved with good intentions. . . .

Next to money and guns, the third-largest North American export is the U.S. idealist, who turns up in every theater of the world: the teacher, the volunteer, the missionary, the community organizer, the economic developer, and the vacationing do-gooder. Ideally, these people define their role as service. Actually, they frequently wind up alleviating the carnage done by their money and weapons, or seducing the "underdeveloped" to the benefits of the world of affluence and achievement. . . .

I am here to suggest that you voluntarily renounce exercising the power which being an American gives you. I am here to entreat you to freely, consciously and humbly give up the legal right you have to impose your benevolence on Mexico. I am here to challenge you to recognize your inability, your powerlessness and your incapacity to do the "good" which you intended to do.

I am here to entreat you to use your money, your status and your education to travel in Latin America. Come to look, come to climb our mountains, to enjoy our flowers. Come to study. But do not come to help.[17]

This thorough rejection of global philanthropy percolated for decades, erupting in the work of scholars such as Colombian anthropologist Arturo Escobar in the mid-1990s.[18] Postdevelopment theory and practice called for an abandonment of "development" and interventions of the Global North in the Global South. For the postdevelopment community, assistance, aid, and philanthropy were part of a geopolitical game that exploited the Global South and destroyed people and places.[19] The solution was to do nothing.

The postdevelopment response reverberated in economics with Dambisa Moyo's influential work lambasting foreign aid for Africa and William Easterly's prodigious research on the failures of aid, Global North expertise, and international financial institutions such as the World Bank and the International Monetary Fund.

The influential journalist and author Anand Giridharadas, arguably as provocative as Ivan Illich, portrays global philanthropy as a charade to maintain the elevated social order of the rich and powerful of a new Gilded Age.[20] Political scientist Rob Reich lays out the systematic argument that the perpetual philanthropic foundations generate greater inequality and are repugnant to the idea of a democratic society.[21] Perhaps global philanthropy should be abandoned altogether.

AN ALTERNATIVE SOLUTION

Like Monsignor Illich, we reject the Philanthropist's Burden mentality of many voluntourists, global philanthropists, and development projects exported to the Global South. However, we also discard the postdevelopment plea to abandon all efforts to try and make a difference. There is an alternative model.

The source of this model comes from the unlikeliest of places: the world of banking, not from venture capital start-ups or large investment banks, which are analogous to the Philanthropist's Burden, but from the world of small community banks and their critical role for their neighborhoods as anonymous, empowering sidekicks. Bankers are much maligned. Only 25 percent of U.S. adults believe that bankers are ethical and honest.[22] For many who see banking as a model for exploitation and the antithesis of doing good, the community bank sector provides an innovative and useful blueprint for global philanthropy.

This book is one of hope. We do not believe that those more fortunate global citizens should stop trying to help those with fewer material resources and opportunities. Indeed, we assert that individuals, NGOs, families, churches, students, and others should do more, not less. To increase the impact significantly, we should first change the way we think about the people we want to help, critically examine the activities that we support or participate in, and reexamine our motivations. With a few basic concepts and recalibrations, we can transform our time, effort, and money into experiences that are much more effective and that celebrate and empower local leaders. Give more. Do more. But reconsider your assumptions and reformulate your strategy. You can make a much more significant difference by acting like a sidekick and not a superhero.

You can help transform communities working like an anonymous community banker and not like a flashy venture capitalist or investment banker.

We spent several years researching and formulating the community bank model (CBM) that would dramatically enhance the impact of international development projects. We believed in the model enough to spend hundreds of thousands of dollars on a demonstration project in Brazil. Rather than being leaders or starting new projects, we would act as anonymous sidekicks. Our demonstration project coincided with a terrible economic and political crisis, creating an extraordinarily challenging stress test for the model. This demonstration project lasted for six years, with a total of thirty-two total cases in one of the most challenging environments on the planet. This demonstration project allows for counterfactual explorations of CBM. We will explain this field demonstration, the cases, and the results in detail in chapters 5, 6, and 7. For now, let us briefly introduce the two pillars for success acting as sidekicks in CBM.

Sidekicks

We all have seen those individuals who were born to lend a hand. They are at an event, the hosts are struggling to get things set up, and the natural sidekick notices that someone needs help and instinctively starts setting up chairs or taking down tables or passing out programs. They are never asked and often never recognized. Sidekicks are the heavy lifters who grease the wheels and make our communities better places.

Sidekicks are also ubiquitous characters in literature, film, and comics. Webster's synonyms for the word *sidekick* include *adjunct, aid, assistant, deputy, helper, helpmate, lieutenant,* and *mate.*[23] In films and comics, sidekicks such as Hermione, Robin, Tinker Bell, Samwise Gamgee, Chewbacca, and countless others are not only trusted and loyal companions but also counter the flaws of the superheroes and are indispensable in keeping the focus on the prime objective when the superhero gets off track. While the term originated at the end of the nineteenth century, sidekicks were featured in literature much earlier.

Don Quixote was the ultimate dreamer, but his illiterate neighbor and squire Sancho Panza was the ultimate loyal companion. Sancho knew that Don Quixote was tilting at windmills and demented, but went along for the adventure and to sustain his friend whenever the world was falling away. As the journey progressed, Sancho Panza adds folk wisdom, wise proverbs, and unshakable faith in his friend's mission to counter injustice and to promote chivalry.

Sidekicks have three essential attributes:[24]

• The first is to get to know and understand the superhero. Superheroes do not have to be older than the sidekick but are actively pursuing a worthy cause that the sidekick believes in. Sidekicks are interested in knowing what motivates superheroes to dedicate their lives to these projects and are drawn to high-character individuals who use creativity, personality, and determination to achieve the extraordinary.

• The second is belief in the superhero and in the goals of his or her project, in spite of the superhero's shortcomings (even superheroes have flaws). Sidekicks are honest with superheroes and may need to challenge them when they go astray.

• Finally, one must understand that the sidekick will receive no credit or public praise because that will accrue to the superhero. For many sidekicks, this is preferable and welcome.

In the domain of philanthropy, we describe sidekicks as loyal, passionate, and mostly anonymous supporters of the local superheroes who are successfully fighting to transform their communities with innovative projects. They understand that local leaders are not perfect but honorable and that the projects and goals are laudable and changing lives for the better.

THE TWO PILLARS OF CBM

The first pillar is to empower the large number of high-character local leaders, who are often marginalized and overlooked. Implicit bias results in mental patterns that associate attributes such as *leader, innovator, trustworthy, superhero, senior partner, precise, charitable, policymaker, brilliant,* and *take charge* with development and philanthropy practitioners in the United States and Europe. Implicit bias also results in mental patterns that associate people in Africa and Latin America with attributes such as *stakeholder, junior partner, sidekick, fan, grateful, subordinate,* and *heavy lifter.* Successful international philanthropy and development projects must actively subvert these implicit biases and the associated hierarchies of power. The current practice of senior partners from the Global North and junior partners from the Global South reproduces implicit bias because young people observe who is the innovative praised leader and who is the subordinate local stakeholder. People of the Global South have great ideas, innovative projects, and impressive leadership. They know what their communities need. Youth in the Global South should see locals who look like them when they think of leaders, innovators, superheroes, or people who had the most significant impact on their lives. If your project includes the phrase "recruit local partner to implement our project and represent local stakeholders," then you are very likely implementing the Philanthropist's Burden. *Ideas, innovation, and leadership must all be local.*

Fully empowering local leaders ensures that demand for projects is generated locally. Philanthropic endeavors must be what the local communities want and not something that others think they want. Ignoring what the local community actually wants reminds us of one of the corny old mommy-mommy jokes. "Mommy, mommy, I don't want to go to Europe." "Shut up and keep swimming." We should not assume that people in communities of the Global South feel comfortable openly and directly challenging us if they don't want a tilapia farm, a jewelry cooperative, or a youth soccer organization. Directly confronting foreigners is often culturally uncomfortable, and it may be difficult to speak up to the brash, enthusiastic, and confident gringo. *Ensure that the projects are demand driven and not supply driven.*

We should also resist the impulse to think that we know what material objects others might want or what would improve their lives. Consider this apocryphal story recounted by James Mittelman and Mustapha Pasha:

> There is the story of the English administrator serving overseas in the early days of empire. He stumbled upon a "native" lolling beside a lake and decided to do the chap a good turn. The colonizer gave the local a swift kick to the ribs, awakening him from a deep sleep, and demanded: "Why are you idling with a dozen or so fish beside you instead of catching more?" The lackadaisical response was: "I have caught all the fish that my family can eat today." Unperturbed, the Englishman didactically informed his acquaintance: "My good man, if you net another string of fish, you can sell it in the marketplace." The local repeated his point: "But we already have enough to eat." So the English official persisted: "With the proceeds of your sale, you can employ other fishermen." By this time, the local was feeling quite dumbfounded. He asked: "What then." "Why," said the Englishman, "then you can retire and sleep all day along this lovely waterfront."[25]

We often feel the urge to blame the locals for our failures, and we have participated in conversations that mostly mimic the English administrator. *If you find yourself blaming the local culture for your flop, you are on the wrong track!*

The second CBM pillar is to demand cost efficiency, or the greatest expected impact. Resources are scarce, and one should seek the highest possible expected return on time and money. In the post-COVID-19 world, marginalized neighborhoods will have even greater needs, and resources will be stretched. More than ever, global philanthropy must avoid long shots and maximize investment. Maximum impact emerges from four elements: cost effectiveness, or the percentage of allocated resources that ends up directly benefitting the targeted recipients; the success rate, or the likelihood that the project will actually come to fruition and remain in operation instead of disappearing or becoming a zombie project; the lag time between the donation and/or investment and the use of that money for good; and targeting the appropriate unit of social change.[26] In far too many projects, the actual impact per dollar donated is wretchedly low. *Always maximize the expected impact of resource allocation to benefit the target communities. Beware of the influence of start-up failure rates and lag times on cost effectiveness.*

We invite you to reconsider the Philanthropist's Burden and make a more significant difference by following these two simple rules: (1) relentlessly ensure that the local leaders are the stars, and support their ideas and innovation,[27] and (2) demand high levels of expected cost effectiveness and resist long-shot hopes for success, especially with start-up projects. We further simplify to four words, *empower locals* and *avoid start-ups.* You will obtain these goals quite naturally if you resist the urge to be a superhero and instead embrace your inner sidekick. Rather than practice global philanthropy like a celebrity investment banker or venture capitalist, adopt the anonymous role of a community banker.

This introductory chapter contains some strong assertions, and the balance of the book uses the historical record, contemporary examples, logic, process tracing, and data to build the case. The thrust of the evidence is the research design and results of a multiyear and multicase demonstration test of CBM. We do not argue that CBM is the only way to have meaningful charitable engagement. Many notable philanthropic projects in the Global South are initiated by citizens of the Global North. We contend, however, that our model is optimal for maximizing cost effectiveness and empowering locals. CBM is not for everyone, and many other practices will continue. If every practitioner or participant could, at a minimum, seriously consider how their efforts vigorously empower local leaders and generate the greatest return on investment, the entire sector and many communities will benefit.

The following chapter features a brief history of international development projects and philanthropy and the forces that led to the considerable growth of these activities in recent years. Chapter 3 details the evidence for our claim that the current model is suboptimal and explores the incentives that keep that model in place despite the dismal record. We do that in part by examining several examples that Harry Eckstein refers to as "most-likely cases."[28] That is, we select and examine multiple global development projects that should produce slam-dunk successes with brilliant teams of leaders, universal praise, innovative ideas, significant awards, and enormous budgets in the hundreds of millions of dollars. We also examine many smaller endeavors. Chapter 4 presents the details of the community bank–inspired model with its emphasis on local demand, resource effectiveness, and local leader empowerment. Chapter 5 details our six-year demonstration project to test this alternative model through the case of Miratus Badminton Association and its founder Sebastião Oliveira. Chapter 6 reimagines impact assessment or program evaluation, converting an antagonistic practice that lowers overall impact and demoralizes local leaders to a cooperative practice that inspires local leaders and increases impact. Chapter 7 presents three additional multiyear projects in Rio de Janeiro and three new cases in northeastern Brazil. The results of this demonstration project are illuminating. The final chapter describes a range of options and examples for being highly effective and empowering in your own life, and encouragement for everyone to do more both abroad and in their own communities.[29]

Before proceeding, it is crucial to clarify three points. The first is that, while global philanthropy can be transformative for individuals and neighborhoods, it is not a replacement for effective local, national, and international public policies. Providing high-quality education, health care, infrastructure, and employment for a large population requires huge sums of money and sustained effective national policies. The largest foundation in the world, the Gates Foundation, expends a mere $3.5 billion per year. This is a drop in the bucket of global development needs.

The second point is that many organizations and individuals already act as sidekicks in global philanthropy. They instinctively empower locals and invest in ongoing local organizations. We are not inventing a new way of acting; we are conceptualizing, theorizing, and testing CBM to encourage others to consider the model and its benefits.

Finally, we do not argue that CBM is the only way to participate ethically in global philanthropy. We contend that it is the best model for achieving the highest expected impact for expended resources and for empowering local leaders of the Global South. Other options are available that may meet other personal objectives and preferences.

2

EVERYBODY WANTS TO CHANGE THE WORLD

The Boom in International Philanthropy

I think I could be a philanthropist. A kick-ass philanthropist!
I would have all this money and people would love me. Then they
would come to me and beg! And if I felt like it, I would help
them and then they would owe me big time! (Thinking to himself)
The first thing I'm going to need is a driver.

—GEORGE COSTANZA OF *SEINFELD* CONSIDERING A CAREER CHANGE

There are philanthropists everywhere one looks.[1] Some 90 percent of American adults participate in the charity industry.[2] It often feels like everyone is embarking on a journey or a project to uplift the lives of people in a place far, far away. How did we arrive at this point of so much overseas uplifting, giving, volunteering, and promising new projects?

Philanthropy has a long pedigree, dating to at least the fourth century BC, when Plato left his farm to his nephew with instructions for using the proceeds to support faculty members and students at his academy. The word *philanthropy* comes from the Greek words *philos*, which means "loving," and *anthropos*, which means "humankind." Philanthropy is literally the love of humanity: not merely the love of one's family, community, friends, or tribe but the universal love of humanity.[3]

Philanthropy refers to a wide range of private-sector, religious, nonprofit, and personal initiatives to uplift the human condition. This excludes government programs such as the U.S. Agency for International Development (USAID), the Department for International Development (DFID) in the United Kingdom, other government programs led by permanent staffers,[4] and development projects from international financial institutions such as the World Bank and the Asian Development Bank. While some see them coterminous, there is an essential and sharp distinction between the words *philanthropy* and *charity*.[5] Philanthropy aims for the sustainable transformation of individuals or communities. Charity is a short-term solution such as alms to a homeless person or soup kitchens for the hungry. Charity would be giving a hungry man a fish, while philanthropy would be providing fishing equipment, training, and a refrigerator to a community near fishing grounds. Philanthropy also differs from a wide range of critical and vital emergency interventions such as natural disaster relief, refugee relief, and responses to famine and epidemics.

Individual giving in the United States is widespread and has deep roots. Harvard, Vanderbilt, Stanford, and other wealthy people followed Plato's example and left considerable amounts of money to support or found universities.[6] Benjamin Franklin was strongly influenced by the Boston minister Cotton Mather, who advocated benevolent spending for education, hospitals, and poverty alleviation. Franklin spearheaded fundraising for a fire company, a library, and the University of Pennsylvania in his beloved Philadelphia.[7]

In this chapter, we first present three early examples of global philanthropy. We then employ a critical juncture and path dependency analytical framework to explain why the United States features such a robust and vast international compassion sector.

EARLY GLOBAL PHILANTHROPY

While the practice was once uncommon, international philanthropic efforts have a long and illuminating record. History reveals episodes of foreigners armed with modern instruments, new ideas, and utopian dreams arriving to rescue some disadvantaged population. The results were often catastrophic, despite the best intentions, state-of-the-art technology, and detailed plans. In many ways, these early efforts foreshadow the grandiose contemporary plans, romantic expectations, and too-common failures of today. The

Philanthropist's Burden Stages

1. Contact/awareness: A trip or an item on the news or the Internet makes you aware of the underprivileged other and their need for intervention (*Your new-caught, sullen people*).
2. Eureka moment for big idea: You imagine a project that will civilize and transform, although there are sometimes ulterior motives (*With dear bought wisdom*).
3. Exceptional effort from exceptional people: The best and the brightest put forth a considerable effort and personal sacrifice to help (*Send forth the best ye breed*).
4. Optimism: There is a burst of confidence in the formulation and the launch. Everyone thinks your idea is brilliant and destined to succeed. Sometimes you win a significant grant or a competition to confirm your expectations. You will change the world and make a difference in the material conditions of others (*Fill full the mouth of Famine, And bid the sickness cease*).
5. Praise: While the sacrifice is for the locals, a bit of recognition and admiration for the leaders is warranted. Campus newspapers, social media, magazines, and others shower you with praise for your sacrifice and big heart. This praise was often delayed in Kipling's time. With social media, it is now immediate. You can even use photos of your sacrifices in impoverished communities with dark-skinned children on your Tinder and other dating apps (*Comes now, to search your manhood. Through all the thankless years . . . The judgment of your peers*).
6. Failure and rejection: In spite of the hard work, great plan, excellent cause, and support of god and men, the project goes awry and ends as a zombie project (largely lifeless but not officially dead) or an outright failure. This leads to finger-pointing and hard feelings with the local community (*The blame of those ye better. The hate of those ye guard*).
7. Blame: When things eventually go awry, you blame locals and their inferior culture for failure (*Watch sloth and heathen Folly, Bring all your hopes to naught*).

process follows seven steps that mirror the progression described by Kipling's "The White Man's Burden": contact, big idea, efforts from the best and the brightest, optimism, praise, failure, and blame.

The three projects discussed below had grandiose plans to civilize, modernize, and elevate the human condition in the Global South. They also incorporated market-based activities to generate revenues, a practice that is increasingly common today and referred to as social enterprise.[8] Practitioners often portray social enterprise as something new and innovative. In fact, it has a very long pedigree.

Jesuit missions to the Guaraní: The Jesuits created the missions of South America to improve permanently the spiritual and temporal conditions of the Guaraní Indians in the Southern Cone.[9] The Spaniards also had the ulterior motive of establishing a series of frontier fortifications to protect urban and political centers from invasion. At their peak, these "socialist utopias" and "Christian communist republics" had 250,000 indigenous inhabitants in 200 communities known as "reductions" and considerable autonomy from the Spanish crown.[10] These indigenous communities exported hides and 300,000 pounds of *yerba mate* tea per year,[11] built fine musical instruments, composed melodious baroque music, and established powerful militias to fight off the Brazilian slave traders known as *os Bandeirantes*. The Catholic priests introduced many trades to the reductions, training coopers, hatters, printers, weavers, carpenters, silversmiths, musicians, and instrument makers. The natives were becoming civilized in the eyes of the Jesuits.

Anyone who has seen Roland Joffé's powerful film *The Mission*[12] knows that this 160-year development project ended in tragedy and blood, with the expulsion of the Jesuits in 1767. Some missions collapsed immediately, and others endured for a time but under very different circumstances. A century and a half of effort came to naught.

Fordlândia in Brazil: A few years after receiving Kipling's poem "The White Man's Burden," Theodore Roosevelt told Henry Ford about his experience as an explorer in Brazil's Amazon. Roosevelt inspired Ford to vertically integrate automobile production by supplying his own rubber. Ford believed that he had the white man's burden to civilize and transform inferior Brazilians through a proper daily schedule, the U.S. work ethic, a diet of oatmeal, a prohibition on alcohol, and mandatory square dancing. Ford acquired a 5,625-square-mile tract of land in the Brazilian Amazon in 1928 and the right to rule it as a separate state.[13] Fordlândia was born.

Ford spent millions to create his jungle social enterprise. He built a city styled on the U.S. Midwest, including a hospital, schools, a library, tennis courts, a golf course, an entertainment complex for film and dancing, and U.S.-style cottages for the workers. Fordlândia managers encouraged the Brazilians to garden and read Longfellow's poetry. Ford prohibited single women and jazz music. Ford wanted to engineer the manufacturing of society just as he had transformed the production of the automobile. He despised local expertise, history, and botanists, and never visited the multimillion-dollar project ($250 million in current U.S. dollars). He finally cried uncle after seventeen years and returned the land to Brazil in 1945.

The abandoned jungle town stands as a testament to the folly of trying to bend both the wilderness and human nature to the will and ideas of a wealthy and stubborn international philanthropist. If a perfect Midwestern town is built in the Amazon, fails, and is abandoned, it had to be the fault of the people who were unable to benefit from Henry Ford's generosity and effort. Not a single ounce of rubber from Ford's Brazilian endeavors made it into a Ford car. In spite of the town riots, worker defections, and other evidence of failure, Ford proclaimed Fordlândia to have been a "successful sociological experiment."[14]

King Leopold II and the International African Association of Congo: In the annals of the white man's burden masquerading as philanthropy, there is likely nothing to compare with Leopold II, who combined the quest for the rubber riches of Henry Ford with the religious zeal of the Jesuits. Leopold, the cousin of Queen Victoria of England, was a wealthy, refined, noble, modern, and educated king. When the European powers divided Central Africa in 1876, the British and French supported the assignment of African Congo to Belgium to serve as a buffer state. Leopold desired to Christianize and uplift the immense region of 20 million inhabitants, proclaiming that "to open to civilization the only part of our globe which it has not yet penetrated, to pierce the darkness which hangs over entire peoples, is, I dare say, a crusade worthy of this century of progress."[15] Instead of treating the territory as a colony of Belgium, Leopold formed a charity to administer the Congo. The International African Association of Congo named Leopold as the chair, and he promised, in turn, to dedicate his vast wealth to uplift the inhabitants and bring progress to the region.

In practice, it was a sham. Leopold used the cover of philanthropy to earn a fortune through the ivory and rubber trades, treating the local population with brutality. The population fell by up to half under Leopold's "benevolent" care, collapsing from 20 to 10 million. Local administrators hacked off thousands of workers' hands because they failed to meet their rubber quotas. Disease, famine, and low birth rates accompanied the "crimes against humanity."[16] Mark Twain, Joseph Conrad, Arthur Conan Doyle, and others led a global campaign against Leopold's personal charitable estate, and Belgium formally annexed the Congo in 1908.

Until the end of his life, Leopold defended his intentions as noble and blamed local administrators for the atrocities. He reportedly spoke out against the widespread dismemberment, "Cut off hands—that's idiotic. I'd cut off all the rest of them, but not hands. That's the one thing I need in the Congo."[17] Like Henry Ford with Fordlândia, Leopold never visited the Congo, and he was adamant that replacing barbaric customs with civilizing practices would be a blessing to the locals.

Leopold needed soldiers for his vast personal estate. He was the largest landholder in the world, and his Congo holdings were nearly eighty times larger than Belgium. To generate a steady flow of soldiers and local bureaucrats, Congo administrators established children's colonies and issued orders to "gather the most male children possible" for the institutes. The Congolese did not send their children to these colonies that were run by Catholic missionaries. In reality, these youth centers were orphanages, but in African societies, "with their strong sense of extended family and clan ties, the concept of orphanhood in the European sense did not exist."[18] There was a great demand for orphans to fill the orphanages and a shortage of orphans, so Leopold's Force Publique conducted deadly raids, collected the survivors, and took the "orphans" on death marches to deliver them to the missionaries. Thousands of children died on the long journeys to the youth colonies, and the death rate was often over 50 percent in the orphanages. "The mother superior of one Catholic colony for girls wrote to a high Congo state official in 1895, "Several of the little girls were so sickly on their arrival . . . our good sisters couldn't save them, but all had the happiness of Holy Baptism; they are now little angels in Heaven who are praying for our great king. """[19]

Cruel demand creating a supply of orphans is one of the most horrific consequences of Leopold's so-called philanthropy. Something similarly sad is happening today. There is an oversupply of orphanage tourists and a shortage of orphans. Two-thirds of UK higher education students believe that volunteering at a Global South orphanage would enhance their career prospects, and 80 percent of the 8 million children living in orphanages are not orphans.[20] Children are being sold to or stolen and placed into orphanages to sate the pressure from orphanage volunteers, a practice that generates huge revenues for voluntourism agencies and some orphanage directors. The author J. K. Rowling recently launched a three-year campaign to discourage orphan voluntourism, stating that "despite the best intentions, the sad truth is that visiting and volunteering in orphanages drives an industry that separates children from their families and puts them at risk of neglect and abuse."[21]

CRITICAL JUNCTURES, THE BOOM IN INTERNATIONAL PHILANTHROPY, AND SUBOPTIMAL PATH DEPENDENCE IN THE UNITED STATES

The Jesuit, Ford, and Leopold II experiences are enlightening, but they also represent something episodic and uncommon before 1950: international philanthropy was rare and reserved for the rich and the powerful. In contrast, legions of individuals and organizations are now implementing projects or volunteering to uplift the human condition in Brazil, Paraguay, the Congo, and the rest of the Global South. What factors led to this growth? Why is the practice inefficient?

Critical junctures and path dependence are part of an analytical framework that helps explain why certain institutions or practices become dominant and why suboptimal practices are so difficult to reform. Scholars point to the QWERTY keyboard as a straightforward example. The top left letter keys on old typewriters and new keyboards are QWERTY, even though keyboards could be arranged in other patterns that would permit faster typing. Why? When keyboards first appeared in 1873, typewriters had keys that would jam if the typist worked too fast. The QWERTY keyboard allowed for efficient typing, but it was not so fast as to jam the keys regularly. Today, with computers and keyboards, there is no jamming, but the decision to adopt the QWERTY keyboard created path dependency whereby the high cost of changing from the QWERTY that we all use to a superior arrangement maintains the suboptimal keyboard.

Some historians quibble with the precise facts of this typeface chronicle,[22] but scholars fruitfully employ critical junctures whereby decisions by powerful actors are pivotal for the selection of one path of institutional development over another path. These junctures are *critical* because once a path is set, the institutional arrangements are difficult to reverse, even if there are more efficient alternatives. Why? Several mechanisms mutually buttress the continuation of the institution or practice, namely, positive feedback, increasing returns, and self-reinforcement.[23] Therefore, even an inferior institution, product, or practice becomes increasingly costly to reform or replace once a path is selected.

Critical junctures and path dependence create a particularly useful analytical framework to explain the origins and enduring legacies of economic and political norms and institutions. Antecedent conditions frame or constrain powerful actors. In the context of those conditions, critical junctures are major episodes of institutional change that generate an enduring legacy.[24] Elite actors contest the outcome of the critical juncture and shape the resulting path. Critical junctures and path dependency help explain the endurance of inefficient practices, including why it is so hard to reform suboptimal health-care systems, why chemical control of agricultural pests endures in spite of claims that integrated pest management is superior, and the continued dominance of fossil fuels for energy.[25]

Scholars use this analytical framework to explain different patterns in the philanthropic and nonprofit sectors across countries.[26] The legacy of path dependence may be enduring, but it is not always permanent. In banking and finance, the Great Depression produced an intense political battle over banking reform and the eventual passage of the Glass-Steagall Act in 1933. The act mandated the separation of commercial and investment banks, which was crucial in preventing financial abuse of commercial banks selling securities. Powerful economic and political forces pushed back in the economic boom years of the 1990s, which led to the repeal of Glass-Seagall in 1999 and the risky practices of complex derivatives and mortgage-backed securities that produced the 2008 Great Recession. The post-1999 fusion of commercial and investment banks produced enormous institutions deemed "too big to fail" and, despite their reckless practices that caused the financial crisis, were bailed out by taxpayers.[27]

Two sequential critical junctures in the tax code set the United States on a path of rapid growth in the nonprofit sector, a path with positive feedback, increasing returns, incentives, and self-reinforcement. In the past fifty years, additional legal, societal, and economic phenomena combined to internationalize philanthropy into a practice that is inefficient, embraces the White Man's Burden, and is incredibly difficult to reform.

ANTECEDENT CONDITIONS: DE TOCQUEVILLE AND AMERICAN ASSOCIATIONS

The practice of banding together in voluntary organizations to help others has a long and well-documented history in the United

States.[28] This activity is one core component of U.S. exceptionalism[29] and forms part of the national identity.

By the time Alexis de Tocqueville toured the United States in 1831 to observe the American political experiment and pen *Democracy in America*, voluntary associations with neighbors pooling their efforts to improve their communities were common. This made a great impression on the Frenchman due to the significant contrast with his European experience. If a road in town needed repair in the United States, the townspeople organized themselves collectively and repaired it; in other countries, citizens petitioned the authorities to make repairs or handled the problem as individuals.

> In America I encountered sorts of associations of which, I confess, I had no idea, and I often admired the infinite art with which the inhabitants of the United States managed to fix a common goal to the efforts of many men and to get them to advance to it freely.
>
> I have since traveled through England, from which the Americans took some of their laws and many of their usages, and it appeared to me that there they were very far from making as constant and as skilled a use of association.
>
> It often happens that the English execute very great things in isolation, whereas there is scarcely an undertaking so small that Americans do not unite for it. It is evident that the former consider association as a powerful means of action, but the latter seem to see in it the sole means they have of acting.[30]

The array of voluntary organizations in the United States evolved into community chests (which in turn became the United Way), fraternal organizations such as the Kiwanis and Optimists, church service projects, and neighborhood organizations. The informal organizing described by de Tocqueville remains a cornerstone of American civic life.[31]

Admirable and widespread as local civic associations are in the United States, we were curious to discover how this local habit evolved into the common practice of so many individuals and organizations going abroad to help those who are not members of one's community, citizens of one's country, members of one's ethnic group, or believers in one's religion.

THE CRITICAL JUNCTURE AND INCENTIVES FROM THE TAX CODE

In his 1899 book, *The Theory of the Leisure Class*, the radical economist Thorstein Veblen condemned the flagrant spending or "conspicuous consumption" of the men that controlled great fortunes. The Gilded Age (1870–1900) witnessed the biggest economic boom in U.S. history, with manufacturing, railroads, finance, real estate, steel, and mining producing spectacular wealth. The four richest Americans ever were all Gilded Age tycoons: John D. Rockefeller, Andrew Carnegie, Cornelius Vanderbilt, and William Henry Vanderbilt.

When Andrew Carnegie gave hundreds of millions of dollars in 1911 and 1912 to build libraries and fund philanthropic activities in the United States, Canada, and the British colonies, he did so without any tax incentives. The people viewed large-scale philanthropy with suspicion. Public intellectuals, activists, elected officials, and voters were hostile to huge fortunes going to universities or foundations. John D. Rockefeller's attempt to secure congressional approval of a $100 million open-ended foundation "to promote the well-being of mankind throughout the world"[32] generated such furor from labor leaders and national Republican politicians that he eventually resorted to a New York State charter to establish his foundation.[33] This was a critical juncture for the charity industry.

Rob Reich (2018) details the depth of the philosophical, political, and societal battle over the sanctioning of perpetual private foundations. The rich and powerful of the Gilded Age eventually won the war and federal authorization, and the number of perpetual private foundations grew from 2,000 in 1959 to nearly 100,000 in 2014 with some $800 billion in total capitalization (Reich 2018, 141–142). This is the first part of the tax code critical juncture. Reich concludes that this outcome set philanthropy on a path that is undemocratic, produces inequality, and subsidizes elites. Reich also describes an alternative path or counterfactual had the battle resulted in an alternative outcome.

In the same year as the launch of the Rockefeller Foundation in 1913, the country ratified the Sixteenth Amendment to the U.S. Constitution, which mandated a permanent federal income tax and eventually income taxes in thirty-three states.[34] It also ushered in lobbying and the approval of tax loopholes and deductions. The first individual income tax deduction for charitable giving became law in 1917. A significant shift occurred in 1954 with a complete modernization of the tax code, including section 501(c)3 for tax-exempt organizations. This is the second part of the tax code critical juncture: now everyone could raise tax-exempt money for philanthropy, the associated travel, retreats, and salaries. The subsequent growth of tax-exempt organizations and philanthropic activity is staggering. Today, there are more than 1.5 million tax-exempt organizations in the United States, and U.S. citizens donate nearly $400 billion annually.[35]

Not only is giving often exempt from federal income tax, it is also often exempt from state income tax. Marginal state tax rates are as high as 13.3 percent. The highest federal marginal tax rate is 39.6 percent, for incomes above $418,400. Higher-income earners in California face a combined marginal tax rate of 52.9 percent.[36] Donating money to international philanthropy only costs the wealthy Californian 47 cents for every dollar donated; other taxpayers pick up the additional 53 cents in lost tax revenue.

Tax deductions are significant incentives for donations to churches, arts organizations, and universities: three pillars of modern American life. Subsequently, the lobbying power and grassroots support to continue with generous tax deductions are considerable. The real beneficiaries are not lower-income taxpayers—who give away a higher percentage of their income than do wealthy people.[37] The charitable tax deduction now only benefits families with itemized deductions greater than the $24,000 standard deduction.[38]

The widespread support for this tax deduction also results from the influential belief in the United States that government is inefficient, and individuals and private efforts to help the poor are vastly superior. President George H. W. Bush used the presidency to push the idea that a "thousand points of light" would help more under-privileged people than could government.[39]

THE FORCES FOR THE PREVALENCE OF INTERNATIONAL PHILANTHROPY

The Global Tourism Revolution

International philanthropy often arises from interactions between more privileged individuals of the Global North and less privileged peoples of the Global South. We often hear stories of families who travel abroad and are inspired to set up a soccer nongovernmental organization (NGO) for girls or church groups who keep returning to Central America to help communities with service projects. The staggering growth of international tourism is a significant cause of the increase in global philanthropy.

The first great modern wave of globalization from 1870 to 1913 brought dramatic changes in transportation, trade, colonization, and immigration. The world was getting smaller, but traveling from the United States or Europe to South America or Africa was still expensive and time-consuming. In 1914, it took forty days to travel from Europe to the interior of Brazil and between ten and twenty days to go from Europe to Mexico.[40]

The second great wave of globalization (1944–1971) witnessed the widespread use of jet airplanes. All-inclusive vacations, paid holidays, and cheap and fast air travel unleashed a wave of international tourism. No longer reserved for the wealthy, soldiers, priests, adventurers, and scientists, vast swaths of the population of Europe and North America now had the time, means, and interest to travel abroad. In 1950, almost all international tourism involved travel from one advanced industrialized country to another.[41] The United States, Canada, and Western Europe received 23 million of the global total of 25 million international tourists at the midpoint of the twentieth century.

The increase in tourism to the developing world is particularly impressive. In 1950, only a couple of million individuals crossed borders as tourists in Latin America. A mere 400,000 international tourists visited Mexico or Central America in that year, while 500,000 visited the Caribbean, and only 400,000 traveled across borders within South America.[42] Today, international tourist arrivals to Latin America surpass 80 million per year (figure 2.1). Many of those tourists are interested in the culture and are inspired to help after witnessing inequality and poverty.

Not only are more tourists traveling to Latin America, Asia, and Africa, but the tourism profile is changing. Beach tourism and enclave all-inclusive resorts were all the rage in the 1980s; they were perceived as a prestigious vacation to show off to family and friends. Today, many tourists shun these generic sun-and-sand vacations and seek authentic experiences in culture, nature, and adventure. Authenticity is increasingly essential for today's travelers, who will

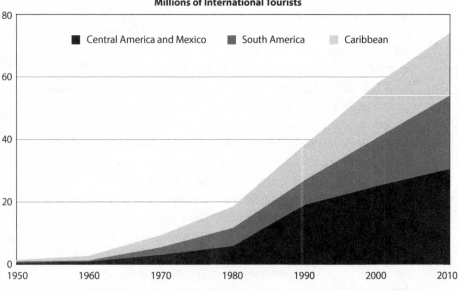

Figure 2.1 Tourist arrivals to Latin America, 1950–2010

backpack off the beaten path, experience slum or favela tourism, and stay away from hotel clusters and tourist-trap restaurants.[43]

These authenticity-seeking tourists are the precise demographic that wants to change the world. Increasing numbers are college students studying abroad. In the 2017–2018 academic year, 341,751 U.S. university students studied abroad.[44] Nearly half of them chose locations outside Europe and North America.

Voluntourists dwarf the study abroad numbers. Voluntourism is a $173 billion industry run by competing religious organizations and other nonprofits.[45] A 2008 study found that 1.6 million people volunteered abroad that year. Every one of them is a philanthropist, giving their time and money to elevate humanity. As good philanthropists, these experiences could be tax-deductible for U.S. residents.[46] Much of contemporary international tourism rejects yesteryear's desirable activities of sitting at a beach or playing golf. Young people want a genuine experience with the locals. According to U.S. tax law, "generally, you can claim a charitable contribution deduction for travel expenses necessarily incurred while you are away from home performing services for a charitable organization only if there is no significant element of personal pleasure, recreation, or vacation in the travel."[47] This segment of voluntourism is getting a tax deduction while experiencing the very type of international experiential travel that people yearn for.

Social Media and the Internet

The third great wave of globalization features the computer, the smartphone, and the personal communications revolution, which incentivize international philanthropy in essential ways. Social media and the Internet significantly enhance our ability to make contact and gain empathy for people in faraway lands. Communication with people around the globe is instantaneous and essentially free through apps like Skype, WeChat, and WhatsApp. Facebook and the Internet are regularly exposing us to opportunities to change the world. A Google search for "volunteer abroad" returns 5,370,000 hits, roughly the same number as "international philanthropy." "Save the world" returns 151 million hits. "Mission trips Africa" returns 3,260,000 hits. A search for "mission trips Honduras" returns more than 1.5 million hits. Costa Rica is much more developed than Honduras and needs far less philanthropy. Yet it is also a popular tourist spot and considered safer than Honduras; therefore "mission trip Costa Rica" returns double the hits as "mission trip Honduras."

More important, the Internet drives the personal motivation to be a philanthropist. Social media such as Facebook and Instagram have turned all of us into public praise addicts.[48] When cyberfriends respond favorably to our posted images and other content, a little shot of dopamine is released in our brains, giving us pleasure. This creates a need to post content that will reward our dopamine habit with a steady supply of positive feedback in the form of likes or hearts or encouraging emojis or gushing comments. In essence, everyone can be a minor celebrity on Facebook, Instagram, and Snapchat.

Nothing confirms our awesomeness to our social media friends more than a picture of us cuddling emaciated dark-skinned children

Figure 2.2 The Global Humanitarian of Tinder
Source: Art Cazé

in some poverty-stricken location far from home (figure 2.2). We instantly share our voluntourism and other philanthropic exploits with families and friends, letting everyone know that we achieved George Costanza's twisted idea of becoming a philanthropist. One observer of this phenomenon derides humanitarians who go so far as to use photos of themselves with poor children of the Global South for dating; such photos can be found on the website Humanitarians of Tinder (www.humanitariansoftinder.com). How can you beat saving the world combined with tax-deductible travel to get awesome humanitarian photos for your Tinder profile?

People can also promote their nonprofit or development project and collect donations through dazzling inexpensive websites. The Internet ratchets up the incentives for participation in the international compassion industry.

The Cult of Technology/Modernization and American Exceptionalism

Many U.S. citizens believe that they are exceptional, they can solve any problem with ingenuity and technology, and their mere presence enhances lives and projects in the Global South. How else do we fully explain the voluntourism phenomenon?

We sometimes receive queries from young people who are going to be in Rio de Janeiro for a few days or a couple of weeks and would love to volunteer for an afternoon or a few days at one of our partner social organizations in the favelas. One of the popular choices for volunteering is with the remarkable social circus, Crescer e Viver. We find such requests perplexing and ask if they have experience with the circus or if they even speak Portuguese. The answer is invariably negative. To young Americans, this is no hindrance because they perceive themselves as educated, technology-savvy, and remarkable leaders and problem solvers. They are constantly reminded at university that they are exceptional and can save the world. We respond with the following: "We have a friend in Madagascar. They do not speak English and have never studied finance or worked in a bank. However, they want to volunteer to come to

Orange County and live with you and help you with your work at the bank." Young Americans often find this suggestion ridiculous but they do not also see the parallel to what they are proposing. Even after a further explanation, they believe they add value with their mere presence at the circus, even without speaking the language or having a single circus skill; a volunteer from Madagascar that does not speak English and knows nothing about banking, however, would be a nuisance.

This conviction results from many sources. The first is the belief in U.S. exceptionalism, a city upon a hill, inspired by God, the best in everything. In the 1950s, social scientists and policy makers elaborated modernization theory, whereby any country could follow a ladder or recipe of development based on infrastructure, technology, taming nature, and good government. As part of the Cold War, the United States would help position allied traditional societies on that path to become prosperous and modern.[49] In the 1950s, the transformative technologies produced dams and roads and other modernizing infrastructure, which required massive expenditures. Today's solutions still include traditional engineering, but they also include inexpensive and accessible technologies such as apps, cell phones, and personal computers. The incredible advances in technology and the rapid spread of smartphones and digital information allow novel high-tech responses to global social challenges. Technical innovation, apps, and computing power can result in important and impressive social good, but technical innovation is not the only option and often not the best option for making a community a better place.

Kentaro Toyama addresses these issues in *Geek Heresy: Rescuing Social Change from the Cult of Technology*. Toyama was a software engineer for Microsoft who was sent to India to harness technology to improve education. His technology-rich solutions won awards and showed promise, but he soon discovered that technology was not the magic cure that everyone believed.

> I grew up in a mentality in which science and technology and engineering are the ultimate salvation for civilisation. And I've come to think that beginning with such an assumption is dangerous, because

it rules out all kinds of other solutions that would seem to be more suited to addressing problems. I routinely hear people say, "You suggest technology doesn't solve social problems"—and then with a completely straight face they add, "But what else is there?" Well, there is no end to other types of solution! It's just that if you think of technology as the primary one, then it's hard to even think of others."[50]

Toyama's beliefs sound heretical given modern assumptions about the social benefits of technology—what Toyama now believes tends to be "empty sloganeering that collapse[s] under critical thinking." Tucked up beyond our laptops, smartphones, and tablets, Toyama writes, "we are unable to entertain alternatives to tech-driven, capitalist, liberal democracy, so we pronounce [technology] the ultimate salvation."

The combined belief in U.S. exceptionalism and the cult of technology is a potent force for the conviction that we can save the world. But it contributes to the incentives for international philanthropy and to the high failure rate of international philanthropic projects. The cult of technology encourages the belief that product innovation is the great savior for poor people. There must be a new high-tech composting toilet or new software or other technology that will bring miracles to an impoverished community. This belief tragically eliminates social innovation or process innovation from consideration. Social innovation often requires speaking the local language, consulting local leadership and listening to their input, patience, and humility. The cult of technology has considerable support from the media. An article in the university alumni magazine about a new technology invented by students that will benefit people in Bolivia is much sexier than an article about a group of students learning the Aymara language to understand culture and development and to support local social innovation.

Some of us are old enough to remember the first time we witnessed a fax machine in action. A person in New York could send a document via fax through a telephone line, and it would magically appear in California, where the recipient could sign the document and send it back. It was as mystifying as someone beaming up to the starship *Enterprise*. We all believed that the wave of digitization and computerization would lead to greater productivity and the need to work fewer hours. In fact, the opposite happened as advances in technology resulted in people working more hours.

New technologies can easily burden individuals and communities with far more work instead of easing their workload. Toyama explains this as one outcome of the law of amplification.[51] Those who want to improve the lives of others should be wary of immediately defaulting to a technological or product innovation solution. Technology can produce impressive results, but our experience indicates that social or process innovation often yields more benefits.

INCREASING INEQUALITY

From the 1930s to the 1970s, a more equitable distribution of income and wealth was a trend in advanced industrialized countries.[52] Since the 1970s, income and wealth inequality increased in the Global North, often quite dramatically. Income remains stagnant for lower- and middle-income families, while income and wealth rose substantially for the top 10 percent. In the United States, the top 10 percent now receives 51 percent of the income each year and holds 77 percent of the wealth.[53] Inequality is a major reason for an increase in overseas philanthropy. Why?

The two most important issues are wealth concentration and competition due to income inequality. The concentration of wealth generated massive fortunes and a modern version of the megaphilanthropist that surpasses the Rockefellers and the Carnegies. The thirty-first issue of *Forbes'* billionaire list found a record 2,043 billionaires worth a total of $7.7 trillion.[54] This equals 233 more billionaires than in the previous year. Led by Bill and Melinda Gates and Warren Buffet, megaphilanthropy of the superrich is a growing phenomenon. Facebook founder Mark Zuckerberg pledged 99 percent of his wealth, nearly $50 billion, to philanthropy, although his strategy received considerable criticism.[55] The Bill and Melinda

Gates Foundation, Wellcome Trust, Howard Hughes Medical Foundation, Soros Foundation, MacArthur Foundation, and many others have expended tens of billions of dollars on health, education, the arts, and development, albeit with mixed success.

Many recent spectacular fortunes were made in the field of technology. The reinforcement of these entrepreneurs of the cult of technology as the only solution for all problems is not surprising. In their view, product innovation trumps social or process innovation.

The superrich are the new celebrities and rich stars in entertainment, the arts, education, and sports. They establish their own NGOs and foundations. Multimillionaire entertainers such as George Clooney, Bono, Angelina Jolie, and celebrity academics like Jeffrey Sachs travel to Africa and South Asia for developmental initiatives. Philanthropy generates positive attention on social media and in traditional media for the rich and famous.

Andy Warhol famously predicted, "In the future, everyone will be world-famous for 15 minutes." With social media and international philanthropy, celebrities easily orchestrate that via a cell phone. And you can, too.

Income inequality has an even more powerful effect than wealth concentration. The division between a high- and a low-paying career has never been so stark and ratchets up the competition to shift professional trajectories upward. Applications to the highest-ranked universities are soaring, and acceptance rates are at historic lows. High school students think they need remarkable extracurricular activities and leadership experiences to feel competitive, and an army of professional coaches now advises teenagers on what experiences look best on college applications and assists in writing college essays. In some cases, families pay astronomical figures for coaches to secure acceptance into top universities by inventing false profiles as athletes or minorities. Parents often pay into foundations or nonprofits for these fraudulent profiles for their children, gaining a tax deduction while gaming the system.

Harvard only accepts 5 percent of applicants. The most common words on their application essays are *experience*, *society*, *world*, *success*, and *opportunity*. Brown favors essays about volunteer work and public interest work.[56] This is not necessarily the case with all universities, but students and parents perceive that international philanthropy work helps students get into top colleges. Parents want their children to be part of the new elite, what Elizabeth Currid-Halkett explores in her book on the aspirational class. Building a résumé with markers of the aspirational class such as playing the violin, student leadership, and international philanthropy is seen as the path to upward mobility, wealth, and status ensuring that children end up on the right side of the ever-deepening class divide.[57]

University admissions staff members appear to be tiring of reading so many similar essays. Some are publicly begging for originality and are publishing the frequent and annoying cliché essay categories as examples of what not to do. Two of the most common types of college essays feature the high school international philanthropist.

> **Poor but happy peasants.** Summer trips and mission tours to exotic locales, both overseas and in the Deep South, have become grist for the college essays of both affluent Americans and their counterparts in countries like France and Singapore, where students still refer to their activities by blunt reference to "charity" work. However good their intentions, or those of the parents footing the big bills, these students' essays often persuade readers that their experiences have been so sheltered that they return home with no deeper understanding of the impact of their unequal access to resources on those they went to serve.
>
> **Take me to your leader.** Given their recruitment pitches, admission officers often have only themselves to blame when they are deluged by essays in which students treat leadership not as a process in which they participate and their hard work is reflected in the regard of their peers, but as a trophy to achieve and display on the mantlepiece that is a college resume.[58]

The competition of getting a great job out of college might be even more intense than acceptance to a top university. There is a powerful incentive for highlighting leadership and saving the world on the college résumé.

Nearly every university has formal programs for leadership. The cult of leadership is almost as strong as the cult of technology, and the combination of the two is formidable. Universities and colleges are full of student organizations. Student organizations are valuable institutions on every college campus and serve a myriad of positive purposes, from finding a tribe, to providing services, to organizing cultural and other activities. Campus organizations also provide rich networks of friends that last a lifetime. They are the life of the modern university, and we strongly encourage students to be active in student organizations. However, our experience indicates that some of the organizations founded each month on college campuses replicate in no small degree existing organizations. Many organizations only have a handful of members and could accomplish more by joining forces with similar existing clubs rather than forming competing entities. One rationale for the replication of clubs and organizations is simple: every club has officers, and every student needs leadership on their résumé. Joining an existing club or organization without a leadership position may be considered less valuable.[59] The university system may be producing too many leaders and not enough heavy lifters, too many superheroes and not enough sidekicks.

Universities are themselves competing for donors, rankings, and the best students. They set up elaborate programs for changing the world. Student competitions for products or technology that are promoted as saving some part of the Global South are ubiquitous on college campuses. Students are constantly reminded of their exceptionalism and capacity as global change agents. Alumni magazines, departmental newsletters, student newspapers, and social media feature stories of students bringing civilization and innovation to the impoverished. Kipling would be proud.

The last fifty years witnessed a global boom in philanthropy. A critical juncture and path dependency analysis (table 2.1) helps explain the emergence of the philanthropy industrial complex in the United States. Subsequent societal, economic, and technological forces led to the explosion of activities in the Global South.

TABLE 2.1

Explaining Global Philanthropy Through Critical Juncture and Path Dependency

Antecedent conditions	• Tradition of voluntary associations and local philanthropy. • Belief in U.S. exceptionalism. • Tycoons in the Gilded Age with vast wealth and the desire to found perpetual private foundations.
Two-part critical juncture	• Part 1: the so-called Andrew Carnegie critical juncture. Contestation by powerful actors over sanctioning of perpetual private foundations. Tycoons win. Today there are 100,000 private foundations with $800 billion. • Part 2: the so-called George Costanza critical juncture. Tax code reform and Section 501(c)3 establishing tax exemptions leading to 1.5 million nonprofits.
Economic, technological, societal forces that incentivized international philanthropy	• Explosion of global tourism. • The Internet. • Internationalization of university activities, including study abroad. • Inequality and growing class divide.
Positive feedback, increasing returns, and self-reinforcement	• Dogma that product technology is the only solution for societal problems. • Technology innovation is rewarded in the media, awards ceremonies, and alumni magazines. • Social media rewarding global philanthropists with praise, dopamine hits, and even dating profile pictures. • Cult of leadership and multiplication of organizations and activities so that everyone gets a leadership position to put on their résumé. • Starting an international NGO or participating in international activities such as voluntourism deemed useful for gaining entry into the best universities and landing the best jobs as a way to join the "aspirational class."
Enduring legacy that is difficult to reform	• The Philanthropist's Burden: enormous philanthropic industrial complex based on our leadership, technology, ideas, innovation, and projects to improve the human condition in the Global South.

It is inspiring that so many people care and participate. Great work is taking place, and people genuinely care about the Earth and its people. Yet the same trends that encourage global philanthropy also create incentives to follow the Philanthropist's Burden model of global help. These incentives are robust, and practicing a more empowering and cost-efficient model requires conscious effort. Much of the global philanthropy effort is suboptimal, but it can be easily improved. To better understand common shortcomings and to build an alternative, the next chapter examines specific examples at various points of scale: contemporary can't-miss megaprojects, medium-sized efforts, and microphilanthropy.

3

LESSONS FROM THE CONTEMPORARY GLOBAL PHILANTHROPY PRACTICE

I don't want a little girl in Ghana, or Sri Lanka, or Indonesia to
think of me when she wakes up each morning. I don't want her
to thank me for her education or medical care or new clothes . . .
I want her to think about her teacher, her community leader, or mother.
I want her to have a hero who she can relate to—who looks like her,
is part of her culture, speaks her language, and who she might bump
into on the way to school.

—PIPPA BIDDLE

The popular parlor game Six Degrees of Kevin Bacon suggests
that any two people on Earth are six or fewer acquaintance
links apart. With the size and ubiquity of global philanthropy, most
of us are a single link away from the global compassion industry.
Many of us can identify lessons in this field from our own experiences or those of a family member or close friend. As part of our
journey to build a model that maximizes the sector's efficiency
and long-term benefits, this chapter identifies lessons from a wide
range of existing practices.

Even if we assume that all international volunteers, organizations, and families participating in philanthropic endeavors have
nothing but the noblest of intentions, the current mindset is problematic. Of course, we all know of scandals where individuals with
selfish purposes exploited poverty, disease, and/or catastrophe to
skim—or in some cases, plunder—money from donors and sponsors. These scams plague local charities and international philanthropy alike. The grand champion of intentional abuse might be the
cancer research charities operated by James Reynolds Sr. and his
extended family. The family reportedly raised nearly $200 million

for cancer research and spent almost all of the money on lavish vacations, extravagant salaries for numerous relatives, luxury homes, and a lifestyle that made them one of the rich and famous.[1] We could fill a book with similar tales of greed and theft. The audacity and frequency of these hucksters undermine confidence in altruistic giving. The United Way, Feed the Children, Wounded Warriors, professional baseball player Alex Rodriguez's A-Rod Foundation, the Lance Armstrong Foundation, and many other high-profile and once widely respected U.S. organizations appear in some hall of fame lists of charity shame.[2] Corrupt practices also tarnish benevolence projects in the Global South.

After sharing examples of deceitful efforts at international philanthropy, we will examine a range of projects where the intentions were pure, the money was sufficient, and the planned activities took place. We will consider three large-scale projects that were considered most-likely cases to succeed and that were going to transform vast swaths of the Global South, with budgets in the hundreds of millions of dollars and the backing of academics, celebrities, governments, and international organizations. These projects provide valuable lessons about the potential shortcomings of current practice. We will then look at a range of small-scale global philanthropy projects and flesh out the faulty assumptions, unrealistic expectations, and potential long-term harm from these widely lauded activities. We do not assert that these actions yield no benefits or that the participants are insincere. Indeed, we respect many of these practitioners and applaud their successes. These cases help challenge our perspectives and assumptions, and generate lessons to reconsider our actions and to contemplate improved approaches to our international endeavors.

INTERNATIONAL PHILANTHROPY SCANDALS

These examples are tragedies because they involved a significant amount of misplaced philanthropic money, the project collapsed before starting, or both. When you donate to international charity, how do you know where your money is actually going? These projects highlight the challenge of determining the cost efficiency around donating to charitable organizations. It is often impossible to know from research or websites where the money is going or how much is actually going to the intended beneficiaries.

The entertainer Madonna adopted two children from Malawi and exhibits a genuine connection with that country. She founded the Raising Malawi Foundation to build schools for girls in that impoverished African nation, including one $15 million school. Madonna donated $11 million of her own money for the school and raised a total of $18 million. The foundation expended $3.8 million on the showcase school, and hundreds of people were displaced from their homes to make way for construction. The entire $3.8 million disappeared without the laying of a single brick.[3] Local Malawi women stepped in with local solutions to the abandoned girls' academy. "The superstar's much-hyped bid to set up a girls' academy failed. Now villagers are ensuring their daughters stay in education, and success is built on small steps—like making sure pupils have lunch."[4] Imagine the increased value that Madonna would have had by funding smaller, locally led initiatives instead of grandiose plans of a $15 million academy. Grand plans are often ill-suited for global development.

Madonna's philanthropic adventure went awry, but there is no reason to doubt her intentions and generosity. The same cannot be said for the efforts of Haitian musician Wyclef Jean and his charity Yéle. After the devastating January 2010 Haitian earthquake, Jean was the face of Haiti, performing at benefits and raising millions. Yéle spent $9 million in 2010, and half allegedly went to consultants' fees, travel, salaries, and office and warehouse expenses. Yéle spent $375,000 on office landscaping and even more on development projects that were overseen by Jean's brother-in-law, projects that never materialized. Millions of dollars disappeared. The foundation closed in August 2012.[5]

We do not suggest that all celebrity philanthropy projects are poorly managed. Sean Penn's J/P Haitian Relief Organization also raised considerable sums of money for Haiti. Of $13 million spent, only 10 percent went toward salaries; consultant's fees; and travel, office, and warehouse expenses.[6]

One of the most perplexing cases of international philanthropy is that of superstar humanitarian Greg Mortenson, the author of the best-selling book and save-the-world manual *Three Cups of Tea*.[7] The book details an inspiring tale of Mortenson being kidnapped by the Taliban on a mountaineering trip and how his generous spirit led to his freedom and falling in love with Central Asia. As he departed, he promised to return and build schools. Mortenson established the Central Asia Institute to raise money and to construct schools for the children of the region and to support and promote his books.[8] *Three Cups of Tea* was a phenomenon—staying on the *New York Times* bestseller list for 222 weeks and published in some fifty languages. President Obama donated $100,000 from his Nobel Peace Prize to Mortenson, and *Into the Wild* and *Into Thin Air* author Jon Krakauer gave generously. Mortenson was a celebrity philanthropist, raising about $80 million and appearing at events around the world.[9]

After donating $75,000 to Mortenson's institute, Krakauer developed suspicions about the facts portrayed in the book and published the investigative journalism piece "Three Cups of Deceit—How Greg Mortenson, Humanitarian Hero, Lost His Way." The CBS news program *60 Minutes* followed up with a damning exposé, further undermining his credibility. Mortenson issued an emotional public apology for his errors and reimbursed $1.2 million to the Central Asia Institute. He continues to have dedicated supporters, including friends who produced a documentary film to rebuild his credibility: "3,000 Cups of Tea: Investigating the Rise and Ruin of Greg Mortenson."

Whether Mortenson is an intentional liar or merely a romantic fabulist is disputed. Whether he was just careless with money or dishonest is also contentious. These controversies miss the point. His project was White Man's Burden redux. It was inefficient, and it enhanced rather than subverted existing power relations. The protagonists were not locals in Central Asia; the protagonist was Greg Mortenson.

The number of schools actually built appears to be significantly exaggerated by Mortenson, and vast sums of money went unaccounted for or were misspent. The Central Asia Institute spent $1.7 million promoting and buying full-priced copies of Mortenson's books to ensure continuation on best-seller lists and to generate royalties: that is $1.7 million of tax-deductible charitable donations to provide fees to Mortenson. U.S. taxpayers are unwittingly paying Greg Mortenson. Even before the unearthing of these questionable practices, there was something entirely untoward about Mortenson's brand of philanthropy, and the appeal of his work reveals much about our attitudes. An interview by the *New Yorker* journalist Peter Hessler of development activist Rajeev Goyal that took place some months before Krakauer's exposé illustrates the point.

Last September, when I was researching a profile of Rajeev Goyal, an American development worker, I asked what he thought about the book *Three Cups of Tea*. Rajeev and I were walking through the hills of eastern Nepal, where he had organized a number of projects over the past decade, including the construction of five schools. *Three Cups of Tea* is one of the bestselling books by Greg Mortenson, a mountaineer whose Central Asia Institute claims to have built or significantly supported more than a hundred and seventy schools in Pakistan and Afghanistan.

Rajeev paused for a moment. "It seemed to be mostly about the author, about everything he accomplished," he said slowly. "And that story is about quantity, about the number of schools built." Rajeev said his own work had convinced him that construction projects are overvalued, and sometimes can even have a negative impact on a community. People might become dependent on outsiders, and corruption can become a problem. Building materials and methods may be inappropriate, especially if money comes from far away and there's little oversight. Foreign-funded structures have a tendency to overuse cement, which can change local construction patterns in environmentally damaging ways, especially in dry parts of Central Asia. Rajeev believed that teacher training and other cultural factors often have more value. "A good teacher sitting under a tree can do more than a bad teacher in a new building," he said. "That's why I don't want to do school construction anymore. It might have been a mistake. It's a good instinct, as you want to help, but maybe it's not the best thing."

I asked about his impressions of Mortenson. "I kind of felt sorry for him," Rajeev said. "That was my reaction reading the book. He must have low self-esteem."[10]

If you read Mortenson's tales critically, you encounter something profoundly unsettling: he claims that it is his burden and his sacrifice to rescue brown uneducated people. All the purported successes are based on his exceptionalism, insights, daring exploits, near-death experiences, awesomeness, and leadership. He is gifted and extraordinary in everything he does. The narrative makes Mortenson superhuman. For example, he is a polyglot and must rapidly learn multiple Pakistani dialects to rescue the country from terrorism. "Glacier was *gangs-zhing*, avalanche *rdo-rut*. And the Balti had as many names for rock as the Inuit have for snow."[11] The overused cliché that the Inuit have fifty or one hundred or four hundred words for snow is a myth,[12] so one is not sure what Mortenson is trying to say, except that he wants the reader to believe that he himself is brilliant and deserving of your awe. Even without the fraud, this example—like so many—is neither cost-effective with donations nor empowering to local leaders.

CONTEMPORARY PHILANTHROPY AND ITS DISCONTENTS: LARGE AND SMALL

We want to believe that most contemporary philanthropy projects are founded and implemented by committed and honest development practitioners. Even so, projects often result in inefficiency, unmet expectations, and blame for the local culture for the resulting disappointments. This section examines three large projects with budgets of hundreds of millions of dollars and several much smaller projects. We are empathetic and understand the dreams, efforts, and courage of the people involved in these projects, having been enthusiastic participants in smaller but analogous endeavors ourselves. These cases are not presented to demean or criticize but to prepare readers to shift their perceptions toward a more efficient and subversive model.

The Large Projects and Their Lessons

Three large international projects showcase many of the problematic assumptions of international development projects and the tremendous costs of the Philanthropist's Burden perspective. Each project fits into what political scientist Eckstein called "most-likely cases" to succeed.[13] Each one had hundreds of millions of dollars. Each was designed and implemented by the best and the brightest. All had the support of major media outlets, governments, and international organizations. Celebrities and universities extended praise and support. The ideas were exciting and innovative. They were can't-miss projects that would transform the Global South. They were well administered without charges of corruption or scandal. We personally followed these projects from the earliest and genuinely hoped for their success, but we were disappointed in the end.

The Millennium Villages Project is one of the most ambitious philanthropy undertakings of all time. Launched by the brilliant, influential, and celebrated economist Jeffrey Sachs, whom we greatly admire, the project represents the boldest and most daring experiment to eliminate extreme poverty. Instead of providing enough continuous foreign aid and charity in sub-Saharan Africa to keep people alive and dependent on permanent assistance, Sachs and his team proposed a bold demonstration project: allocate $120 per person per year for five years to eradicate extreme poverty permanently. The investment was significant, but it replaced the continuous foreign aid that kept people alive and dependent with a more substantial temporary intervention that would end after five years. Sachs and his colleagues at Columbia University and the Earth Institute elaborated a detailed 147-page, single-spaced operations manual written by twenty-nine academics. Following the manual would simultaneously increase agricultural output through high-yield seeds and fertilizer, reduce mortality with state-of-the-art mosquito nets, improve human capital with better schools and health care, improve the water supply with better wells and protected springs, and so forth.[14] The money and programming would come from a small army of experts in New York and be implemented with African leaders in fourteen village clusters with a total population of half a million people. Sachs and the Earth Institute hoped that the initial project would follow the very detailed five-year plan and the success would lead to 1,000 Millennium Villages by 2009,[15] eventually covering the entire continent of Africa.

Imagine the significance of permanently eliminating the scourge of extreme poverty in five years for a total cost of $600 per person: the world would be transformed! Not only would this lift hundreds of millions out of extreme poverty, it would also reduce conflict and diminish global migration. Sachs is persuasive, confident, and dogged, and he raised $120 million for his demonstration project. Angelina Jolie joined him early to make the documentary *The Diary of Angelina Jolie & Dr. Jeffrey Sachs in Africa*, which captures the enthusiasm for this innovative philanthropy that was going to wean the poor in Africa from permanent dependence on foreign aid. The musician Bono proclaimed that Sachs was "the squeaky wheel that roars."[16]

The project style is strangely similar to a hybrid of the detailed five-year economic plans of the former Soviet Union and the anti-Communist modernization manifesto of W. W. Rostow's stages of development.[17] Provide enough high-quality seeds and fertilizer in year one and that will lead to a calculable increase in income and food in years 2, 3, and so on. Provide enough insecticide-treated mosquito nets and a working medical clinic, and child mortality will decline by x amount. Drill enough wells, and the terrible consequences of water shortages will disappear. Follow the detailed manual prepared by the smartest people working in global development, and in five years the villages will have permanently eliminated extreme poverty. It was axiomatic; it was theory and math; it was predictable in great detail over five years.

To keep the villages on track, Sachs's team selected an African with a PhD to lead each cluster of villages and a national advisory committee in each of the participant countries. The money flowed in, the high-quality seeds and fertilizer arrived. The clinics were built and staffed, wells were bored, and the world and high-profile donors hoped for the best. We joined them in optimism and antici- pation. The Millennium Villages showed great promise at first, crop output increased significantly, and for a romantic period there was real optimism that one five-year concentrated effort could end the human misery associated with extreme poverty where people live on less than $1 per day.

What so often happens, however, is that the perfect idea and most meticulously detailed plan eventually run into the unexpected hurdles and setbacks that every start-up faces. There are good rea- sons why business start-ups in the United States fail at such a high rate—unforeseen and unknowable setbacks. International devel- opment projects are often led by academics, students, ministers, Peace Corps volunteers, and others that can see only the rosy and optimistic outcome of their work: they play a mental game of con- nect the dots between implementing their brilliant idea and total success. When personal conflicts, drought, storms, political insta- bility, market disruptions, shipping delays, and other real-world events disconnect those dots, the outcomes are often unexpected and disappointing.

In her book *The Idealist: Jeffrey Sachs and the Quest to End Poverty*, Nina Munk details her six years shadowing Sachs and immersing herself in two of the Millennium Villages. This extensive research allows her to remain impressed by Sachs while vividly documenting the project's flaws. Here are just a few of the unpredictable disasters that hit a single village, none of which were covered in the manual from New York City. The Millennium Village of Dertu experienced a devastating drought that killed most of the animals and wilted the crops. The borehole for the well broke down, and both generator- driven water pumps went out at the same time. The value of the U.S. dollar fell, making everything more expensive, and the budget of $120 per person per year was no longer sufficient. The effect on agriculture was extensive because the cost of fertilizer increased almost fivefold. To battle a drought, the villagers planted sorghum, which is more drought-resistant than corn. Unfortunately, a swarm of red-billed quelea, or locust birds, devoured the seeds. "They darkened the land like storm clouds, huge ominous flocks swooping in to devastate the fields."[18] In addition, farming tools were stolen. The locals didn't plant the 5,000 seedlings to grow antidrought trees that the program gave them. A kitchen gardening program, meant to encourage the women of Dertu to grow kale and tomatoes in burlap sacks, hadn't worked either. "The high saline content of Dertu's groundwater was to blame, some said. The women had received no proper training, someone else explained. Somalis didn't like kale, another person told me."[19] Put simply, there are always unexpected setbacks in any start-up venture, and these can be devastating in new global development initiatives. Detailed plans go off the rails with unpredictable setbacks, and desperation leads project officers to make it up as they go along, often with regrettable results.

In addition to the kale, other projects failed due to a lack of understanding of particular local preferences. The local Millennium Village administrator Ahmed was a Somali Muslim from the region, but even so, he was viewed as an outsider in Dertu, with his pleated pants and starched shirts. He tried to convince the locals of the benefits of hay, of cutting the tall grass in times of plenty to save for times of drought. The people refused, saying that God provides the grass, and the people have no right to cut it.[20]

Sachs remained undeterred, however, and extended the experiment from five to ten years. By 2008, the Millennium Village Project was no longer flush with cash, and agriculture was losing money. Sachs hired an expert in social enterprise who asked each Millennium Village local leader to submit a business plan to generate profits and raise venture capital. Local leaders like Ahmed had no training in entrepreneurship or business, and now they were asked to think of an agricultural product to present to venture capitalists. Imagine the problems that could arise from asking local leaders with no experience in entrepreneurship to generate commercial profits immediately from high-value crops. Local program leaders are often blamed if they are unsuccessful in doing something incredibly difficult and for which they have no expertise. Munk describes the results from the village of Ruhiira, Uganda:

> When it came to increasing people's incomes, however, [local leader] Siriri saw nothing but failure. Pineapple couldn't be exported after all, because the cost of the transport was far too high. There was no market for ginger, apparently. And despite some early interest from buyers in Japan, no one wanted banana flour. "I have been failed by the markets," he said soberly. On one level, the cardamom crops had exceeded Siriri's expectations: the crop thrived in Ruhiira's moist valleys. However, as soon as Siriri tried to sell it, he hit a roadblock. "We proved it could be grown," he said, "but when I took it to the buyers they asked me, 'Is it organic?' and I had to tell them 'No! Of course it is not organic!' In Ruhiira we have run-off fertilizer that comes down the fields in the hills above—so no, I am sorry to say it is not organic."[21]

There is something unsettling about the relationship between the team of experts in the United States and the locals in the villages. Sachs has the integrity and the track record to avoid being confused with Greg Mortenson. Both men, however, exhibit a similar messianic dimension and an attraction to the aura of celebrity. This is part and parcel of the Philanthropist's Burden.

The local leader in the village of Dertu was a man named Ahmed Mohamed, a Somali from Kenya's North Eastern Province who, through a combination of intelligence, hard work, and good fortune, left the desert and earned a PhD in Belgium with a dissertation on natural resources management in drylands.[22] "It was Ahmed Mohamed's job to lift the people of Dertu out of extreme poverty. Hired by the Millennium Villages Project in March 2006, one year after completing his PhD in Belgium, Ahmed was responsible for implementing what he referred to, admiringly, as 'the Great Professor's Ideas'—the Great Professor being Jeffrey Sachs."[23] Four years after Ahmed began working and after Dertu experienced what Sachs himself referred to as the geographic equivalent of biblical Job—"Just one disaster after another: droughts, floods, Rift valley fever, rinderpest, you name it"[24]—the Great Professor fired Ahmed.

It is easy to admire Sachs for his optimism, big ideas, intelligence, integrity, and ability to make people believe. In spite of the disappointments and setbacks, the project improved many lives with better education, improved health care, a reduction in malaria, and enriched diets. Still, the Millennium Villages Project morphed from the goal of sustainable development after five years of massive intervention to ten years of intervention, to something much more permanent. Some critics observe that those gains could have happened with far less money. Simon Bland, a senior adviser in the United Kingdom's Department for International Development (DFID), summed up the endeavor: "I know that if you spend enough money on each person in a village, you will change lives. If you put in enough resources—enough *mzungu* [Swahili for "white skin"], foreigners, technical assistance, and money—lives change. I know that. . . . the problem is, when you walk away, what happens?"[25]

We highlight two critical lessons from the Millennium Villages Project:

Lesson 1: Even with the brightest people in the world, the most meticulous plans, and hundreds of millions of dollars, start-up development projects in the Global South almost always fail to reach their original stated objectives. Poor countries are not laboratories and are messy and chaotic, and all start-ups face a host of unexpected and unknown challenges and disasters.

Lesson 2: It is unhealthy when leaders from the Global North are seen as superheroes and "Great Professors," and the locals serve as junior partners and sidekicks. Locals take the blame for all that goes wrong and get little of the credit when things go well.

The Roundabout PlayPump was going to improve the world in spectacular fashion. Like the Millennium Villages Project, this venture was going to transform the poorest parts of Africa by delivering the scarcest of crucial resources: water. There is something so appealing and glorious about the idea of the PlayPump. It was invented in Africa, and the first PlayPump installations are on that continent. This innovation was not concocted in a lab at the Massachusetts Institute of Technology (MIT) or at Georgia Tech. It was also a charming story, with compelling images of smiling kids play-ing and happy locals with plenty of water.

Simply put, the PlayPump is a water pump attached to a merry-go-round. Children play by pushing and riding the merry-go-round, which pumps enough water into the attached 2,500-liter tank to provide daily water for a town of 2,500 people. The world went crazy for this idea! The initial installations were huge successes, attracting politicians, celebrities, and the media. Play-Pump won the World Bank Development Marketplace Award, received $16.4 million at the 2006 Clinton Global Forum, was praised and supported by Laura Bush and billionaire philanthro-pist Steve Case, and was portrayed glowingly on a 2005 episode of *Frontline* from the Public Broadcasting Service (PBS).[26] By 2008, there were 1,000 installed systems, and 4,000 were expected to be installed by 2010. This was proof that indigenous technologi-cal innovation could be a game-changer for Africa and other arid locations.

Imagine this PlayPump system in practice. Not for an hour media celebration, but all day, every day. What could possibly go wrong? Think of yourself or kids you know on a merry-go-round. After how long does pushing a merry-go-round in the heat shift from play to child labor? Is it play to push a PlayPump hour after hour, day after day, year after year? Suddenly, the story was not about happy kids pumping water through play; it was about aban-doned PlayPumps, broken systems, and angry locals. The *Guardian* revealed that in the average community, children would have to push the merry-go-round 27 hours per day to pump 2,500 liters.[27] *Frontline* aired a second story on PlayPump in 2010, reversing its praise.[28] Local women, who were not consulted prior to Play-Pump installations, complained that they were forced to push the merry-go-rounds when the children wouldn't, and traditional hand-pumps were much more effective and cheaper.[29] PlayPump is now the poster child for the idea of the tendency to oversell technology to address complex development problems. It was cool technology, or so we wanted to believe, but the PlayPump gave us the third great lesson.

Lesson 3: The fancier the technology and the cooler the idea, the greater we romanticize both and want to believe in the success. Simpler solutions are usually the best solutions.

Development planners are wise to remember Occam's razor and the law of parsimony. Just as the simplest explanation is often the best, the simplest solution is also usually superior. This presents an important paradox: the simplest solutions are often the best for development projects and locals, but the complicated high-technology solutions catch the eyes of alumni magazines, international financial organizations, celebrities, donors, and politicians.

The final crucial lesson from the PlayPumps experience is that of scaling up. PlayPumps worked in the first couple of installations; then the world assumed that the idea could scale up massively like Subway sandwich franchises with a couple of thousand installations right away. This is the great fallacy of the venture capital mentality of development: that there will be lots of start-up failures in global philanthropy, but it is worth it because eventually a project will succeed, and that single success can be scaled up massively. However, each installation of a project like PlayPumps faces an entirely new set of potential setbacks. Perhaps the first couple of installations were located near a high-quality and shallow aquifer. Perhaps there was unusually good local leadership. Perhaps the effect of a steady stream of dignitaries and celebrities coming and praising the first two towns resulted in extraordinary morale and play ethic among the kids. PlayPumps did not scale up, and we must be very wary of the assumption that lots of failures are okay because the isolated success will scale up and have a continental or global impact.

Lesson 4: Development projects do not scale up easily.[30]

One Laptop per Child (OLPC) is the third miraculous megaproject that was going to reshape the Global South. The idea was simple and very appealing to Global North philanthropists and officials: provide a rugged laptop computer costing $100 to every child, and education will dramatically improve. This idea was hatched in 2005 when laptop computers were far more expensive than they are today. It is the *Field of Dreams* model of philanthropy: If you build the computers and pass them out, education and development will come.

The computers were visually appealing, and the idea enthralled those in the halls of MIT, the United Nations, and the World Economic Forum. The project leaders were charismatic and compelling, and the cult of technology as the source of all solutions is widespread and powerful. OLPC raised hundreds of millions of dollars to further the cause and distributed hundreds of thousands of computers to children.

How did this project turn out? The best test case is Uruguay, a democratic country of 3 million inhabitants with high human capital that distributed 400,000 laptops to nearly all of the students. After nearly a decade, what were the results in Uruguay? A survey revealed that more than 27 percent of the laptops were abandoned due to malfunctions or a lack of technical support. Research showed that the laptops provided zero measurable improvements in reading and mathematics. The whole notion that the mere presence of technology would spontaneously produce for educational and developmental gains is the arrogance that accompanies the cult of technology.[31] When the project was first announced in 2005, African women leaders criticized the program as Western-centric, inefficient, the wrong technology for Africa, and an exploitation of government resources. The local leaders were ignored.

By 2009, international development practitioner Alanna Shaikh penned a touching eulogy for OLPC:

Americans wanted the OLPC. We fell in love with its tremendous promise and adorable shape. (Note: I own an OLPC.) We were the first market it conquered. OLPC launched a give one–get one promotion that let individuals pay $400 to donate one laptop and receive one for themselves. It was a huge success, except that OLPC wasn't set up for that kind of customer order fulfillment. Laptops arrived far later than promised, and several thousand orders were simply lost.

Once the laptop finally started arriving in the developing world, its impact was minimal. We think. No one is doing much research on their impact on education; discussions are largely theoretical. This we do know: OLPC didn't provide tech support for the machines, or training in how to incorporate them into education. Teachers didn't

Figure 3.1 Half a billion dollars

understand how to use the laptops in their lessons; some resented them. Kids like the laptops, but they don't actually seem to help them learn.

It's time to call a spade a spade. OLPC was a failure. . . .[32]

Throwing fancy technology at a problem is not a solution (figure 3.1).

The Small Projects

Most international philanthropy is on a much smaller scale than the three projects already described in this chapter. Perhaps big is not better, and greater success can be found in simpler local projects?

This section is uncomfortable for us because we know so many wonderful individuals who have participated in church mission trips and school-sponsored voluntourism, the Peace Corps, and more. Some of these activities are beneficial, but a great many are inefficient and patronizing to locals they are meant to help. We look at three types of small low-scale philanthropy: the discrete projects such as Engineers Without Borders (EWB) and the U.S. Peace

Corps, the voluntourism sector, and starting an international non-governmental organization (NGO) to bring a youth project to an impoverished community of the Global South.

DISCRETE PROJECTS There are many types of smaller international development projects, from EWB to the Peace Corps. The common denominator in these projects is the enthusiasm and can-do-spirit of young people from the Global North volunteering to give of themselves and install development projects in Global South communities. These volunteers are among the noblest and most enthusiastic people that we have met, and we praise their desires and intentions. Their activities generate valuable lessons.

The Peace Corps was founded as part of the U.S. response to the Cold War. Since its creation in 1961, more than 220,000 Peace Corps volunteers have served in 141 countries.[33] There are many supporters and detractors of the program. The supporters maintain that the program is an inexpensive form of soft power and diplomacy, whereby locals from Malawi to Fiji get to know Americans and their values. Detractors point to the neocolonial thrust, to episodes of violence and sexual assault against volunteers, and to many projects that were unsustainable in the end and that led to hurt feelings and disappointment in the communities.[34]

On balance, we believe that the Peace Corps is positive due to one critical benefit. Peace Corps volunteers spend a full two years and three months in a country, learning the language, absorbing the culture, and altering their perspective. Peace Corps alumni often love the people they serve, and many end up dedicating their lives to development. Many choose to stay and live in the countries or regions where they served. The Peace Corps builds much of the high-quality human capital working in global development and diplomacy.

Peace Corps volunteers do a number of things, including educating, teaching English, and supporting local organizations. We wish to address only one type of Peace Corps mission: that of establishing local development projects. This could be anything from a community garden in Mali, a tilapia farm in Fiji, a women's jewelry cooperative in India, and so on. Volunteers are encouraged to find their project and change the world! The idea is that eager and enthusiastic recent college graduates spend two years in a community where they develop, initiate, and nurture a local project. They also train locals to maintain the project after they leave. There is tremendous initial enthusiasm because the volunteers genuinely want to make a difference. An example of one such project is to organize local women to make jewelry and handicrafts and to sell the products locally to tourists or through the Internet and social media. As one might expect, these projects rarely meet the expectations of the locals or volunteers, and then the finger-pointing and the hurt feelings follow.

Systematic data on the percentage of projects that succeed or fail are hard to come by, but here are some important data from Fiji. The Peace Corps functioned in Fiji for thirty years, from 1968 to 1998, when it shut down its operations until reopening in 2003. A total of 2,496 volunteers served in this tropical paradise, working in the small villages that dot the emerald islands.[35] When the Peace Corps closed in 1998, the program hired one of the volunteers, Victor Bonito who taught high school biology, to survey and document what locals felt about the Peace Corps. The locals often had fond memories of the volunteers. However, Victor could not remember a single project that was still functioning after the volunteers who started the projects had departed.[36] These were all start-up enterprises, and start-ups often fail. As Bonito added in correspondence about his experience:

I spent several months in 1998, after completing two years as a Peace Corps teacher in Fiji, helping with a close-of-service report as Peace Corps was closing their Fiji program after 30 years of operation. My role was to help collect photos and stories about PCVs [Peace Corps volunteers] and the programs they were involved with over the years. Over the years, PCVs went from filling roles in the civil service (forestry, fisheries, teaching, health, etc.) to more being placed in communities and left to develop their own projects/initiatives. While the former can be helpful to some degree when appropriate personnel aren't available, the latter is much less helpful. It takes people a year to get settled and find something they want to do—it may or may not align with local goals—then the second year they try to implement some sort of project. In the third year, a new volunteer comes, and the process repeats. What people were left with was memories about the PCV (what they were like—strange/funny/nice things they did) and where they were from, not whatever project they came to do—and I don't recall seeing any projects that were still running."[37]

Lesson 5: Enthusiasm, youth, and noble intentions are not enough.

EWB organizes and installs water, transportation, sewage, and other engineering-intensive projects in poor communities. There has been some criticism about the failure rate of the projects that see engineering as the solution to every problem and the inability to foresee potential issues that can derail projects in the Global South. One innovative and admirable response from EWB is the Admitting Failure project.[38] The idea is that much can be learned from failure; if the organization can catalog the reasons for the failures, those can be avoided in future projects. We encourage you to spend a few minutes reading the heartfelt admissions of failures and the lessons discovered by these philanthropists: There was not enough funding, the equipment was too sophisticated and hard to repair, we had the wrong seeds, there were personality clashes, and so on. We praise EWB for this effort, and we admire EWB for bringing some real expertise to solving water and other problems.[39]

However, the idea that one can learn from failure includes the questionable assumption that there is an identifiable set of causes for each failure and that correcting for those causes will mean that the project will be successful in the next iteration. Engineers are incredible problem solvers and think this way: If a bridge collapses, find out why and fix it. In fact, EWB projects are more akin to start-up businesses and not bridge construction, and there are unknowable and different potential causes of failure in each attempt. Developmental start-ups are high-risk projects no matter how many times one tries to control for previous mistakes. This is a variant of the scale-up fallacy.

Lesson 6: No matter how many times you correct for the cause of past failures, the failure rate is still high in international start-up projects.

SHORT-TERM VOLUNTOURISM, SCHOOL GROUPS, AND MISSION TRIPS The short-term international volunteer sector is massive. A Google search of "Volunteer change world" results in nearly 9 million hits as companies and organizations vie for the billions of dollars being spent by the young and old alike who travel abroad to save the world. A 2010 survey found that 90 percent of Americans believe that it is important to be personally involved in projects that improve the world.[40] This attitude leads to what Robert Lupton refers to as the "compassion industry." Lupton is a Christian minister who led many a church mission trip until he decided that "vacationaries" were hurting more than helping.

Lupton's book, *Toxic Charity*, systematically exposes the flaws of one sector of voluntourism or vacationary philanthropists, the short-term international mission trips that make up a multibillion-dollar industry.[41] Tourism scholars put the total voluntourism sector at $173 billion.[42] We often speak with college students about short-term international voluntourism. It is all the rage on college and high school campuses across the country, though temporarily paused due to COVID-19. Students argue passionately that the experience was quality philanthropy, that they were improving the lives of poor people around the globe. Participants make two core arguments.

The first is that the thousands of dollars spent to visit orphanages in India or to paint a school in Mexico is cost-efficient. It was efficient first because the school would not be painted, and the orphans would not be played with and hugged without the group of voluntourists. This argument falls flat on two counts. First, there are very likely unemployed or underemployed painters in the village in Mexico that could paint the school for a small fraction of the cost of a group of young people flying to Mexico and touring for ten days. Lupton recounts the stories of an actual church in Mexico painted six times during one summer by six different mission groups and a church in Ecuador built by volunteers but never used because the community did not need it.[43] Imagine what the local community in Mexico could have accomplished with the money spent by six groups of voluntourists traveling internationally to paint that church.

International service work is often incredibly inefficient. Lupton notes that no businessperson would accept the investment return from missionary trips. "Otherwise they would see the obvious: if the money spent on travel, lodging, food, and staff time were directly invested in the people being served, far more could be accomplished with greater effectiveness."[44]

The second argument that voluntourists make is that the short-term experience of traveling to Honduras and interacting with locals makes a permanent change in the participants that will have a significant long-term benefit. Scholars at Trinity Evangelical Divinity School tested this assertion and discovered that these short-term experiences do not result in long-term change. Voluntourists revert to their original assumptions and behaviors within six to eight weeks after returning home from the trip.[45]

Voluntourism can also be a form of neocolonialism and undermine local development. Vacationaries create "a welfare economy that deprives people of the pride of their own accomplishments. . . ."[46] Group after group come to towns in Costa Rica, work on a service project for a few days, take selfies with poor brown kids for their Instagram or Tinder posts, visit the rainforest and the beach, and head home. This does not result in favorable impressions for the locals. As Lupton summarizes, "contrary to popular belief, most mission trips and service projects *do not*: empower those being served, engender healthy cross-cultural relationships, improve local quality of life, relieve poverty, change the lives of participants, increase support for long-term mission trips. Contrary to popular belief, most mission trips and service projects *do*: weaken those being served, foster dishonest relationships, erode recipients' work ethic, deepen dependency."[47]

The bottom line for the compassion industry is simple: Who is the major beneficiary of the billions of dollars being spent? Is it the poor community? Is it the vacationary who travels abroad? Or is it the compassion industry and the network of businesses and leaders that organize the trips and take their healthy cut of a multibillion-dollar industry?

Voluntourism shortcomings are not merely found in religious service trips. Mission trips are most often secular ventures with groups of high school or college students or individuals of all ages that really want to make a difference in the Global South. Pippa Biddle caused quite a stir with her 2014 blog "The Problem with Little White Girls, Boys and Voluntourism."[48] This inspiring piece not only reinforces some of the problems with huge segments of the voluntourism sector but also provides useful and concrete suggestions for improving the outcomes.

Biddle was typical of the millennial generation, generous with her time and talents and believing that she could change the world. She started her global voluntourism activity in high school, paying $3,000 to travel to Tanzania as part of a school trip and where she spent a week at an orphanage and half-built library, followed by a week on a safari. The group spent the week at the orphanage laying bricks as part of the construction. Can you imagine the quality of that bricklaying?

Biddle is extraordinarily observant and able to think deeply about what is best for the communities she serves and not what is best for her. With that perspective, she readily identifies the two major problems with the modern Philanthropist's Burden. The first is the ridiculously low efficiency and massive waste:

> Turns out that we, a group of highly educated, private boarding school students, were so bad at the most basic construction work that each night the men had to take down the structurally unsound bricks we had laid and rebuild the structure so that, when we woke up in the morning, we would be unaware of our failure. It is likely that this was a daily ritual. Us mixing cement and laying bricks 6+ hours a day, them undoing our work after the sun set, re-laying the bricks, and then acting as if nothing had happened so that the cycle could continue. Basically, we failed at the sole purpose of our being there. It would have been more cost effective, stimulative of the local economy, and efficient for the orphanage to take our money and hire

locals to do the work, but there we were trying to build straight walls without a level.

The second is the hierarchical and neocolonial nature of privileged people of the Global North delivering progress and projects to poor people of the Global South:

> I don't want a little girl in Ghana, or Sri Lanka, or Indonesia to think of me when she wakes up each morning. I don't want her to thank me for her education or medical care or new clothes. Even if I am providing funds to get the ball rolling, I want her to think about her teacher, her community leader, or mother. I want her to have a hero who she can relate to—who looks like her, is part of her culture, speaks her language, and who she might bump into on the way to school.

This part is crucial. When Americans or Europeans come into a village or poor neighborhood with their swagger, exceptionalism, money, and modern gadgets, they suck up all the oxygen and snuff out the important flames of local leaders and role models. Locals must be the superheroes and role models.

Biddle goes much further, helping to identify the roles that volunteers and philanthropists should take on and those that they should avoid:

> It turns out that I, a little white girl, am good at a lot of things. I am good at raising money, training volunteers, collecting items, coordinating programs, and telling stories. I am flexible, creative, and able to think on my feet. On paper I am, by most people's standards, highly qualified to do international aid. But I shouldn't be. I am not a teacher, a doctor, a carpenter, a scientist, an engineer, or any other professional that could provide concrete support and long-term solutions to communities in developing countries.

In the end, there are lots of opportunities for voluntourists and many programs are excellent. Before you participate as a voluntourist, you should carefully consider the organization and activities.

The most important question is, Is the entire voluntourism activity a false façade? The oversupply of voluntourists produces fake projects. There are so many westerners volunteering to hug orphans in India, southern Africa, or Cambodia that local entrepreneurs buy or rent children as fake orphans.[49]

Voluntourists need to think very seriously about their real motivations for doing this work. Do they want the best for themselves with travel and social media and feeling like they are saving the world or do they want the best for the local communities? Do they have specific essential skills for the project that cannot be replicated by locals? Health teams traveling to Mongolia or Appalachia providing dental work, cataract surgeries, and so on, are some of the many examples of exceptional, efficient, and laudable voluntourism that changes lives. Locals should be painting schools.

What if you are not an eye surgeon or a dentist? Should you voluntour? Many roles for voluntourists are appropriate. For example, support the local English teacher, a critical skill all over the world. Raise money for an exceptional organization. Help build a webpage. Volunteer as a sidekick and not as a superhero. Always elevate the local leaders, teachers, and parents, and be humble about what you can do. Never take photos of children without the permission of their parents, and please don't use a picture of yourself with a child in need for your social media or your dating app.

WHAT ABOUT THE PROGRAM WITH UNIVERSAL PRAISE: MICROCREDIT FOR WOMEN

One international philanthropic program seems to have universal appeal: microcredit for women. Modern microcredit gained global attention in Bangladesh with pioneering work by Muhammad Yunus and his Grameen Bank. Yunus was awarded the Nobel Peace Prize in 2002. We were fortunate to listen to Yunus speak a few years ago at Emory University. He was passionate, charismatic, and compelling. Yunus's idea is to give small, short-term loans to women and include societal pressures for repayment of the loans.

The women would use the money to become entrepreneurs, freeing them of the control of their husbands, building female camaraderie, and reducing poverty. The growth of microcredit in Bangladesh was dramatic, and with a spokesperson like Yunus, the idea spread rapidly across the Global South. Policymakers and funders viewed microcredit for women as the latest panacea for poverty eradication. Microcredit empowered local women. It enhanced entrepreneurship. It was sustainable because the repaid loans were recycled to other women. At its peak in 2007, there were 3,522 microcredit institutions reaching 154,825,825 clients. Of the poorest borrowers, 83.4 percent were women.[50]

Silicon Valley executives heard Yunus speak in 2003 and founded Kiva, a microcredit organization that has provided a million microloans and a billion dollars in a total of eighty countries. You can go to Kiva.org and make a loan to the pool of borrowers, although not to individuals. It all sounds so appealing. A number of books extolled the virtues of microfinance, with titles such as *The Miracles of Barefoot Capitalism: A Compelling Case for Microfinance*; *A Billion Bootstraps: Microcredit, Barefoot Banking, and the Business Solution for Ending Poverty*; and *Saris on Scooters: How Microcredit Is Changing Village India*.

By 2010, scholars and practitioners began to think more carefully about microcredit and to examine outcomes systematically. Lamia Karim published *Microfinance and Its Discontents: Women in Debt in Bangladesh* in 2011, offering a sobering account of societal pressures, suicide, and a cycle of debt for women in that country. A number of critical articles and books followed, including *The Rise and Fall of Global Microcredit: Development, Debt and Disillusion* in 2018. Esther Duflo and her colleagues at MIT conducted the first controlled experiment on microcredit in Hyderabad, India, concluding that "microcredit had mixed effects on business activities and little to no effect on women's empowerment or children's education."[51]

While people give loans to Kiva interest free, this does not mean that the women in Guatemala or the other seventy-nine countries are not paying high interest rates. The local administrators for Kiva in Guatemala and other countries are charging rates that many consider exorbitant. According to its website, Kiva quotes interest rates as the "self-reported average rate charged by the Field Partner to the entrepreneur." Of the 1,530,180 Kiva loans as of November 2018, more than half charged an interest rate above 30 percent, while over 51,000 loans charged in excess of 60 percent annual interest.[52]

One of the most persuasive critiques comes from Hugh Sinclair in his 2012 *Confessions of a Microfinance Heretic: How Microlending Lost Its Way and Betrayed the Poor*. Sinclair worked for a decade in all aspects of microcredit and in Africa, Asia, and Latin America. He ultimately concluded that, due to high interest rates, socially aggressive collection techniques that bring shame and dishonor, and negligence on the part of the local banking partners, microcredit resulted in greater harm than good. In their 2011 feminist review of the literature, Nalini Visvanathan and Karla Yoder conclude, "Program designs, particularly Grameen-based, use group members as social collateral and exert undue pressure on borrowers to make payments on time. These pressures result in women borrowing from moneylenders so they do not fall behind and get penalized. The recourse to new loans to repay old ones on time creates a spiral of indebtedness for women to survive and improve their lot."[53]

If someone in New York City lends money with interest rates of up to 200 percent per annum[54] and with extreme social pressure and public shaming to repay the loan, we would accuse them of being a loan shark. If a company near a military base puts soldiers in a cycle of debt with high-interest, short-term payday loans, we call for regulation. And yet the appeal of high-interest, short-term credit to women in poverty that often leads to cycles of debt, public shaming, depression, and high suicide rates continues unabated, even after all the mounting research showing the limited benefits, at best, of microcredit.

Jason Hickel summarizes the cultural affinity that we have for microcredit and our enduring faith in this market-based solution to poverty.

I'm always amazed at how many students show up each year in the classrooms of the London School of Economics, where I teach, quivering with excitement about microfinance and other "bottom-of-the-pyramid" development strategies. Like eager young missionaries, they feel they've stumbled upon the One Idea that is sure to save the world.

Would that it were true. What's so fascinating about the microfinance craze is that it persists in the face of one unfortunate fact: microfinance doesn't work. Of course, there are some lovely anecdotes out there about the transformative power of micro-loans, but as David Roodman from the Center for Global Development put in his recent book, "the best estimate of the average impact of microcredit on the poverty of clients is zero." This is not a fringe opinion. A comprehensive DFID-funded review of the extant data comes to the same conclusion: the microfinance craze has been built on "foundations of sand" because "no clear evidence yet exists that microfinance programs have positive impacts."

In fact, it turns out that microfinance usually ends up making poverty worse. The reasons are fairly simple. Most microfinance loans are used to fund consumption—to help people buy the basic necessities they need to survive. In South Africa, for example, consumption accounts for 94 percent of the microfinance use. As a result, borrowers don't generate any new income that they can use to repay their loans so they end up taking out new loans to repay the old ones, wrapping themselves in layers of debt."[55]

Some claims about microfinance doing more harm than good go too far. We do agree, however, that we are predisposed to embrace any practice that spreads the gospel of entrepreneurship and capitalism. Due to the basis of empowerment for women, we find microfinance particularly appealing and wish it were a great success. Sadly, the evidence is at best mixed that the $80 billion microcredit experiment empowers women and alleviates poverty.[56] Hoping for a development panacea to succeed does not make it so.

Development practitioner Joseph Hanlon and his colleagues take a very different approach to providing cash, arguing that the benefits from just giving money to the poor are far superior to microlending and other assistance programs with extensive bureaucracies and hoops to jump through.[57] Millions of people have been lifted out of poverty in the Global South through government conditional cash transfer programs, where mothers receive money each month in exchange for their children attending school and getting their vaccinations.[58]

The conviction that poor people would spend unconditional cash transfers wisely and that simply giving cash greatly reduces the program costs and social stresses of microlending led Paul Niehaus to found GiveDirectly in 2009. In the past decade, GiveDirectly provided $160 million in cash to 170,000 families living in poverty. Just giving people money without forcing them to pay it back rubs many Americans the wrong way. We hold stereotypes of poor people that they will waste the money on temptation goods like alcohol and tobacco. In fact, the poor do not systematically waste cash, and the positive impacts are long term.[59]

PERHAPS YOU WANT TO START YOUR OWN INTERNATIONAL PROJECT?

Everywhere we travel, we encounter self-sacrificing individuals and families who felt inspired to start a development project as an act of international philanthropy. A large number of these projects resulted from a trip or experience in a foreign country, caring deeply for the local youth, and wanting to provide a transformative experience to those young people. Families and individuals think about those activities in Oregon or South Carolina that positively changed their children, friends, or themselves and want to replicate that in Vietnam or Bolivia.

This desire is incredibly noble but misguided. Let us take one example. A family once told us about a trip to Cambodia, which is a beautiful country with an energetic population, a tragic past (think of the Khmer Rouge and the Killing Fields), and a growth in tourism. It is easy to be enchanted and to want to be part of the ongoing recovery. The members of this family told us that they were so touched that they wanted to set up a soccer program for girls. This effort is a lovely sentiment. It is also imprudent.

In the first place, the likelihood of this project underperforming, failing, or becoming a zombie project (barely alive) is very high, as is the case with many start-ups. More important, there is very likely an existing sports program for development on the ground already, one that is led by locals. Wouldn't it be more efficient and much less neocolonial to partner with the existing local organization that is using sports or art or dance for girls in Cambodia?

When we ask this question of people involved in U.S.- or European-based projects, the answers we receive follow similar patterns: (1) We did not look for or identify any existing successful organizations already on the ground (that can always benefit from additional support). (2) We can't trust those locals with our money. (3) We like the personal benefit of having our organization and our webpage and our credit/praise.

If you look, you will find numerous local organizations and individuals all over the world with long track records of success in helping local youth. It shows the worst of the White Man's Burden to assume that they are corrupt, dishonest, and untrustworthy because they are from the Global South.

Lesson 7: You are not superior in character because you are from the Global North. There are large numbers of locally led organizations doing exceptional work all over the world. Join forces with them if you want to make a real difference in youth programs.

We applaud and respect people who genuinely want to play a part in making this world a better place. There are inspirational examples of success in many of these practices, but international philanthropy must be far more cost efficient and locally empowering.

We have participated in these efforts, and made some of the same errors and encountered the same pitfalls and failures as others. This exploration leads to some valuable lessons. Following these lessons can be difficult because the incentives from alumni magazines, career ladders, social media, and peer pressure are powerful. Nevertheless, if you want to have the most significant impact, the following seven lessons, repeated from the chapter, are worth remembering:

Lesson 1: Even with the brightest people in the world, the most meticulous plans, and hundreds of millions of dollars, start-up development projects in the Global South almost always fail to reach their original stated objectives. Poor countries are not laboratories and are messy and chaotic, and all start-ups face a host of unexpected and unknown challenges and disasters.

Lesson 2: It is unhealthy when leaders from the Global North are seen as the superheroes and "Great Professors," and the locals serve as junior partners and sidekicks. Locals take the blame for all that goes wrong and get little of the credit when things go well.

Lesson 3: The fancier the technology and the cooler the idea, the greater we romanticize both and want to believe in the success. Simpler solutions are usually the best solutions.

Lesson 4: Development projects do not scale up easily.

Lesson 5: Enthusiasm, youth, and noble intentions are not enough.

Lesson 6: No matter how many times you correct for the cause of past failures, the failure rate is still high in international start-up projects.

Lesson 7: You are not superior in character because you are from the Global North. There are large numbers of locally led organizations doing exceptional work all over the world. Join forces with them if you want to make a real difference in local development programs.

These seven lessons guide the design of the community bank model of philanthropy. We present the model in detail in the following chapter.

4

THE COMMUNITY BANK MODEL
OF INTERNATIONAL PHILANTHROPY

Nine out of ten start-ups will fail. This is a hard and bleak
truth, but one that you'd do well to meditate on. Entrepreneurs
may even want to write their failure post-mortem before they
launch their business.

—NEIL PATEL

The inspiration for this book came from our failure with
international philanthropic start-up projects. While the lessons that we learned have an application to many forms of global
giving—including voluntourism, microcredit, and megaprojects—
the original stimulus was the realization that traveling around the
globe to start an initiative from scratch to lift up the locals is both
a wonderful sentiment and a terrible idea.

Imagine that you study abroad in Rwanda or travel with your
fraternity to surf in Colombia. You explore Vietnam with your
family or visit a refugee camp in Jordan with a student organization. You fall in love with the generosity of the people, the smiles
of the children, the spirit in the music, and the sharing of food.
You also witness the poverty, the depth of the unemployment,
the real challenges for children to escape cycles of poverty and
violence. You want to make a permanent positive impact. You are
privileged and grateful, with an excellent education, resources to
travel, connections, and optimism. What do you do? What can
you do?

With the unprecedented growth in international travel, study
abroad, traveling church groups, international business, gov-
ernment-sponsored interchange, and the transporting power of
the Internet, more and more people are asking themselves these

questions. While COVID-19 interrupted this trend, it will likely return and grow in the future. It is the most beautiful expression of human nature. We yearn for an opportunity to create something to change a deprived community. We want to make a difference. It may be agricultural like a community garden, entrepreneurial like a social enterprise selling local products online, or educational like tackling literacy or a college entrance exam preparation program. Programs for youth, such as a boxing program to keep students away from drugs, arts-oriented programs teaching filmmaking or painting, a rigorous music program, soccer academies, and many more, are particularly appealing and prevalent.

Individuals often remember programs in their own community that enriched their lives or those of their children. There is widespread acknowledgment that intensive youth participation in demanding, high-level performance activities such as dance, sports, chess, arts, and music can dramatically alter the habits and trajectories of children and adolescents, and people want to share those same benefits with young people in the Global South.[1] People feel a calling; they are fortunate and want to share. Many of us genuinely want to make this world a better place.

Imagine that you traveled with that fraternity to surf on the Pacific coast of Colombia. The coast is one of the poorest and most troubled regions of that beautiful, promising, yet violence-prone country. Surfing changed your life in Southern California, and you are sure that an effective surfing project could make a difference for underprivileged Colombian kids. You have a community that you have fallen in love with and an emotional connection to the people there. You believe in the power of surfing activities to transform young people. You are going to use high-level performance to help those Colombian children stay off the streets, avoid illicit activities, thrive in school, gain confidence, get in shape, and all of those positive benefits that the sport brought to your life. Close your eyes and think; how would you do that? Connect the dots between the initial eureka moment to bring a surfing program in Colombia to the actual functioning program. What steps would you take? How could you best help those youth?

The decision to help a community in the Global South with your favorite youth activity often results in an international philanthropic start-up (IPS); the process likely includes the registration of a nongovernmental organization (NGO) and securing tax-free status, raising money, building a webpage, purchasing equipment, securing local employees or volunteers, acquiring permits, and spending some months on the ground. Nothing could be nobler, and nothing could be more misguided. Why?

THE ALLURE AND WEAKNESS OF IPSS

The IPS is a large segment of the global compassion industry. Individuals, families, clubs, college professors, foundations, corporations, Peace Corps volunteers, international organizations, churches, and NGOs initiate IPSs with increasing frequency around the globe. Some of them succeed in delivering long-term benefits to the locals.

Everyone who starts a new enterprise, whether philanthropic or profit motivated, expects to succeed, and they want it to be theirs. The founders maintain control over the organization and get to shape it. They may experience the unbridled joy of watching young people thrive in their program. They also can get a lot of accolades, praise, and awards.

Unfortunately, IPSs deliver too little average return for the investment and often undermine local leadership. If you really want to help children in coastal Colombia, then you should maximize the expected impact of your investment in time and money (figure 4.1).

Philanthropic resources are scarce and must be maximized. Overall impact contains four elements. The first is the cost effectiveness. In our example, it would be the percentage of funds that goes to deliver the surfing project to children on the Colombian Pacific coast. The most common factors that reduce resource effectiveness are fundraising costs, overhead, and salaries—sometimes bloated—to directors. Even if these costs are low, many other components can significantly reduce the percentage of total resources

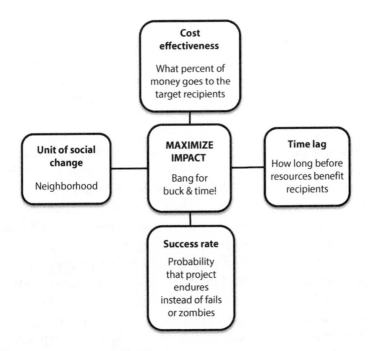

Figure 4.1 Impact: cost effectiveness, or return on expended resources

that reach the target recipients. If the project is a start-up, just preparatory work for the program has many costs. In many countries of the Global South, licensing, legal fees, and other bureaucratic hurdles are nearly impossible to navigate and excessively expensive.[2] There may be considerable barriers and unexpected expenses to import surfboards, to lease or build a secure space to store the surfboards, and to get permission to train minors in a sport with nontrivial risks. Wiring money to your NGO in a foreign country often involves unexpected taxes and losses due to exchange rates. One's enthusiasm for a project in the Global South often crashes before the actual activities even begin.

Any IPS involves many start-up costs that occur long before a single child hangs ten on her or his first wave, if ever. If you donate $100 to a friend at the idea stage of an NGO to help children learn to surf in Colombia, how much of that money is having a direct impact on the children in that Colombian community? What is the bang for your buck?

Second, one must consider the realistic likelihood that the program will sustainably deliver the envisioned services because *start-ups have a high failure rate*, even in the best of circumstances. Many never get off the ground. We have considerable observational experience and anecdotal evidence of the high failure rate of international development projects, but rigorous datasets on the failure rates of IPSs do not exist.[3] Fortunately, there are excellent data on start-up failure rates in comparable industries in the United States. We assume—and can find no logical reason to think otherwise—that a philanthropic start-up in a community in the Global South with a different language, culture, legal system, bureaucracy, and infrastructure will have at least as high a failure rate as a business start-up in the United States.

Imagine that you are considering investing in a new restaurant start-up in the United States. The restaurant owner offers you a return on investment of 12 percent preferential interest per year for ten years and then your money back. Is this a profitable investment? Unfortunately, you must also include in your calculations the risk of the restaurant never opening or going bust after one or more years and losing all or most of your money. The most comprehensive examination of restaurant start-ups finds that 60 percent fail within the first three years.[4] Does the risk-adjusted return of 12 percent in a new restaurant based on the above failure rate compensate you for that risk?[5]

Perhaps restaurant failure rates are higher than rates in other sectors. In fact, despite the common myths, restaurant failure rates are not higher than many other industries. High-growth technology start-ups have a 90 percent failure rate, and software start-ups fail between 75 and 90 percent of the time.[6] Whenever you fund a start-up, whether a restaurant or a software start-up or a social project in the Global South, you need to include the failure rate in any calculation of the expected return on your expended resources.

What about the most glorified sector and one that inspires many entrepreneurs, that of high-promise Silicon Valley start-ups? High-promise Silicon Valley start-ups have at least $1 million in investment and operate in an area with the brightest people, the best networking, the highest concentration of successful companies to serve as examples, and top-quality mentorship programs. Harvard Business School professor Shikhar Ghosh conducted a survey of 2,000 high-promise start-ups between 2004 and 2010, those with at least $1 million in investment and in the Silicon Valley. Of those 2,000 high-promise start-ups, only 5 to 10 percent met their projections, and only 25 percent returned at least the initial investment but with no additional return.[7] As Ghosh notes, "In Silicon Valley, the fact that your enterprise has failed is actually a badge of honor."[8]

If the failure rate by experts in start-ups in high-promise environments and $1 million in funding is in the range of 75 to 95 percent, we can expect an even higher failure rate of start-up NGOs in the Global South founded by idealists from the Global North with limited start-up experience; incomplete knowledge of the local customs, language, legal framework, and business culture; and an inability to access the elite local networks often based on long-term kinship networks or reciprocal favors.

The reality is far worse. Start-up failure rates do not account for the time and money spent on the ideas and projects that never make it to the launch. Of every 3,000 commercial ideas, 125 will become projects that consume significant resources. Of those 125 projects, only two will formally launch, and just one will become a commercial success.[9] The chances of long-term success with the IPS surfing project in Colombia are unacceptably low (figure 4.2).[10]

Even if there are low fundraising and administrative costs in a philanthropic venture, imagine what happens if the project never gets off the ground, closes down quickly, or exists in a zombie state (a zombie organization is one that is still registered and maintains its NGO status but does not function in any meaningful way) and never results in the long-term surfing lessons to underprivileged

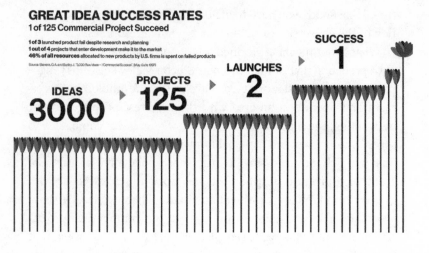

GREAT IDEA SUCCESS RATES
1 of 125 Commercial Project Succeed

1 of 3 launched product fail despite research and planning
1 out of 4 projects that enter development make it to the market
46% of all resources allocated to new products by U.S. firms is spent on failed products

Source: Stevens, G.A. and Burley, J. "3,000 Raw Ideas = 1 Commercial Success", (May-June 1997)

IDEAS
3000 ▶ PROJECTS 125 ▶ LAUNCHES 2 ▶ SUCCESS 1

Figure 4.2 Great idea success rates

children. The payoff for these expended resources is zero! Imagine the discouragement of the participants—who are excited by the program and committed to the hard work—if the program never delivers or ceases to function after a few months or a year.

Third, the time lag must also be included in your calculations of value or impact, particularly for programs in Africa and Latin America.[11] Starting an NGO is quite easy in the United States and parts of Europe. Sometimes all it takes is a few hours to fill out the forms. Registering a corporation in most U.S. states can be done online in a matter of minutes. Things are far different in the Global South, even in relatively advanced countries like Brazil.

How hard is it to open a start-up in Brazil? French chef Pierre Cornet-Vernet wanted to open a small store to sell confectioneries in the Rio de Janeiro neighborhood of Copacabana. Working full-time and employing an attorney, a forwarding agent and an accounting specialist, this process took eleven months. "It's like a game," Cornet-Vernet notes. "You need a document. However, to have that document, you need to hand in another seven documents. And to get each of these seven there's a different demand."[12]

In Brazil, it takes thirteen separate procedures and 169 days to open a business or philanthropic start-up.[13] It is not the worst case in the Global South. According to the World Bank's "Doing Business 2018," much of the Global South is mired in red tape, with multiple hurdles to open any business (or NGO) and often requiring favors from bureaucrats and politicians that result in incentives for corruption and bribery. If you need to construct a small building to store your surfboards in Colombia, obtaining the building permit takes at least 132 days. That is quicker than the 434 days in Venezuela and Brazil and the 347 days in Argentina. If some corporation donates surfboards and ships them to Colombia, they may remain stuck in customs for months or years. In the best of circumstances, your surfing start-up in Colombia won't be getting children on the surfboards for a long time.

Now that we have discussed the importance of cost-effectiveness, sustainability, and the time it takes to start an organization, let alone operate it, the final element is to target the optimal unit of social change. Research indicates that targeting neighborhoods as the unit of social change radically alters one's perception of how transformations take place and endure.[14] As David Brooks notes in a review of the literature:

> You've probably heard the starfish story. There's a boy on the beach who finds thousands of starfish washed ashore, dying. He picks one up and throws it back into the ocean. A passer-by asks him what's the point of that. All these thousands of other starfish are still going to die. "Well," the boy responds, "I saved that one."
>
> Many of our social programs are based on that theory of social change. We try to save people one at a time. We pick a promising kid in a neighborhood and give her a scholarship. Social programs and philanthropic efforts cream skim in a thousand ways. Or they mentor one at a time, assuming that the individual is the most important unit of social change.
>
> Obviously, it's possible to do good that way. But you're not really changing the structures and systems that shape lives. . . .

Thinking in neighborhood terms means radical transformation in how change is done. It means escaping the tyranny of randomized controlled experiments in which one donor funds one program that tries to isolate one leverage point to have "impact."[15]

Our experience confirms the centrality of the neighborhood. In this sense, we believe that William MacAskill and others miss the point by asserting that impact is calculated by "how many people benefit, and by how much."[16] Imagine that a particular project benefits 300 young people spread over 300 cities. Imagine another project with the same total cost that benefits 200 children in a single neighborhood. Which would have a higher expected, long-term impact? Real sustained transformation comes one neighborhood at a time.

IPSs have a woefully low expected impact due to the failure rate of start-ups everywhere, the enhanced difficulty of start-ups in the Global South, and the long lag time between eureka idea and full operation. Yet people remain enthusiastic about starting new projects that will save the world. We'll examine why this is so in the next section.

FAILURE DOESN'T MATTER; THE EVENTUAL SUCCESS IS WORTH IT

In the world of venture capital for start-ups, 75 to 95 percent failure rates are accepted and even celebrated. Failure is a badge of honor. The next venture might be a billion-dollar unicorn or a trillion-dollar Amazon or Apple. An eventual success may scale up to transform an industry.

This embrace of start-up failure and venture capital thinking is dominant in the United States and is pervasive in the global philanthropy world. People with this mindset say that they don't mind if a venture in a village is quickly abandoned or becomes a zombie project. The principals will learn from their errors and succeed next time, and that rare successful project may scale up to alter the whole world dramatically. A few donors lose their money, but there is no real harm.

This "failure-doesn't-matter" attitude is erroneous for IPS for three essential reasons:

1. The myth of the occasional colossal start-up success that scales up. Silicon Valley regularly produces venture capital success stories that make investors very rich and that transform markets and our lives. Many billion-dollar companies began as start-ups in high-tech cities and some even became trillion-dollar companies. These stunning successes compensate investors for a string of failures. There are no analogs to Amazon and Apple in IPSs, and shrugging off failed projects because a colossal success is somewhere just over the horizon is merely wishful thinking. Some may counter that a successful project in one location can be replicated again and again in other sites, like a franchise. This is erroneous thinking, too. Franchises bring with them many of the dynamics of a start-up, and the failure rates can be extremely high. In the restaurant industry, stand-alone start-up restaurants have a three-year failure rate of 60 percent, while franchises have a three-year failure rate of 57 percent.[17] We learned from the PlayPump experience that development projects do not easily scale up.

2. Failed IPS are very costly and painful. While failed start-ups in Silicon Valley are badges of honor with limited collateral damage other than to the investors,[18] failed or deserted development projects in the Global South leave behind hurt feelings, demoralized local leaders, development fatigue, the physical carcasses of abandoned infrastructure, fractured communities, abandoned young people, and a cloud of personal and communal failure (figure 4.3). We should not seek to fail forward.

3. Marginalized communities need help now. Most important, there are young people on Colombia's Pacific coast that you care about and want to help. Your big idea will most likely fail, and you will not help the people you most want to help.

Figure 4.3 The carcasses of failed IPS

A COMMUNITY BANK STRATEGY CAN RAMP
UP SUSTAINABLE SUCCESS

Let us return to the Colombian coastal community with good waves and underprivileged youth. The Philanthropist's Burden response is to think that this community needs outside help, outside leadership, outside big ideas, a start-up project, and a Global North work ethic.

Is there a better way to maximize impact and cost-efficiency for the youth of that community? What if you walked through that coastal community with a completely different mindset and a very different perspective? In other words, it is not about you and your big idea. It is not about your leadership or your project. It is about helping the children cost efficiently, sustainably, and quickly.

Instead of examining the situation with a start-up mentality, try thinking like a community banker. The scene is the same: good waves, low high school graduation rates, high crime levels, and lots of young people hanging out on the streets. The surf-loving community banker's first thought is: are there any local organizations with high-character local leaders and existing high-quality surfing programs for youth in this community or a nearby town that I can help expand? From the remote beaches of Bureh, Sierra Leone, to the gang-infested neighborhoods of Alto, Peru, to the isolated coastline of Termales, Colombia, surfing NGOs with considerable local initiative and leadership already exist, and many have a long track record of success. You can ramp up the impact and the cost-effectiveness dramatically with something immediate and with a high likelihood of success by using your limited resources to expand an existing and ongoing local project. As an added bonus, you will be elevating and empowering local role models.

COMMUNITY BANKS AS SIDEKICKS

Start-ups and venture capital are sexy and grab headlines. Many of us can recite celebrity names from the start-up world and venture capital arena because the returns can be so spectacular. Can you think of a celebrity community banker?

There are over 5,000 community banks in the United States. The bankers in these banks are largely hidden and embrace their anonymity. Their business is not sexy. They don't have famous social media footprints and won't be interviewed regularly for the *Wall Street Journal*. Yet their business model is enlightening when it comes to international philanthropy, ramping up the impact, functioning as sidekicks, celebrating the locals, and reducing the lag times for delivering services to those in need. How is all of this done?

Let us first briefly describe how these banks work. Community banks safeguard customer deposits. The banks lend the funds in those deposits at a higher rate than what they pay on their deposits, and the gap between the cost of funds and the interest earned from the loans results in the bank's gross margins. The lower the cost of funds, the better; checking accounts pay no interest, so the cost of those funds is zero. Deposits on a bank's balance sheet show up as a liability but are converted into an asset by lending the money to customers. Think of George Bailey in the classic movie *It's a Wonderful Life*.[19] The money is not in the bank. Miss Davis deposits the money in Bailey's Building and Loan Bank, and then that deposit is converted to an asset by lending it to the Martini family to buy a new house. Deposits come from the community and are then reinvested in the community through loans. Margins are extremely slim in community banking. The typical net interest margin[20] is around 3 percent, and a good return on assets for a community bank is approximately 1 percent. This leaves little room for error or defaults. Assuming you make 100 loans at the same dollar amount, a single bad loan wipes out the profits from the other ninety-nine loans. Community bankers should not take high risks, and with a low cost of funds, they do not need to.

To ensure low default rates and profits, community bankers eschew new business ventures and provide loans to entities with a long track record of success, good leadership, and strong relation-ships and reputation in the community. While start-ups have failure rates between 60 and 95 percent, community bank loans are almost always repaid, with default or failure rates of 0.4 to 3 percent. Even in the worst of times, for example, during the Great Recession of 2008, the net charge-offs were 2.72 percent, meaning that over 97.28 percent of customers were still expected to perform on their loans. In the economically healthy third quarter of 2017, community bank charge-offs were 34 basis points (0.34 of 1 percent), meaning that 99.66 percent of loans were still considered collectible.[21]

The relationship between risk and reward is one that all bankers know and understand. The more risk, the greater the reward. The higher the rate of return, the greater the inherent risk. Commu-nity banks invest depositors' funds and cannot afford to take a loss. Depositors want their deposits and excess liquidity protected from loss. Businesses take risks by developing new products, investing in equipment, buying real estate, expanding into new markets, and growing their accounts receivable and inventory by adding cus-tomers or new markets. The idea of risking their excess cash at a bank in a checking account with no real return is foolish. Hence, they just want to protect their liquidity in a safe place, like a strong community bank, so they can use that money later for their busi-ness and a better return.

On the other hand, venture capitalists invest in start-ups and can expect a much higher return on their investments and assets to offset the greater risk of loss. Equity is the most expensive form of capital and has the highest percentage of loss, whereas bank debt is the cheapest form of capital and has the lowest percentage of loss.

How do community bankers lend money and achieve such positive results? The goal is the same: deploying funds as efficiently and effectively as possible and trying to get the best risk-adjusted return. International philanthropy with scarce resources should also avoid high risks, and philanthropy can learn some key strategies on how to do this from community bankers.

When reviewing a credit request, the community bank lender wants to determine the likelihood of repayment based predominantly on historical performance. Trends are important, and if someone has demonstrated historical cash flow for several years to cover debt and interest payments, the chances are good that it will continue. Most community banks will not lend money to businesses without at least a three-year track record because start-up lending is too risky for community banks (up to 90 percent of start-up businesses fail). A multitude of unforeseen events can happen during the first three years of the life of a company. The more years of historical performance that can be analyzed and then extrapolated into projections, the more predictable financial trends such as cash flow and ability to repay will be in the future. This does not mean that there are no failures in established successful businesses. A company that has been in business for twenty years with no losses can suddenly experience a change in its market or cost structure due to outside forces. This is the reason banks typically renew lines of credit every year so they can monitor and consider these unforeseen changes.

THE FIVE Cs OF CREDIT AND IDENTIFYING SUPERHEROES

The banking world uses the five Cs of credit for considering loans: character, capacity, capital, conditions, and collateral.[22] Correct application of the first four Cs is useful for identifying superhero partners in the Global South, reducing international philanthropic losses, and maximizing impact. We eliminate the fifth C, collateral, from our discussion because it is typically used to determine a secondary source of repayment and is a way to minimize a bank's loss in the event of a default. Because our model is for donating funds and our return is based on the impact of improving lives, we determined that collateral is not useful for our model.

Character is defined as the mental and moral qualities distinctive to an individual. Knowing how people react to adverse or challenging circumstances is paramount to underwriting a loan. Do they keep their word? Have they failed to pay their debt before? How do they react in challenging situations? Do their peers find them honest? What is their track record? What is their reputation among their business partners over a long period?

People with good intentions make promises, but people with good character keep them. A person that keeps their word looks you in the eye and says they will pay you back. And they do: Even if it is difficult.[23]

One of the main reasons the U.S. community banking system works and can compete with the big-money center banks is that huge banks are not structured to assess and make decisions based on character. All the credit decision-making is centralized and taken out of the hands of local bankers who know their customers. Personal relationships are the best way to understand someone's character; community bankers have local decision-making authority and know their customers, their standing and reputation in the community, and their lifelong commitment to honoring their word and paying back loans. If the business does get into trouble and the borrower has a good relationship with the community lender, the loan will often be worked out and the bank will be paid back to preserve the relationship and the business's standing in the community. It is much more difficult to renege on a commitment to a person you know well than to renege on a loan to a big institution. Community banks in the United States are unique in the world because many countries have a limited number of large banks and few, if any, smaller community banks. Access to credit is very difficult in those countries because character is omitted from the underwriting, and it is merely formulaic. The advantage of community bankers is that they live in the town, know the borrower's family and friends, and can make good judgments about character. Big-money center investment banks already have a huge market share and make a significant percentage of their revenue in fees by selling products and services and are not always motivated to grow loans. Community banks, on the other hand, earn very little in fees and instead make most of their revenue in interest earned from lending the money in their community. The big banks have more products and services and a lower cost of funds, yet community banks still thrive and grow because they can make loans based on the character of the borrowers.

Capacity refers to the ability of the borrower to repay the loan. Lenders often look at the length of time that a business has been in operation and its history of repaying previous loans to measure capacity. The more consistent the historical positive cash flow—income after all expenses in a business—the more predictable the capacity of a business to support and make payments on its loans. Less consistency means lower reliability. Capacity in lending assesses the company's ability to support the debt service. Capacity is impossible to access in a new venture with no historical data, experience, or cash flow.

Capital: If the borrower has significant skin in the game, or a substantial personal investment in the business, the chance of default decreases. That is why individuals with a large down payment have an easier time securing a mortgage and can pay a lower interest rate. Being completely committed, both emotionally and financially, makes it more problematic to walk away if things get difficult. Capital also gives the banker an idea about how fast the business can grow. Companies often leverage the business's balance sheet through debt by borrowing more money than they have in equity, and the more leverage, the greater the risk. Too much growth can be a huge risk in a business if the debt is significantly greater than the capital. The greater the leverage, total debt to equity, of a business, the less the margin for error.

Conditions: It is always important to know the intended uses of the funds and how the funds will be paid back. For example, are the funds going to finance short-term assets, like working capital, or long-term assets such as equipment?[24] If the borrower fails to meet the conditions of the loan, subsequent disbursements or loans are threatened.

COMMUNITY BANK MODEL OF PHILANTHROPY:
BE A SIDEKICK

Adapting the lessons from community banking to international philanthropy is simple and follows a few basic steps:

1. *No start-ups*. This is fundamental and non-negotiable.
2. Identify existing *locally led* philanthropic organizations with a long track record of success.
3. Take stock of the *character* of the local leaders. Identify high-character leaders from the referrals of high-character contacts. Spend time with the organization and listen to its members describe the history of the organization, the benefits to recipients, the steps they took to overcome challenges in the past, the reasons for starting the organization, and so on. Communicate with other NGO leaders in that community, journalists, bloggers, U.S. consulate officials, alumni of the program, and neighbors of the organization to learn their opinions of the character of the organization leaders.
4. Determine the *capacity* of the organization to maximize the impact of new funds. Can the existing infrastructure employ additional resources rapidly and efficiently? Does the organization need the money to cover its overhead or for new projects? What are its fixed costs? Can it scale those expenses up or down depending on the level of its income? How has the organization performed in the past and in different environments? Organizations with a long track record of success have a higher capacity than start-ups for several reasons. First, they are fully functioning and have a long history of covering their overhead with existing facilities, an experienced staff, proper equipment, licenses, and so

on. Second, they have demonstrated that they can manage their cash flow for many years. They know their fixed and variable cost structure and their local resources. We work with an organization in Brazil that required seventeen years for the construction of its facilities. Its leaders were local, with decades in the community. They have strong networks and established respect that are essential resources to employ capacity.

5. Detail the *capital* that the leaders have invested in the philanthropic organization. Often this may not be much, but it may be all they have, and the rest will be in the form of sweat capital. Some individuals have injected sweat capital and their savings into an organization for many decades. Founders of social organizations often forgo compensation to ensure the survival and sustainability of their community project. They will have war wounds from fighting for the organization during difficult times. Another form of *capital* in these organizations is "hugs capital." One can quickly see the bond and love between the leaders and the recipients when you spend time with successful philanthropic organizations led by community residents in the Global South. This hugs capital allows them to call in favors, get special deals, cut corners, and survive in the most difficult times. Leaders have witnessed the transformations of many people over many years, and extensive hugs capital results in great satisfaction and a desire to continue to help, even if that takes Herculean efforts. It also builds a group of people who are loyal, committed, and connected to the individual and organization and will lend a hand if needed. Hugs capital creates community. Sweat and hugs capital helps to certify them as donation (credit) worthy. Also, it is important to understand the NGO's balance sheet and financial ability to manage and accomplish its objective. Giving too much money can outstrip its ability to deploy funds efficiently and effectively. No matter how competent and effective the management, there is only so much a small organization can do.

6. Make sure both parties agree on the *conditions*. How will the money be used to benefit the program participants? What is the overall impact? What precisely will they do with the additional resources? What is the cost associated with it, and when and how long until it will be utilized? In a social enterprise in a tumultuous favela in Rio de Janeiro, those conditions may change over the course of the grant period. Meeting the conditions is important for subsequent grants.

TABLE 4.1

The four Cs of credit adapted to global philanthropy

	Community Banking	Global South Philanthropy
Character	Lend to businesses led by leaders with integrity and proven leadership.	Provide resources to social organizations with leaders with proven integrity.
Capacity	The ability of the company to repay the loan.	The ability of the social organization to use the funds efficiently and rapidly for a big impact on participants.
Capital	The borrower has a significant investment in the business and won't easily walk away.	The leaders have considerable investment in the business, sweat equity, hugs equity, and commitment to the community and participants. They won't easily walk away.
Conditions	The conditions include the terms of the loan for repayment. Meeting those conditions is critical for the continuation of lines of credit and other loans.	The conditions include a commitment to using the grant money as specified. Meeting those conditions, even if renegotiated, is important for subsequent grants.

Steps 3 through 6, which include the four Cs, are detailed in table 4.1.

The community bank model (CBM) is very simple: identify local organizations with a long and verifiable track record of success and led by high-character locals, and invest in them through donations to improve lives and communities rapidly and efficiently. Instead of starting your own IPS with a high failure rate and the long lag time between the original idea and delivering benefits, you can have an immediate impact by helping an ongoing enterprise. The impact is even more significant because the fixed costs are typically already covered in these organizations: Your donation is likely to bring the highest return on the variable costs. The expected return on investment (donation) in CBM is many times higher than that for the Philanthropist's Burden or IPSs.

There is an incredible side benefit of CBM. Remember that there are two pillars to real success. The first is to demand cost efficiency or maximum impact with your contributions to philanthropy. The second is to empower local leaders relentlessly and to avoid reinforcing existing unhealthy global power relations. Local leaders know their communities and know what they need. By investing in or donating to their efforts, you are elevating the status of these local social activists; certifying the value of their years of hard work; acknowledging their innovation, creativity, and ideas; and subverting centuries of power relations and hierarchies whereby the great leaders and innovations come from the Global North.[25]

It is useful to think about superheroes, who get all the fame, credit, respect, money, and praise. Then there are the unsung sidekicks, who support the superhero but never steal the limelight and are respectful and deferential to the superhero. Community bankers feel at ease in the anonymity of the sidekick role. They have helped countless entrepreneurs and businesses grow and become successful, and they have assisted millions of consumers in realizing their dreams by financing their first house or car. They are happy to stay in the background. Upgrading and improving the compassion industry merely requires thinking as a sidekick to support a local superhero and not as a superhero seeking a local sidekick as a junior partner. The traditional model has the superhero from the Global North and the sidekick from the Global South. We invite you to subvert that mindset and the accompanying power relations by inverting the existing paradigm (figure 4.4).

LEARN FROM WARREN BUFFETT

Warren Buffett, the Oracle of Omaha, is widely known for getting a great return on his investments. Buffett pledged the greatest share of his $90 billion net worth to philanthropy. He could easily start one of the world's largest foundations, rent a fancy building, hire administrators and staff members, put his name on everything, and get all the fame. But he didn't. Instead, he provides vast sums of

INVERT
THE MODEL

Figure 4.4 Invert the model

money to existing philanthropic organizations such as the Bill and Melinda Gates Foundation because it is far more cost-efficient to expand existing well-functioning organizations than to start something from scratch. Even Warren Buffett is a sidekick and puts his ego to the side. We can all learn from that.

BE EFFICIENT AND SUBVERSIVE

Wonderful and praiseworthy projects and social organizations are founded by individuals living in the Global North, and they benefit people of the Global South. However, the overall failure rate of those types of organizations is too high, and they reinforce existing power relations. If you really want to make the greatest expected impact, give up the Philanthropist's Burden and start-ups, and adopt the framework inspired by community banks (table 4.2). Identify successful local organizations with a long track record of success and leaders with high character. Assist those organizations

TABLE 4.2
Comparison of CBM with the Philanthropist's Burden

	CBM: Build on Local Success	Philanthropist's Burden: Start-Up
Time needed to achieve a positive impact	Immediate because the program is fully functioning.	Years to build infrastructure and start the program. Lots of cash and funding lost.
What can be accomplished with small amounts of additional money	A significant impact because all fixed costs are already covered, and this money goes only to variable costs, such as team tournament travel.	Small amounts of money are not very useful because of the high fixed and start-up costs needed.
Expected impact	The expected impact is high. The lag time is short, and the likelihood of continued success is high with an organization with a long track record and high-character leader.	The expected impact is low. The probability of start-up failure is high, and there are long lag times and lots of start-up costs. The probability of abandoned or zombie projects is high.
Lifting or empowering local leaders	All ideas, leadership, credit, and acclaim stay local. Locals are the superheroes, and outsiders are the invisible sidekicks. This model erodes hierarchies and enhances local role models for communities.	Senior partners and superheroes are from the Global North, who seek junior partners or sidekicks from the Global South. This approach reinforces hierarchies and devalues local leaders.
Innovation	By knowing the community and local resources, local ideas will be more innovative and community appropriate.	With little knowledge of the community and local resources, Global North leaders blame the local culture for any failure instead of innovating to meet their needs.
Final result	Positive, reinforced relationships. Transformed individuals and communities.	Hard feelings, unfulfilled promises, abandoned projects.
Acclaim and fame	Always for the local leaders, volunteers, and participants.	Often for the senior partner from the United States or Europe.

as a sidekick while empowering locals as leaders and role models. Inspire others around the world about those organizations through word of mouth and the media. Maximize your impact while empowering local actors.

This sounds great, but does it work on the ground? The following chapters present a six-year demonstration project of the model in marginalized neighborhoods in Rio de Janeiro and northeast Brazil.

5

RISE UP & CARE

The Demonstration Project

I can't take kids away from the drug dealers once they begin. When they
are young is the time to act. It's like a branch or tree trunk; you can't
shape it. But a twig you can!

—SEBASTIÃO OLIVEIRA

Does the community bank model (CBM) work in practice? Is it
efficient with a high success rate and return on investment?
Does it empower locals?

Critiquing existing models is easy. It is more demanding to propose an alternative model. The real challenge, and one that is rarely
executed, is putting the alternative to a real test. If you believe in an
idea, demonstrate that it works. Armed with our two guiding principles (achieving the biggest and timeliest expected impact, and
empowering locals), we decided to assess the model with a demonstration project by funding and executing a multiyear experiment,
Rise Up & Care.

When we told people about our idea, claiming that the benefits of international philanthropy could be greatly improved with
a model based on community banking, we were challenged most
often on two fronts. First, some believe that there is a shortage of
locally led, successful philanthropic projects. Individuals from the
Global North often go to the Global South and do everything from
voluntourism to international philanthropic start-ups (ISPs) in part
because they believe that there is a scarcity of local champion leaders and viable local projects with long track records. If this were
true, then CBM would be inconsequential.

The second common concern is that the Global South is characterized by high levels of corruption, as certified by organizations such as Transparency International. According to the 2017 Transparency International Index, of the seventy-four countries in Africa and Latin America, only five are in the best fifty cases globally on corruption.[1] The other sixty-nine countries, including Brazil, exhibit moderate to high levels of corruption. Where corruption is endemic, the argument goes, a culture of corruption is pervasive, and one cannot trust local leaders with philanthropic dollars when the leaders are embedded in a highly unethical environment.

Both of these concerns are reasonable. For any demonstration project to be persuasive, these concerns must be accounted for. Our research design required that we identify a number of organizations that met precise criteria, that we use the sidekick strategy to select four organizations, and that we donate $25,000 per year to each over multiple years.[2] This strategy provided fourteen original cases. The criteria were straightforward:

1. The organization must be fully functioning with a successful track record for at least ten years: no start-ups. This is the maximizing impact/efficiency dimension.
2. The leadership, ideas, and innovation must be local. This is the empowering/subversive dimension.

To take the pair of critiques seriously, we decided to focus on a single niche type of community organization in a single location, in part to demonstrate that these organizations are plentiful. Indeed, one of our biggest surprises was the large number of impressive local organizations to choose from. We could have selected many sectors, including the environment, culture, education, health, women's issues, animal rights, civil society, democracy, and so on. We decided to focus on organizations that use high-level performance to transform youth.

Intense performance activities for youth are an intervention that is extensively validated by both theoretical and empirical evidence. The established benefits of these activities go far beyond improved health from regular exercise. Enthusiasm for these activities dates at least to the ancient Greeks, where Galen proposed that exercise not only resulted in health and a harmony of parts, but also virtue in the soul.[3] The practice of sports, dance, circus, music, the arts, and theater; the nature of competition and teamwork; the achievement of goals; and the time spent on physical exertion rather than other potentially nefarious activities results in individual and group social change, reduced delinquency, greater success in school, achievement orientation, and more.[4]

Participants in high-level performance exert themselves nearly every day of the week and for several hours each time. They have clear goals for elevating their performance and publicly demonstrating that achievement. They are surrounded by others who are striving to reach challenging goals. Multiple high-achieving older individuals started in the organization as young kids and serve as palpable examples and role models. There is a tangible ladder of success with low rungs that young people who are starting can achieve, and individuals can see steps for reaching their dreams through commitment and hard work. There are satisfying rewards along the way. Rather than spending their afternoons on the streets, often getting involved in the drug trafficking or other illicit activities that are prevalent in many communities, youth in high-performance social organizations spend their afternoons and evenings in organized activities requiring exertion, discipline, and concentration led by community leaders and surrounded by others with dreams of success. They gain status in school with medals, travel, and publicity on social media. Their families are proud and encouraging.

The evidence of the benefits of high-performance activities for youth is extensive. Our favorite evidence comes from Iceland. When Icelandic youth suffered the highest substance abuse rates in Europe, officials turned to American psychology professor Harvey Milkman for a solution. Milkman's research in the early 1990s focused on addiction, and he demonstrated that young people are naturally hardwired for addiction. Trying to repress alcohol addiction was likely to fail. Replacing alcohol addiction with a positive addiction would be much more successful.[5]

"We didn't say, you're coming in for treatment. We said, we'll teach you anything you want to learn: music, dance, hip hop, art, martial arts."[6] Indoor soccer pitches were built, as were badminton courts, swimming pools, and music performance centers.[7] With 364,000 inhabitants, Iceland now has 345 soccer pitches, and the men's national team qualified for the 2018 World Cup.[8]

Far better news than the soccer success is the dramatic reduction in substance abuse, as seen in figure 5.1. Addicting young people to performance activities works. Numerous academics examined the Iceland experience. The research and data were vetted and tested at conferences and appeared in peer-reviewed journals. This evidence confirms and adds to the existing body of research on the value of such activities for youth.

William MacAskill provides an additional and perhaps cold-hearted suggestion for maximizing impact, the quality-adjusted life year (QALY). QALY implies that impact should be measured by the quality or percentage of life improvement multiplied by the number of years of expected remaining life expectancy. An intervention

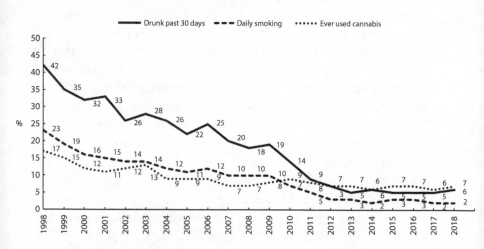

Figure 5.1 Annual percentage of self-reported substance use among Icelandic adolescents, 1998–2018
Source: Kristjansson et al., 2019

that improves by 20 percent the remaining life of a ten-year-old with a life expectancy of seventy years results in twelve QALYs (60 years × 20 percent improvement). In contrast, an intervention that improves by 40 percent the quality of life of a sixty-year-old with the same life expectancy results in only four QALYs (10 years × .4).[9]

We selected Rio de Janeiro as the location of this experiment for four reasons. First, Brazil exhibits high levels of corruption, and this location controls for the influence of a corrupt society on the potential of CBM in the Global South. Second, we wanted to discover if there really exists a large number of these target social organizations that are locally led and functioning for at least a decade. Third, we had spent time in the city, had some connections, and understood the culture and the language. Finally, we intentionally wanted a difficult environment where organizations are stressed and challenged, what Eckstein calls "least-likely cases."[10] With a mix of hopeful confidence and wild curiosity, we selected the favelas of Rio de Janeiro in Brazil as the perfect setting to put the model to the test.

Rio de Janeiro is a very challenging environment. Successful programs for youth in the favelas are of critical importance given the inequality and violence. To give you an idea of the difficulties of life in the favelas and the need for transformative organizations, Amnesty International reports that from 2005 to 2014, on-duty police officers killed 5,132 people in the city of Rio de Janeiro, mostly young people in the favelas. The pressure of young men to join drug trafficking and criminal gangs is potent. Secondary school graduation rates are low, while incarceration rates and violent death rates are high. These locations are particularly challenging in recent years as Brazil entered an unprecedented economic, political, and social crisis.

THE SETTING

There is a common saying in international business consulting: Brazil is not for beginners. Brazil has always been a tricky place in which to maneuver, but that has been even more true in recent years. According to the international media, no country has gone from boom to bust faster. In 2001, economists at Goldman Sachs placed Brazil in the club of the BRICs (Brazil, Russia, India, and China), the large countries with a significant upside for local consumption and untapped export potential with their natural resources. The economies of the BRICs were ready to soar! With the popular progressive president Luiz Inacio "Lula" da Silva governing for eight years, Brazil experienced impressive economic expansion, and innovative social policies spread much of that expanding economic pie to the most impoverished Brazilians, lifting 40 million people out of poverty.[11] *The Economist* published the cover image of the Corcovado Christ statue taking off like a rocket in November 2009,[12] and the 2014 World Cup and 2016 Olympic games were projected as the crowning glory of Brazil's transition from the butt of the joke that "Brazil is the country of the future, and always will be" to a global economic power and consolidated democracy. How quickly things can change: The news from Brazil and Rio de Janeiro over the past few years is appalling.

The string of disasters hitting Brazil and the coverage in the press are truly unparalleled. The Bento Rodrigues dam burst in November 2015, killing sixteen people and releasing 60 million cubic meters of iron waste into Brazilian rivers and the Atlantic Ocean. A corruption scandal within the state-controlled Petrobras oil company and private construction companies could top $300 billion in fraudulent practices and resulted in the jailing of many of Brazil's top corporate leaders and the indictment of or criminal charges for dozens of politicians from across the political parties. A dengue epidemic was followed by the zika virus outbreak, which infected over 1 million people in Brazil and resulted in babies born with microcephaly and other grim consequences of the disease. The country entered the most significant economic recession in memory, with millions of newly unemployed and a government unable to provide basic health and other services. A congress mired in massive levels of corruption impeached President Dilma Rousseff on a technicality. Four former governors of Rio de Janeiro state spent time in prison,[13] as did former President Lula. The previous president, Michel Temer, was linked to corruption and had an approval rating of 4 percent.[14] The highly touted police pacification of Rio de Janeiro's crime-ridden favelas collapsed, and violent crime is surging. A drop in the price of oil has decimated the budgets of Rio de Janeiro state and city, and at the worst possible time. The state of Rio de Janeiro is close to bankrupt, and public employees, including police, health workers, and teachers, have endured periods without paychecks. The 2018 presidential election runoff featured two candidates with high rejection rates. The country elected a president with a history of racist and misogynistic statements, and President Bolsonaro's family was linked to the paramilitary death squads that terrorize poor neighborhoods.[15]

Within this challenging city and country, the most negative portrayal in the media is reserved for the favelas. Social, geographical, and political circumstances divide the city of Rio de Janeiro into two distinct parts, which are juxtaposed as the city versus the favela, the asphalt versus the dirt, and the legal versus the illegitimate. This shapes the conditions of invisibility, rejection, and caste that in turn drive the leaders and participants of the favela-based social movements and civil society to create change.

To understand the demonstration project, one must first understand the historical, political, and social context of the favelas. Favelas are often described as Brazilian urban slums, but this description is inaccurate.[16] A favela is simply a community of more than fifty-one dwellings where the homes do not have legal title. Approximately 20 percent or nearly 1.5 million individuals of Rio de Janeiro city live in anywhere from 700 to 900 favelas. Their origins emerge from the combination of the end of slavery, the founding of the Brazilian republic, and the unfulfilled promises of the Brazilian state to their most vulnerable citizens.[17]

Brazil was the largest recipient of African slaves in the world, with some 5 million slaves brought from 1501 to 1866 to work as servants and in agriculture, forestry, and mining. Slavery was much more extensive in Brazil than in the United States and lasted until 1888. Of the 12.5 million slaves that left Africa for the Western Hemisphere, 10.7 million survived the dreaded journey, and a mere 388,000 landed in all of North America. Rio de Janeiro received five times more slaves (2 million) than did all of North America.[18] Emancipation in Brazil occurred just before the end of the monarchy, and the 1889 transition to a republic was anything but smooth. Brazil is an enormous country, larger than the continental United States, and the population of the country in 1889 was less than 30 million, most of them clinging to the coast like crabs.

The new republic had limited control and power in the vast hinterlands, and breakaway settlements sprouted. One of these was Canudos, in the semiarid backlands in the northeastern state of Bahia. Led by the mystical religious leader Anthony the Counselor, who claimed to predict the end of the world, the settlement attracted tens of thousands of disaffected black and mestizo outcasts. Canudos was perceived as a threat to the new republic, and three military expeditions—each larger than the previous—attempted to destroy the town. Each failed. Humiliated and looking weaker and weaker with each defeat, the national government finally had enough, and the minister of war and federal cabinet planned an overwhelming assault of troops, dynamite, and cannons to destroy the counselor and demonstrate the power of the new Brazil. After three disgraced military defeats against the rag-tag spiritual community, the government in Rio de Janeiro took no chances. Recently emancipated slaves were lured into the expeditionary forces with a promise that, if the campaign were a success, the national government would provide housing to the triumphant troops.[19]

The final campaign was a massacre, resulting in the utter destruction of Canudos and the death of up to 25,000 inhabitants. The former slaves in the republican forces were now victorious troops and returned to Rio de Janeiro in 1897 to receive their promised reward, a house. They camped on a hillside close to downtown Rio de Janeiro, sleeping in improvised tents formed by hanging blankets over small bushes. In the semiarid region of Canudos, the plant used for these tents was the favela bush, and the name was adapted to the new community of returning victorious soldiers, the Favela of Providencia. The former soldiers lived in the Favela of Providencia and petitioned the government for their promised rewards. Their descendants are still waiting 124 years later!

From that original favela, the number of squatter communities has grown to over 700. The variation is significant. Some have as few as fifty-one dwellings, while Rocinha and Maré each have more than 120,000 inhabitants. Many are mature communities, existing for more than a century, while others are recent. Some, such as the eighty-year-old Vidigal perched on the seaside hill between the wealthy neighborhoods of Leblón and São Conrado, inhabit some of the most desirable real estate in the country. Others are far from jobs, the beaches, and downtown, requiring up to two hours of transportation to reach the city center. Some favelas are controlled by drug traffickers, others by gangs of former police known as *milícias*, and still others by occupation and pacification forces of the official police.[20] All of these communities and the people that live there share a common identity plight since the return of the Canudos soldiers: they are invisible, stigmatized, illegitimate, ignored, and partial citizens.

This sharp division between being a favela or asphalt person is crucial to understand the vitality of the individuals and social organizations working within the communities. For example, these favelas are homes to the famous samba schools that parade in the Sambadrome every carnival, delighting millions of Brazilians and tourists with their music, dance, floats, choreography, and messages. Until very recently, however, maps of Rio de Janeiro identified the hundreds of favelas as uninhabited green spaces.[21] Because the homes in the favelas were not titled or registered, the city and state felt little responsibility to provide a census, running water, proper sewage, or security, so it was easiest to omit them from the maps. Elites are embarrassed by favelas and their residents. The favelas developed their own improvised systems of protection, essential services, and transportation. From the returning soldiers in Providencia 124 years ago to today, most people of Rio de Janeiro want to pretend that these citizens are defective or do not exist.

As squatters, inhabitants of the favelas have limited rights and are subject to expropriation and land seizures even many decades after constructing a home and living on a piece of land. When land prices surge in Rio de Janeiro, real estate moguls, construction companies, and government officials use a host of mechanisms, from violent intimidation to property condemnation over safety issues, to expropriation to seize high-value favela properties and to relocate the former inhabitants far from the city center, far away from where most of the jobs are located. A surge in seizure and confiscation took place in the buildup to the 2016 Olympics.[22] To be a favela resident is to face uncertainty and the possibility of being uprooted and moved at any time. Such residents are considered by outsiders as expendable. Residents of favelas supposedly make the city dirty and give the city a bad image; their sewage flows into the Guanabara Bay, and the drug dealers ruin youth. These communities desperately need courageous and innovative local leaders and successful social projects, particularly for young people.

One of the consequences of this divide is the difficulty of comprehensive social mobility out of the favela and into the asphalt. One of the common traits of all the leaders we encountered on this journey is that their own educational and professional success was not enough to erase the perception of *cariocas*—another name for the inhabitants of Rio de Janeiro—that they were inferior. One could get an advanced degree and still be looked down upon.

Brazil, like much of Latin America, experienced a lengthy bureaucratic authoritarian military regime during the Cold War. Generals ruled from the 1964 coup to 1985, and fully democratic elections did not take place until 1989. With the return of democracy came a new constitution that provided, for the first time, financial incentives for nongovernmental organizations (NGOs) in Brazil, as well as a newfound pride in the Afro-Brazilian movement and advances in civil society in the favelas. Thousands of organizations formed, some by ambitious foreigners bringing their ideas to Brazil, and others established by elites in Brazil wanting to help the people of the favelas. Other NGOs were formed unfortunately by elites to divert money to themselves or their relatives. The most impactful organizations were those led by social entrepreneurs from within the favelas that wanted to encourage young people to succeed and avoid joining the gangs and drug traffickers.

How did we find the potential cases for our experiment? The most important thing was to locate local superheroes who founded successful long-term organizations. These high-character individuals had dedicated their lives to transforming their communities. The process involved interviews with bloggers; activists; journalists; government officials, including the secretary of culture for the city of Rio de Janeiro; U.S. consulate officials; and participants in the sports for development and NGO communities. We also used social media such as LinkedIn. We conducted interviews with leaders; volunteers, staff members, and alumni were consulted to assess the character of the leaders, trajectory of the organization, track record, impact on the community, and expectation for continued success.[23] This involved multiple visits to each organization and extensive observation. The objective was to identify four innovative local organizations that implemented organic local innovation to transform young people and their communities dramatically and that had been functioning for at least a continuous decade.

We identified over a dozen organizations that fit the criteria and selected four as partners and recipients of grants. Each vetted organization was invited to submit a one-page application that detailed how it would use a one-year US$25,000 grant. If the organization fulfilled its objectives for each grant and provided documentation of how it used the money, it could apply in a one-page proposal and receive up to three additional awards of up to $25,000 each. Rise Up & Care provided a total of twenty-nine grants of varying amounts to Rio de Janeiro organizations during a seven-year period.

THE CASE THAT CHANGED OUR LIVES: SEBASTIÃO OLIVEIRA AND THE MIRATUS BADMINTON ASSOCIATION

Miratus Badminton Association was our first partner organization, and it best exemplifies the characteristics, challenges, innovation, and success of locally led programs. The founder, Sebastião Oliveira is the son of a maid. Like many children of maids in Rio de Janeiro, his mother was forced by her employer to abandon him, and he ended up at age seven in the state juvenile detention center, the Funabem. The Funabem was like a low-security prison, riddled with violence and abuse. Oliveira represents a minority of Funabem cases, one who eventually became a successful professional (educator) and who did not end up in prison or dead.

Oliveira identifies two men who were instrumental in intervening and transforming his life, and he wanted to do the same for other children:

> Two events influenced me; my mother's boss Antonio Alfrânio did not allow me at age six to live in his house where my mother was a live-in housekeeper. He sent me to a state orphanage or detention center, where I lived from 7 to 18 years. Lost inside this institution with 1700 inmates, I was fortunate to find an angel, Master Izaías, my instructor of autobody work, who gave me attention, affection, and guidance that changed my life. Most of my fellow inmates are now either dead or in prison, so my life is a miracle and a gift from the personal attention from Master Izaías.
>
> As I did not like what I went through inside this institution, being excluded from living with my mother and facing lots of violence and threats, I work now to match young people and opportunities, following the positive attitudes of my teacher. To repay part of what happened to me, I leave the comfort zone of my family, to find and give passion and a path to the excluded children of the favela.
>
> I do today what one enlightened man did for me inside Funabem [state orphanage], what saved my life. That allowed me to choose between the right path and the wrong way to go, actions that made me dream, and materialize my dream, where today the results of my work allow me to tell my story of dedication and overcoming.[24]

Oliveira married a woman from the small and humble favela of Chacrinha, Rio de Janeiro. With his job, he could afford to live out of the favela, on the asphalt, but that presented a dilemma. Should he relocate to his wife's favela or start a new chapter away from the chaos? He would always be considered a favela person, and he was driven to make a difference in the underprivileged community. He decided to move into Chacrinha and spent his spare time motivating youth and transforming the neighborhood.

To understand Oliveira and the sidekick model fully, we encourage you to watch the short trailer of the documentary film about Miratus and Oliveira, *Bad & the Birdieman*, at www.badbirdieman-movie.com.

Oliveira was a good swimmer, and he decided to build a swimming pool to transform youth. After constructing the pool, he decided that this was a terrible idea because success in swimming requires the right biotype, and swim training is monotonous and isolating. He attended a conference on youth sports, and someone suggested badminton, a game that Oliveira had never played. He was convinced that badminton was perfect as soon as he swung the racquet. It was instantly enjoyable. It required little equipment. It was a growing sport in Brazil with lots of tournaments. Kids of any biotype could enjoy the game. Most important, the game was fun and addictive for very young kids. Oliveira knows that if he could get children as young as three to start and keep them motivated through high school, he could permanently change their lives. "I can't take kids away from the drug dealers once they begin. When they are young is the time to act. It's like a branch or tree trunk; you can't shape it. But a twig you can!"

Oliveira started to recruit players, gather equipment, and set up a space in a swamp. From there, he moved to rooftops (figure 5.2). Unfortunately, it rains a lot in Rio and practice was often disrupted. Oliveira had a dream that he would construct a world-class badminton facility in the favela with four indoor courts, a computer center, library, cafeteria, and dormitory. He secured some land with his savings and started digging holes and constructing. He hit a hurdle when the holes were so deep that he could not lift the rocks and dirt out by himself. He called his one friend from Funabem, Ramos, and asked him to help. With their four hands, they have constructed, brick-by-brick and day-by-day, a magnificent facility with all the features that he had dreamed about, and it took seventeen years.

Figure 5.2 Miratus training on the rooftops of Chacrinha in 2006

Once the first court was playable, the children started serious training (figure 5.3). They loved badminton, and Oliveira is a motivating and charismatic leader. One hundred and sixty children from Chacrinha and nearby favelas participated in the program named Miratus. They trained hours every day. The day of reckoning arrived, and the children of Miratus got crushed at their first tournament. Worse yet, they lost to elite, privileged kids with private clubs and coaches. Oliveira was disappointed. The favela had to show that they could compete. The kids had to win for their dreams and to keep playing.

Miratus consulted outside experts to train the kids for success and began a training program with lots of jumping rope and push-ups. Oliveira knew right away that this training would bore the kids, and he dismissed the traditional training program and thought about alternatives. How could he train the kids in a fun way that also produced champions? "Everything Sebastião [Oliveira] does is crazy. People can't believe it. . . . Everything he does works out. . . .

Figure 5.3 Sebastião Oliveira coaching in 2016

I've never seen such determination. . . . On weekends, I go out to dance and have fun, but he stays. It's no coincidence he built his house on top of the courts. He lives for Miratus" (Funabem friend Ramos).

Life in the favela is all about unconventional solutions, about process innovation. After months of thinking, Oliveira developed an innovative training program based on a five-step process of samba dancing: Miratus would use samba dancing to teach badminton! The children would first learn samba dancing to develop lightning-quick footwork that mimicked the movement of players on the court. Then they would incorporate the movement of the racquet with the movement of samba dancing. Finally, they could play and practice, but always with periods of samba dance exercises. Within months, the Miratus team began dominating Brazilian badminton tournaments.

The children started to improve and win, and a ladder of success took shape. Many players earned monthly badminton sports stipends from the Brazilian government of US$250. This encouraged others to try harder. The team was invited to tournaments farther and farther away from its home base. For a ten-year-old to travel to another state, when their parents have never left Rio de Janeiro, is a transformative activity. Some even traveled to Canada, Chile, China, Denmark, the Dominican Republic, Malaysia, Mexico, Peru, and Spain. As the best players improved, the Badminton World Federation awarded monthly stipends of US$500 per month to eleven Miratus players. Suddenly, they were stars in the favela, their home, and their school. Their grades improved.[25] Their self-confidence blossomed. They paid to expand their family homes with their badminton stipends.

Between 2006 and 2019, Miratus players won seventy-five medals at the Junior Pan-American Games, including 65 percent of the Brazilian gold medals. Players from Miratus represented Brazil in the Nanjing Youth Olympics in 2014. Two players won silver medals in the Pan-American games in 2015. Two players from the favela, trained with samba dancing, represented Brazil for the first time in the 2016 Olympics just a few kilometers from the impoverished favela where they were raised. In 2019, Miratus's Ygor Coelho won Brazil's first gold medal ever in badminton at the Pan-American Games (figure 5.4).

The Miratus case and Oliveira clearly demonstrate the power of high-performance programs for at-risk youth and the advantages of having local leaders and local ideas. Only a local would think of using samba dancing to train badminton champions. There is a ladder of success that gets the children addicted to the physical activity. The youngest players can actually see a six-year-old who travels to tournaments, a ten-year-old who is ranked number one for under-eleven players in Brazil. They also see many players who receive monthly sports stipends, players who win Pan-American medals, two players who competed at the Olympics, and players who are now full-time professionals. These older players are idols and role models in the club and motivate the newer players as they can visualize where the Olympic player was just a few years ago. They have been featured in the *New York Times*, the *Washington Post*, and on the *Today* show; on television and media throughout Brazil; and on other media around the world. Miratus and Oliveira

Figure 5.4 Ygor Coelho: Miratus player in the 2016 Rio de Janeiro Olympic Games
Source: Gwen Maitre

are featured in an award-winning documentary film.[26] They have a higher status than the drug dealers. Their successes reach their peers through social media.

There is a marked difference in the lives between the Chacrinha neighborhood children who participate in Miratus and those who don't. Oliveira and all of our superhero partners are diverting hundreds of young people from a life of crime, prison, and early death. Drug trafficking and criminal gangs are omnipresent in the favelas of Rio de Janeiro. Most of those who join a drug trafficking gang do so between the ages of 12 and 15 years. Of those who join gangs, 93 percent drop out of school before graduating; 97.4 percent of drug traffickers are male and 63 percent are Afro-Brazilians.[27] Education is often discarded as a way to a good career: 82 percent of all favela residents have less than eight years of formal education.[28]

The drug traffickers provide prestige and a tribe, but at a high price. The likelihood of violent death before age thirty in Rio de Janeiro favelas is between 18 and 23 percent![29] What organizations like Miratus embark on is deadly serious: 36.5 percent of adolescent deaths in Brazil result from murder,[30] a number that is much higher among black youth in the favelas. Police killed a record 1810 civilians in Rio de Janeiro in 2019, an average of five per day.[31] High-performance neighborhood youth organizations offer an alternative addiction, a different path, and a better outcome. Of the 400 young people who have participated in the Miratus program over the years, only one has joined the drug gangs and only one has died of violence (figure 5.5). As former Miratus participant and coach Aleksander notes, "I was the only one of my large extended family

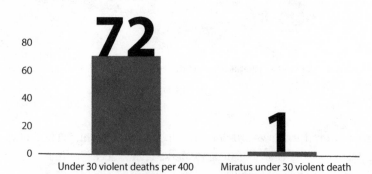

Figure 5.5 Expected violent deaths in favelas for people under the age of thirty versus Miratus violent deaths per 400 for people under the age of thirty

that entered Miratus. It saved my life. All of my cousins are now dead. Life here is complicated. Very complicated."

Miratus exhibits incredible and constant innovation in addition to samba dancing. It shows videos of new training techniques regularly on its Facebook page. Miratus also exhibits the motivation and attitudes of leaders who come from the favelas and understand those challenges and their limitations. Their biggest motivation is to help the youth of their community. Their desire to prove the critics wrong and to show what the favela is capable of (figure 5.6) is an additional motivation that results in Herculean efforts that last for decades.[32]

Oliveira uses the facilities and his status as a community leader for activities and projects outside sports, including eye exams and free eyeglasses, language courses, and math. Miratus sponsors a program for students to prepare for the rigorous university entrance exams in Brazil known as the *vestibular*. Passing the *vestibular* provides free education in the public universities.

Figure 5.6 Sebastião Oliveira carrying the Olympic torch

Oliveira is as proud of these students as he is of his badminton champions:

> The PRE VESTIBULAR MIRATUS, an initiative of the pedagogical team of the Miratus Association, once again achieved an expressive mark: More than 77 percent of the students passed at UERJ [Rio de Janeiro State University]. Three students scored number one on their vestibular tests!

Rise Up & Care was honored to award Miratus four $25,000 grants and some smaller donations. The impact of those contributions has been incredible. The money went to finish the girls' locker room, build a computer room, and fund additional player travel to domestic and international tournaments. Oliveira meticulously accounted for every dollar, including regular photographs of every player who was able to travel and compete.[33]

> We were able to take dozens of young people to tournaments thanks to Rise Up & Care. One player went unranked to the 2016 Jr. Pan Am Games in Peru and won the tournament, securing a US$2,500 stipend from the Pan Am Badminton Federation to participate in the Jr. World Championship in Bilbao, Spain! Imagine how that changes his life! No single experience transforms a youngster from the favela as much as traveling and competing at a distant tournament.[34]

Miratus also provides vital evidence about the threat of corruption. Oliveira knows that corruption is rife in Brazil and that he, as a black man in the favela, is an easy target if he were to be guilty of corruption. He errs on the side of transparency and caution!

Imagine that, instead of awarding additional funds to Oliveira, we had the big idea to start our own badminton program in the Chacrinha favela. Which model would be superior?

> Rise Up & Care has been a new gift in my life, providing resources that send these young athletes to compete in tournaments around Brazil and around the globe. Traveling, competing, and succeeding

against the top athletes expands the horizons of these beautiful kids and provides incentives to work harder and to imagine a different future that they can achieve. Kids need dreams![35]

MIRATUS IN THE ERA OF COVID-19

On March 7, 2020, the exclusive Rio de Janeiro Country Club hosted the social event of the year, the engagement party of Pedro Alberto de Orléans e Braganza, the great-great-great grandson of Brazil's last emperor, Pedro II. The créme de la créme of *carioca* high society flew in from their homes in London, Belgium, Italy, and the United States to attend the event, just a few meters from Ipanema beach. These globetrotters unleashed the coronavirus on Rio de Janeiro, with more than half of the seventy people at the lunch later testing positive for COVID-19. The maids that work in the affluent guests' penthouses were infected and carried the disease to the favelas.[36]

President Jair Bolsonaro, the right-wing populist known as the Trump of the Tropics, dismissed the virus as a media trick, referring to COVID-19 as a little flu. Bolsonaro claimed that Brazilians were immune to the disease, "Not least because Brazilians need to be studied. They never catch anything. You see some bloke jumping into the sewage, he gets out, has a dive, right? And nothing happens to him."[37] President Bolsonaro fired his health minister, Luiz Henrique Mandetta, on April 17, 2020, for defending quarantine measures. Mandetta's replacement, Nelson Teich, resigned four weeks later because the president demanded widespread use of hydroxychloroquine in coronavirus patients. COVID-19 infections and deaths surged, especially in the densely populated favelas. With tourism jobs eliminated and the informal sector frozen by the quarantine, many go hungry. The situation is critical.

Rise Up & Care considers grants upon request from partners; a one-page grant proposal must include specific uses of the money. What would happen if Rise Up & Care just gave unsolicited money to high-character leaders with long track records of service to their communities? Would the recipient use it on a vacation, a car, or temptation activities like gambling or alcohol? On March 27, 2020, when total COVID-19 deaths in Brazil reached ninety-two,[38] Rise Up & Care sent Oliveira and Miratus $2,500 in an unsolicited donation and with zero conditions. Rise Up & Care simply informed Oliveira that the wire was sent and that he could use the money as he wished in these difficult times.

Oliveira is a superhero, but he has flaws. He can be stubborn. He believes in doing the impossible. He sometimes has wild ideas that don't work out. But that stubbornness and his oversized dreams led him to build a world-class badminton facility by hand over seventeen years to train Olympic athletes in a sport he did not play. He kept Miratus alive through Rio's many periods of economic collapse and political upheaval. We were not surprised to hear Oliveira's response to the unexpected and unsought small donation. He was going to feed all of the families in Chacrinha who had nothing to eat due to the virus.

Leveraging $2,500 to feed hundreds of families for months is quite a feat. Oliveira used the money to get matching funds from local businesses and organizations and from a network of friends that stretch from Canada to Switzerland. There were no more badminton tournaments, so the athletes volunteered to help prepare monthly food baskets. The four-court badminton facility turned into a massive distribution center. By June 25, 2020, the Miratus Badminton Association distributed 110,000 pounds of food to a total of 1,800 families (figure 5.7).

Rise Up & Care was nothing but a sidekick, providing a small seed to a dynamic and respected local leader. That modest seed money was magic in the hands of Oliveira and his badminton athletes. And when children in that community think of a role model, they will not think of someone from the United States; they will think instead of someone like them.

From December 2015 through March 2020, Rise Up & Care funded nine Miratus Badminton Association grant requests. Oliveira always used the money exactly as he said he would, and he was able to leverage the money to increase efficiency and return on

Figure 5.7 Sebastião Oliveira overseeing COVID-19 relief
Source: Gwen Maitre

investment. Miratus would regularly take more kids to tournaments than that specified in the grant request. Oliveira is accountable and documented every expenditure. Rise Up & Care has a small fund set aside to assist Miratus athlete travel when tournaments resume after the pandemic recedes.

6

REIMAGINING IMPACT ASSESSMENT

We should not ask circus clowns to produce impact evaluations.

—VINICIUS DAUMAS, CIRCUS CLOWN

N ow that you have read the story of Sebastião Oliveira and Miratus and watched the short trailer about the documentary film *Bad & the Birdieman* (www.badbirdiemanmovie.com), we need to address the critical issue of impact evaluation. If you have not watched the trailer, we urge you to do that now. You may even want to watch the documentary. We will refer to Oliveira and Miratus repeatedly in this chapter.

The community bank model (CBM) partner selection process is simple. The minimal requirements are:

- Character: Local leaders with integrity and a track record of success.
- Capacity: organizations that can efficiently and rapidly use the funds. They know their cash flow and their fixed and variable costs.
- Capital: leaders with sweat and hug equity in an organization and enduring connection to the community. They are all in, financially and emotionally, and will not walk away in the face of difficulties.
- Conditions: Agreed-upon commitment for how the money will be spent, and accountability in documenting that use.
- Subversive: Ideas, leaders, role models, and innovation are local, elevating the status of local role models and subverting the implicit bias legacy of the White Man's Burden.

One additional requirement is critical for maximizing impact or the return on donation. Substantial existing research must support the benefits of the organization's primary activity. As one example, chapter 5 included a thorough presentation of the historical, theoretical, and empirical support for the benefits of high-level performance activities for youth.

We regularly explain our work with Oliveira, the established benefits of high-performance activities for at-risk youth, the dedication of Miratus to squeeze every penny from each donation, and Oliveira's stewardship in documenting the destination of each dollar. The first question we often hear is, "Where is the impact assessment showing that those specific dollars paying for participation in those particular tournaments directly resulted in better school grades or reduced violence or some other measurable outcome in that year?"

This question is understandable but this view of impact assessment paradoxically results in substantially diminished impact. This is particularly important for modest grants to smaller organizations. Asking Oliveira to spend thousands of dollars from a modest grant and hundreds of hours verifying that high-level performance activities like badminton are good for children in marginalized neighborhoods would be imprudent. Few would dispute the benefits of high-intensity performance activities for children as long as the children choose their own activity. That money and time would be much better spent training kids in badminton and the associated life skills. We agree with those who find that local project champions are the key to development success in the Global South.[1]

Donors, researchers, and implementers in global philanthropy and development have a natural harmony of interests. All are passionate about improving the human condition. The current best practice of impact assessment often turns that harmony of interests into adversarial relationships. In this chapter, we critique the current impact evaluation system, explain the roots of a different approach for smaller interventions, and provide a cooperative alternative that will restore the harmony of interests and ramp up overall impact of philanthropic work. We then provide a specific example of the approach from our next set of projects.

BEST PRACTICES, WORST OUTCOMES

The need for impact assessment is obvious.[2] We must support what works and maximize returns on scarce resources. Donors rightfully want value for their money. If an organization claims that its activities make a difference, you want to donate to support or expand its endeavors. And you want to know the impact of that donation.[3]

In the real world, this is extraordinarily difficult and requires extensive research design, proposal writing, implementation, preintervention measurement, postintervention measurement, management, data analysis, report writing, vetting, and independent review. Completing these activities on the cheap or without highly trained practitioners produces questionable data. Following rigorous procedures could easily consume tens of thousands of dollars, often much more. Even then, would those evaluations reliably measure what you want? Or would they simply create work? Scholars point out at least ten weaknesses in traditional philanthropy impact assessment.[4] Four critiques are particularly salient for small grants to small organizations:

1. *Huge opportunity costs.* Every dollar spent on grant proposals, impact assessments, and reporting is one less dollar going to the target population's critical needs. Every hour spent by a community activist on the steep learning curve and lengthy production of rigorous evaluation is one less hour spent on the actual mission.
2. *Fuzzy lag times for some outcomes.* In many cases, it is improbable that you can match the timing of the intervention with the change in the outcome. If Rise Up & Care provides $25,000 in 2016 to Miratus Badminton Association and one potentially measurable indicator is improved high school graduation rates, in what year will Miratus Badminton Association see improved high school graduation rates for its athletes?

3. *More alternative explanations than cases.* Providing an intervention and later measuring the amount of change is based on the faulty assumption that all other factors remain constant except for the intervention. This is rarely true in marginalized communities of the Global South. Favelas are continually shifting, with dramatic changes in socioeconomic conditions, violence, government policies, access to health care and transportation, and so on. Therefore, you cannot necessarily attribute any change in an indicator to any single intervention. In statistical terms, you do not have any degrees of freedom.

4. *Conflict of interest and bias.* Just as every parent can explain why her or his children are above average and gifted, every organization in every sector will produce self-assessments that confirm the miraculous positive effect of their work. Universally positive impact evaluations cloud the entire self-assessment enterprise.

Nobel Prize–winning economists Abhijit Banerjee, Esther Duflo, and Michael Kremer have long argued that the standard method of assessment is largely a waste of time and money: one cannot estimate the impact of a program intervention without a control group. "The critical objective of impact evaluation is therefore to establish a credible comparison group. . . . This group should give us an idea of what would have happened to the members of the program group if they had not been exposed, and thus allow us to obtain an estimate of the average impact on the group in question."[5] The gold standard in assessment requires an often quixotic quest to find two organizations that are nearly exactly the same, in similar communities and conditions, and randomly select one for the intervention and use the other as a control group.[6] Estimates of a single "low-cost" randomized impact evaluation range from $50,000 to $300,000.[7]

These economists and other randomistas conduct brilliant and enlightening research on poverty, education, and health with randomized evaluations (REs).[8] For nearly two decades, they have also recognized and affirmed that "not all programs can be evaluated with randomized evaluations,"[9] even with a limitless budget. Others, such as Dani Rodrik, argue that these randomized evaluations

(RE) in development can be applied only to questions of very narrow scope and are inappropriate for nearly all of the interesting practices.[10]

If there is a single control case and a single treatment case, there are still many alternative potential explanations for a difference in outcomes. For Miratus, imagine we have two badminton training centers in similar communities. One organization gets $25,000 for additional player tournament participation, and the other does not. A generous foundation donates an additional $50,000 or more to conduct a low-cost RE on badminton and school performance. Could we attribute any change or outcome to the randomized intervention? With only two cases, it would be impossible to know. Perhaps one of the local schools changed administrators or closed. Maybe a new criminal gang took over one community and the schools were closed thirty days of the school year, or a community suffered from one of the particularly devastating floods that are common in Rio de Janeiro. There are far more potential explanations of the outcome than there are cases, which renders any hope of causal inference impossible.

One potential solution to this problem is to replicate the program in many different settings, perhaps by selecting thirty paired programs and communities. This would have enough cases for causal inference, but it is far beyond any conceivable budget and has its own set of critics.[11] One poverty intervention with multiple high-quality and high-cost REs is microcredit. Banerjee and colleagues examined six of those RE field experiments with treatment and control groups and found a "modestly positive" pattern "but not transformative, effects."[12] Hundreds of thousands of dollars, perhaps millions, were spent on multiple iterations of microcredit, with the gold standard of assessment, and the jury is still out on its benefits.

Finally, tricky ethical questions surround these social experiments with real people and children. How would you feel as a parent of a badminton player at the control center that did not receive the intervention for tournament travel, but the impact assessors want to track your child's progress at school and her or his behavior? There is already enough envy, resentment, and violence between favelas in Rio de Janeiro. What about the opportunity costs? Wouldn't that $50,000 or more for the RE to determine if it is better to have children playing badminton twenty hours a week and competing in tournaments rather than hanging out on the streets be better spent training more kids in badminton and sending them to tournaments?

The widespread recognition that randomized evaluations (REs) are neither generalizable nor appropriate for many types of interventions has not stopped donors from adopting RE as the standard best practice. According to the U.S. Agency for International Development (USAID), "The impact evaluation must be able to show that change occurred on the outcome of interest and it must be able to demonstrate that the change it measured would not have occurred . . . in the absence of a particular USAID intervention. In most cases this involves a comparison of what happened to the beneficiary (or treatment) group to what happened at another."[13]

USAID is not alone in expecting rigorous measure-intervene-measure self-evaluations, with or without control groups, for even small grants. Foundations, government agencies, consultants, and bureaucrats glorify a tiny toolbox of impact assessment methods even when they are prohibitively expensive, burdensome, inapplicable to many interventions, and biased. The open secret is that program directors, community activists, and nongovernmental organizations (NGOs) know that this style of impact assessment is inappropriate.[14] They eventually tire of trying to explain why, and they surrender, wink, and simply insert intervention-flattering numbers the best they can.[15] If we recognize that current practices of evaluation are inefficient at best and cause harm at worst, then the time has come to admit that we are plowing the sea. How can we do better?

IRON LAWS AND BULLSHIT JOBS

While working in the British Foreign Service, Cyril Northcote Parkinson observed the expansion of colonial bureaucracies even as the empire was shrinking. He later became the editor of *The Economist* magazine, where he published Parkinson's Law in 1955. This law simply states that work expands to fill the time available for completion.[16] Parkinson uses the law to deduce that bureaucracies will naturally multiply subordinates and multiply work. The multiplication of officials, no matter how great, will never leave anyone idle because work is elastic in its demand on time. Corporations, universities, government agencies, and nonprofits will continuously need more staff members.[17]

A half-century later, Jerry Pournelle proposed the Iron Law of Bureaucracy, which asserts that bureaucratic organizations are populated by two types of people: those who are devoted to the actual mission of the organization and those dedicated to the organization itself.[18] In all cases, the second group of people gains control of the organization. The result is a risk-averse and brand-conscious organization devoted to the perpetuation of the organization rather than its stated mission.

Combining these two laws of bureaucracy, we should expect staff members and administrators to multiply and spawn layers of subordinates, gain control of any established public or private institution, and fill their days mandating layer upon layer of paperwork; training seminars; regulations; make-work; workshops to discuss mission statements; retreats to repeat the same things as last year's retreat; online certifying of compliance with the latest policies; organization-wide adoption of jargon and buzzwords; articulation of new policies to replace last year's policies; committees that rarely accomplish much except forming subcommittees; regularly scheduled meetings where the same four people pretend to look smart;[19] and, above all, assessments. These activities and mandates are often justified by using the magic words *best practice*. Organizations can avoid these mandates only with great and deliberate care.

David Graeber formalizes the causes and ramifications of Parkinson's Law and the Iron Law of Bureaucracy in his best-selling book, *Bullshit Jobs: A Theory*.[20] Graeber documents how and why enormous swathes of people "spend their entire working lives performing tasks they secretly believe do not really need to be performed. The moral and spiritual damage that comes from this situation is profound. It scars our collective soul."[21] Bullshit jobs reproduce at rapid rates in bureaucracies, and the modern university is no exception. In the University of California (UC) system, there were almost twice as many faculty members as administrators in 2000. Administrators multiplied like rabbits since and, by 2015, there were 10,539 administrators and 8,899 faculty members.[22] Bain & Co. consultants discovered eleven layers of management between the chancellor and the faculty at UC Berkeley.[23]

Many young people dream of making a difference by working in philanthropy. They are willing to earn lower salaries for meaningful work. They are often disappointed by performing make-work and feel disconnected from the activities that first attracted them to a career in philanthropy. David Wertheimer admits, "One of the reasons I left being a nonprofit executive director was that I realized that I was consistently putting the needs of my organization above the interests and needs of the clients we were serving."[24]

One of the refreshing characteristics of Miratus and Oliveira is the absence of bullshit jobs, and the tiny staff volunteering and working at the badminton center prioritize the children over the institution. We discovered the same dynamic in local organizations throughout the favelas of Rio de Janeiro. Bureaucratic bloat and make-work *can* be avoided; Parkinson's Law and the Iron Law of Bureaucracy are not predestined.

A MODEST PROPOSAL FOR A BETTER ASSESSMENT PROCESS

Vinicius Daumas is a gifted and beloved clown (figure 6.1). As a young man, Daumas discovered the power of circus to captivate, charm, arouse dreams, and change young people. His dedication and work have touched many.

> The clown is free because he is not afraid of the ridiculous. To be a clown is to see the world in reverse, with different lenses than those that people normally see. That is why I am a clown 24 hours a day.[25]

Figure 6.1 Vinicius Daumas
Source: Photos by Gustavo Malhieros

Let's reimagine impact assessment through different lenses. When we first asked Daumas if he would be interested in a small grant of $25,000 for the social circus Crescer e Viver, he surprised us with the answer. He was only interested if the grant provided significantly more benefit to the children than the costs of time and money for grant proposal preparation, impact assessment design, impact assessment implementation (that he knew was probably of questionable value), and final reporting. He did not want the money if the consequence was the creation of bullshit jobs. Daumas wanted to avoid opportunity costs; he wanted to spend his precious time and exceptional skills working with at-risk children. He felt that the circus clown should not be tasked with designing, implementing, analyzing, and reporting high-quality impact evaluations.

The stakes are too high for us to demand make-work and low-value project evaluations. All of our partners serve their communities with long hours and bare-bones staff. They rightly bristle at the idea of using valuable resources to generate mountains of low-value data. Impact evaluation practices can be greatly improved; repurpose considerable amounts of money to actual interventions; rescue Daumas and thousands of others from the misery of soul-destroying bullshit jobs; and let them spend that time as circus instructors, badminton coaches, dance teachers, and theater directors. The key to improved efficiency and value in assessment comes from a classical theory of economics.

Adam Smith published *The Wealth of Nations* in 1776. Smith's first sentence foresaw the dramatic increase in productivity and wealth from the *division of labor*. Ten workers, each focusing on their specialized task in a manufacturing process, could produce 48,000 pins a day, while an individual doing the whole process alone could make only 20 pins in a single day (ten workers could make a maximum of 200 pins). Division of labor and specialization generate a 24,000 percent increase in impact.

We propose the following *cooperative division of labor* for global philanthropy for smaller interventions of $50,000 or less (the cost of a serious impact evaluation would otherwise cannibalize a large proportion of the resources). University researchers and labs, large charitable institutions like the Bill and Melinda Gates Foundation, government agencies like the National Institutes of Health, and international organizations like the Inter-American Development Bank and UNESCO use their large budgets, peer-reviewed publications, vetting, conferences, specialized expertise, research communities, advanced methods, greater objectivity, and decades of experience to support and conduct research on what works and what does not work in global philanthropy and development, including health, education, youth, gender, poverty, the environment, human rights, and so on. Research is their comparative advantage and highly specialized skillset. They very often partner and cooperate with donors and social entrepreneurs in this work, but they take the lead in the independent basic research on what works.

Donors and grantors should support those interventions for which the evidence of their benefits is already established, avoiding activities where research shows an adverse effect or a questionable benefit. As William MacAskill explains, development economists have rigorously evaluated the intervention of sending donated textbooks to Africa. In the absence of teacher training, donating textbooks has no discernable effect on the performance of school-children. Consequently, there are higher return interventions for donors' money.[26] As expected, the organizations that collect and ship donated books to Africa always find a robust positive impact in their self-assessments, as does every other organization in every other self-assessment.

Local community activists and social entrepreneurs in the Global South have a passion and talent for engaging with at-risk popula-tions. Their comparative advantage and extraordinary skills are in delivering the interventions. As good stewards, they must also be accountable and document how resources were deployed and what activities took place. How was the money spent? How many chil-dren participated in tournaments? How many children regularly practiced at the badminton center? How many medals did the ath-letes win at the national championships? How many participated in samba classes? Oliveira taught himself enough architecture and contracting to build a world-class, four-court badminton center. He developed a methodology of using samba dancing to train cham-pions at local and international badminton tournaments. Given enough years of dedicated study, he could learn advanced statistics, survey methods, research design, and REs. If he were convinced it would help the children, he would conquer the 1,198 pages in the *Handbook of Field Experiments: Volume 1* and *Volume 2*, to gain pro-ficiency in topics such as "Heterogenous Treatment Effects and Pretreatment Variables." This particular topic does not give him a comparative advantage. Gaining proficiency in it and other top-ics would mean massive opportunity costs and would dramatically reduce impact. It would crush Oliveira's soul. It is disturbing that so many consider this "best practice."

Duflo and Banerjee, the magnificent economists who co-edited the *Handbook of Field Experiments: Volume 1* and *Volume 2*, could pos-sibly construct a world-class badminton facility in a favela, learn Portuguese, train young people to compete at the highest level, and then conduct impact evaluations. All of this would probably take a decade or two. Everyone in development and philanthropy would laugh at the idea. It is not their comparative advantage or their passion. That would waste their time and talents. A division of labor is much more productive.

Let's take a different type of intervention as an example. Suppose that you love coral reefs. You want to make a tiny difference in coral reef health. Foundations, universities, and government agencies have conducted significant research on coral reef health, and there is agreement on the benefits of some interventions. The healthy mangrove forest is one intervention that has strong consensus support for healthy reef ecosystems, as long as the right species is planted in an appropriate location. You conduct research and confirm that there is wide agreement that planting mangroves provides many environmental benefits, including coral reef well-being. You vacation in Fiji and meet village leaders who lead a campaign to plant 10,000 mangroves. You observe the healthy mangroves planted in previous years. You are impressed with the community and the leaders. You make a donation and even spend some time carrying mangrove propagules to the planters. You might even snorkel on the adjacent reef that benefits from low coastal runoff.[27] Because there is often cooperation between donors, basic research practitioners, and local implementers, a university marine biologist present may be researching survival rates of different planting techniques.

The local organization plants mangroves and reports on how many were planted and how many survived x years in previous plantings. Planting mangroves is their specialty, and they have lots of experience. It would be inefficient and a duplication of effort for the Fiji mangrove planters to attempt to demonstrate scientifically the precise positive effect of planting those specific mangroves on that particular reef. Their efforts would likely result in questionable reports suffering from inherent biases, insufficient budgets, inexperience, and an absence of expertise. This *evaluation syndrome* dismisses the productivity gains of the division of labor.

We want to share how we are incorporating this model of impact evaluation (figure 6.2) in our next project. We are presently updating

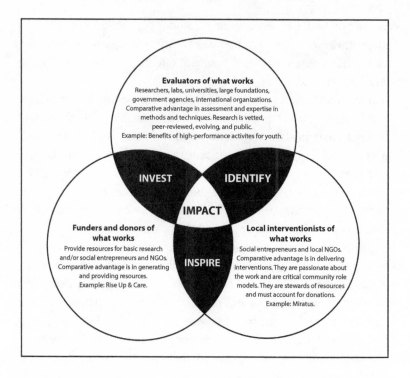

Evaluators of what works
Researchers, labs, universities, large foundations, government agencies, international organizations. Comparative advantage in assessment and expertise in methods and techniques. Research is vetted, peer-reviewed, evolving, and public. Example: Benefits of high-performance activites for youth.

INVEST   IDENTIFY

IMPACT

Funders and donors of what works
Provide resources for basic research and/or social entrepreneurs and NGOs. Comparative advantage is in generating and providing resources. Example: Rise Up & Care.

INSPIRE

Local interventionists of what works
Social entrepreneurs and local NGOs. Comparative advantage is in delivering interventions. They are passionate about the work and are critical community role models. They are stewards of resources and must account for donations. Example: Miratus.

Figure 6.2 Cooperative division of labor for global philanthropy impact assessment

and replicating our Brazil demonstration projects in a new location, Colombia. One of our discoveries in Brazil was the power of imagery and media on stereotypes and implicit bias. The media negatively portrays favela residents and Afro-Brazilians as lazy, poor, vice-ridden criminals. Role models and admirable leaders look different in the media. We celebrated Oliveira and featured him as a superhero in a documentary film and in a children's book written explicitly to combat stereotypes, and we noted a shift in attitudes and social media posts about Oliveira as a leader and role model. On the day of the launch of the children's book, *Scout's Superhero Search: The Birdieman of Rio de Janeiro* (www.scoutheroes.com), a launch that was attended by prominent national political leaders, local government officials, and community members, Oliveira sent us a simple WhatsApp message, "I feel like an important person."

Changes in attitudes are measurable, and we want to measure the effect of the targeted interventions on implicit bias and attitudes in future cases. There are three actors or partners in the cooperative division of labor. The first is the research partner, in this case, Georgia Tech. A vertically integrated projects (VIP) team of undergraduate students, graduate students, and faculty members are identifying and selecting partners in Colombia with similar characteristics to Oliveira and Miratus: high-character local leaders in poor communities with a long track record of using high-performance activities for youth in neighborhoods. The VIP team is also designing and building attitude surveys and implicit bias tests about self-esteem, role models, leaders, and life expectations. The Georgia Tech team will partner with filmmakers in Colombia to produce the documentary film about each selected leader and organization, the children's book with the local leader as a superhero and illustrated by a local street artist, digital games, and other interventions that will celebrate the local leaders in the selected Colombian communities. Georgia Tech researchers and students will also organize the attitude and implicit bias tests of the community population and youth participants before the interventions and again after the interventions, working with locals in Colombia to administer the surveys. This work is technical and requires specific research and digital media skills—both of which are part of Georgia Tech's comparative advantage.

The second actor is the philanthropic partner that will provide the modest expansion grants to the targeted organizations using high-performance activities to transform youth. In our case, it is Rise Up & Care. Rise Up & Care will cooperate actively with the Georgia Tech team and the local organizations in Colombia.

The final partner is comprised of the local organizations using high-level performance for youth and their leaders. They will cooperate with the Georgia Tech team in the administration of the attitude surveys and implicit bias tests before and after the interventions, in the production of the documentary films, and in the creation and free distribution of the children's books throughout the community. These organizations will also receive small grants to support or expand their work. They will not be expected to use their time or those small grants to develop, administer, and report rigorous impact evaluations. They are expected to use their passion, talent, and comparative advantage to work with youth and transform their neighborhoods.

This cooperative division of labor for assessment replaces the existing antagonistic practice with a more harmonious impact evaluation process. Funders and researchers invest time and resources in finding what works and improving methods and applications. Researchers and local change agents work together to identify policies and practices that uplift the human condition. Local social entrepreneurs maintain great flexibility and autonomy in customizing interventions to best suit their community (an example is Oliveira creating a five-step program of samba dancing to create excitement and skill in badminton in Rio de Janeiro). Donors and local change agents jointly inspire each other and the world about programs that uplift the human condition. The model is dynamic because our understanding of what works in development and philanthropy constantly evolves. Reimagining assessment produces a substantial improvement in the current practice and increases the overall impact.

In chapter 7, we will present additional Rise Up & Care partners, their inspiring work, and their stewardship and accountability.

7

ACTORS OF RESISTANCE

Life is only possible if it is reinvented.

—GUTI FRAGA

The Sebastião Oliveira story melts cynicism in our troubled world. It is hard to imagine anyone more inspiring. We may assume that Oliveira is singular or extremely rare in the tough neighborhoods of Rio de Janeiro. In fact, the entire area is teeming with indomitable, creative, and motivating leaders. Our greatest difficulty, and the source of considerable grief, came from narrowing down the potential full-partner organizations to four because there were many outstanding candidates.

Maré, unlike many favelas located on hillsides, sits on the steamy flat plains near the Guanabara Bay. Maré is enormous, with over 140,000 residents, 138 supermarkets, 307 beauty salons, and zero banks.[1] Maré is subdivided into smaller zones, controlled by different violent gangs, mafia-like militias of former police, or current militarized police.[2] There is a constant threat of open gunfire as these heavily armed groups try to expand or protect their territory, and the locals wryly told us that they refer to the area as Bosnia. It is all too common to see young civilians with semiautomatic weapons, to have military police aim guns at you while you eat lunch, and to hear a burst of gunfire (figure 7.1). Maré is also home to numerous laudable social entrepreneurs.

In Brazil, until 1998, there was no national college entrance exam like the SAT.[3] Even now, individual university departments

Figure 7.1 A day in Maré
Source: Photo by Jon Wilcox

often produce their own custom entrance exams, called the *vestibular*. The best universities are typically public universities, and passing the *vestibular* is largely possible through attendance at selective private high schools and participation in expensive test prep courses called *cursinhos*. Consequently, students from the favelas face long odds to gain entry into a top university. Eliana Sousa Silva grew up in Maré and achieved the nearly impossible: she scored high enough on the college entrance exam to enter a high-quality and tuition-free public university. She later earned a PhD in sociology.

Sousa Silva noticed that there were almost no students from her background at the university because so few could pass the *vestibular*. Instead of leveraging her PhD to enjoy a comfortable life as a scholar, Sousa Silva felt the calling to make a difference in her community. She organized a group of colleagues to found Redes de Maré in 2007. Their first project was to prepare teenagers from her community to pass the entrance exams. Twelve hundred of their students subsequently succeeded and entered the university.[4] We met many such students who participated in the *cursinhos* at Redes de Maré, passed the *vestibular*, graduated from university, and returned to work for Redes in community action. Rise Up & Care gratefully contributed to the Redes de Maré *cursinho* program.

Sousa Silva and her colleagues did not stop there. Redes de Maré conducted a census and named all the streets; they set up libraries, day-care centers, arts spaces, a women's home, and more. One of Sousa Silva's creative writing students was Marielle Franco, the first person ever elected to political office from Maré, who was assassinated in 2018 by a former police officer with ties to both the militias and to the family of the current president of Brazil.[5] Both women's names appeared on a leaked kill list, and Sousa Silva regularly receives death threats.[6] Eliana Sousa Silva is a superhero, and she is not the only one. There are many in Maré.

Lia Rodrigues is one of Brazil's most celebrated contemporary dancers and choreographers. After a couple of years working in France, she returned to Rio de Janeiro to found the Lia Rodrigues Companhia de Danças. In 2004, Lia decided that she wanted to have a greater social impact, and she moved her dance company from downtown (Centro) Rio to Maré (the map of Rio in figure 7.2 gives a sense of the difference). Lia told us that it was both incredibly difficult and incredibly rewarding. Some days, rehearsal must be canceled due to excessive gunfire. The dancers are exceptional and have toured the world. Lia Rodrigues is an inspiration.[7]

The Integrated Program for Music (PIM) on the outskirts of Rio de Janeiro dazzled us. Master musicians Claudio and Celia Moreira founded the program in 2000 in order to bring classical musical instrument training to the underprivileged of the region. PIM trains 450 future musicians from ages four to ninety-one, and many graduates of the program are now professionals in Rio de Janeiro, Recife, and France. PIM is a labor of love for Claudio, Celia, and their colleagues and is touching many lives.[8]

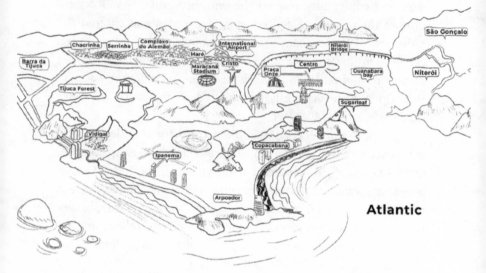

Figure 7.2 Map of Rio de Janeiro
Source: Art Cazé.

The community activists of Rio de Janeiro use all manner of high-performance activities for youth development, including soccer, tennis, boxing, filmmaking, orchestra music, circus performance, surfing, theater, and dance. Here are some of the change agents who have short films or film trailers that provide an inspiring window to their courage and efforts.

Tuany Nascimento was born in the Complexo de Alemão agglomeration of favelas and trained as a gymnast and a classical ballet dancer who represented Brazil in world competitions. She now dedicates her life to teaching ballet to the girls of the Morro de Adeus favela of Alemão and is featured in the short film *Bullets and Ballet*.[9]

Alan Duarte lost nine family members to gun violence in the Complexo de Alemão, and rebuilt his life through boxing. His gym offers boxing, kickboxing, and personal development training to the youth of his community. Alan is featured in the film *The Good Fight*.[10]

Mércia Britto and Luis Lomenha participated as teenagers in the casting process and production associated with the film *City of God*. They subsequently founded Cinema Nosso, a cultural institution that trains young people to participate and lead in the audiovisual production chain in Rio de Janeiro. More than 4,000 have taken the courses, and many are now professionals in film, video game design, and cultural production. Rise Up & Care partnered with Cinema Nosso in the production of several documentary films and donated $75,000 for film equipment used in their work. *Magic Movie Motion* tells the heartwarming story of determined and creative youth using film to reach their dreams.[11]

The police entered the favela of Vigário Geral in August 1993 and massacred twenty-one innocent people. Instead of seeking revenge, Anderson Sá and José Junior created a movement based on art, culture, and the music of their band AfroReggae. Universal Music signed the band to a record deal, and the AfroReggae Cultural Group is now one of the most prominent social organizations in the city. AfroReggae is the subject of the award-winning documentary, *Favela Rising*.[12]

The number of locally led organizations in the Global South with high-character leaders, innovative methodologies, and long track-records of success is astonishing. Rise Up & Care could, unfortunately, select only four Rio full partners to receive multiple donations.

CRESCER E VIVER CIRCUS

Vinicius Daumas and Junior Perim (figure 7.3) grew up in one of the poorest and most violent communities in greater Rio de Janeiro, São Gonçalo. Both were outstanding students and active in politics. With time, they went their own ways. Perim worked in politics and community activism; Daumas joined a traveling social circus for four years as a clown. In those four years, he witnessed the beauty and challenges of all of Brazil, and also the importance and potential of the circus for social transformation. Daumas seized on the power of the circus for young people to reimagine themselves, their

Figure 7.3 Vinicius Daumas and Junior Perim, founders and directors of Crescer e Viver

lives, and their futures, and he wrote a proposal for a social circus for São Gonçalo. He encountered his old friend Perim in a bar, and they decided to combine their strengths and open a social and professional circus to transform youth first in their hometown and later in the small favelas near Praça Onze, in downtown Rio.

We urge you to view the short trailer of the documentary film about Perim, Daumas, and Crescer e Viver circus, or the complete film, at www.giracircusmovie.com. The trailer will give you a real feel for the organization, leaders, and participants. To survive in the favela is like juggling while balancing on a tightrope.

The three core principles of Crescer e Viver (the name of the organization translates in English as "grow and live") are designed for youth to reimagine their lives and their future[13] by countering stereotypes and implicit biases through actions:

1. I AM (Who are you? You are someone with an identity, and you matter.)
2. I CAN (You can achieve anything you set your heart, mind, and body to.)
3. I WANT (What do you want? What are your dreams? Know them and go after them!)

Crescer e Viver has been transforming lives in Praça Onze for sixteen years. The story of D'Jeferson exemplifies these core principles. D'Jeferson approached Daumas and Perim when they first erected the circus tent on squatted land. As an overweight, black, illiterate, gay man, D'Jeferson faced discrimination and prejudice in Rio de Janeiro. He wanted to be a trapeze artist and had been rejected for years by multiple circus schools. Crescer e Viver embraced D'Jeferson's dream, and he trained with them for four years. He is still overweight, black, and gay, but he has toured Sweden and Italy as a trapeze star (figure 7.4). "I've fulfilled my dream. This is where I live my dream. I've been to places I never imagined going, received applause I never imagined receiving."[14] Similar discourse is common in all the organizations. Success in high-level performance makes the participants somebody important when societal discourse emphasizes that they are nobody or that they are invisible.

Figure 7.4 D'Jeferson on the trapeze

Circuses have long been important social activities around Brazil and in underserved communities. Crescer e Viver initiated the annual Rio de Janeiro International Circus Festival in 2013 to showcase circuses from around the world and to solidify their vision of circus as transformational. This warm acceptance of all desiring individuals as potential circus stars despite their biotype or other perceived limitations is showcased in the Crescer e Viver's circus training and performances for the disabled under the big top.[15] The circus not only provides training, mentorship, and healthy food, it also provides an alternative to other activities and a safe environment. The neighborhoods surrounding the circus tent are precarious and challenging. "If it weren't for our circus," notes Vinícius, "I can honestly say that many of these teenagers would be dead. For sure some would be in a trafficking gang."[16]

As an organization with considerable infrastructure and programs, many years of continuous success, energetic and charismatic leaders, and a high level of respect from a range of actors, Rise Up & Care invited a proposal from Crescer e Viver. Daumas and Perim requested money to support the training of the youngest children, to produce annual professional shows to give the participants experience, and to generate income through social enterprise. They fulfilled all goals and proposal objectives, and Rise Up & Care made six grants to date. Crescer e Viver unceasingly documents their stewardship with social media posts, photographs, and reports.

When Rise Up & Care first visited us at the circus the two representatives entered the conference room saying that Junior and I were superheroes and they wanted to be our invisible sidekicks. This made us laugh, because lots of people visit with lots of big talk. But, to see these individuals that we just met laying out the program of how they provide funds and that they wanted to partner with several organizations, it was magic! The most incredible part was the degree of personal confidence that was established so quickly. The biggest benefit was not the money, but the sensation of confidence, reciprocity, solidarity. . . . We must also mention the film, "Gira & the Circus of Life," directed by Kátia Lund and Lili Fialho, and produced by Rise Up & Care. This film opened so many doors for the Crescer e Viver Circus, so that the world could know what we do and whom we do it for.[17]

Imagine that, instead of awarding additional funds to the Crescer e Viver Circus, we raised funds to start our own circus program in Praça Onze. Because we trusted and invested in the vision, talent, and skill of the existing organization, we maximized our return on investment, and everyone benefited.

Many grants have so many restrictions that they can cost more to administer than the benefits they provide. There are also grants that come with conditions for the creative and technical aspects of teaching circus. They push us aside and don't fully respect what we do and how much work we have put into developing our training programs. Rise Up & Care believed in us and trusted in us, and only wanted to support our work and our initiatives. The application form was only one page, and the annual reporting was straightforward. Rise Up & Care only seeks to help in areas that we need the most, and they give us all the glory. They always say that they only want to be sidekicks, and we are always the superheroes. We did not understand that at first, but we do now.[18]

On March 26, 2020, Rise Up & Care sent $2,000 to Crescer e Viver as a small, unrequested grant without conditions or stipulations to use as they chose. COVID-19 and the Brazilian economic collapse threaten their community. The Crescer e Viver circus leveraged those $2,000 of unrequested funds to work miracles. Perim unleashed his force of personality and networking prowess to multiply resources with foundations, banks, and suppliers. With these resources, the circus provides debit cards to 1,600 at-risk families near the circus tent, with enough money on each card to buy a monthly basket of food for each family. The circus also coordinates the production and distribution of masks and hand sanitizer.

Perim is a superhero, partly because he can be stubborn and demanding. People will tell you that he can drive everyone crazy.

Superheroes are never perfect. Because of these traits and his dogged tenacity, Perim is able to accomplish great things for the neighborhood.

GUTI FRAGA AND NÓS DO MORRO

Nós do Morro ("We of the Hill" or "We of the Favela") and the extraordinary Fraga are spectacular partners. For a multisensory picture of Fraga and the high-energy favela of Vigidal, we invite you to watch a two-minute introduction, and the complete documentary film featuring Fraga, at www.gutidreamsmovie.com. Nós do Morro is the oldest of our partner organizations and has brought culture and opportunity to Vidigal for thirty-four years. Fraga is from a poor family in the interior of Brazil and came to Rio de Janeiro as an actor some forty years ago. A successful director and actor of stage, television, and film, Fraga's defining experience was a trip to New York City, where he saw community theater way off Broadway, in some of the marginalized neighborhoods. Fraga created the community group Nós do Morro[19] in 1986, with the goals of training young people in the performance arts such as acting, music, and dance and to bring culture to the favela.

> I always say that I was a poor person who had every opportunity in life, and maybe that somehow influenced some decisions in my life. This question of opportunity was what moved me all the way to unimaginable experiences. Art gives you this power to travel unbelievable journeys. In 1985, on a trip with my friend Maria Pera to New York, I encountered the popular culture of the ghettos instead of the traditional Broadway shows. I almost always went far off-Broadway and there I saw things that moved me, they were small spaces where one worked in an alternative way and with a lot of quality, and this ended up inspiring me and then I thought: "Man, this is what I want to do!"[20]

Fraga has an original and creative methodology of giving each cohort of young people an all-encompassing project that combines months of grueling physical work with performance. The first project was to convert a donated house into a theater. This required thousands of person-hours to chip away and remove a huge boulder to make room for a stage. Literacy was a problem, so a reading program emerged. As one alumnus of the program notes: "Guti and Nós do Morro are always starting over. If there is a rock blocking the path, Fraga stops and studies the rock. He doesn't go around. Instead, he breaks it. . . . That's Nós do Morro's philosophy."[21]

Soon, a variety show began each Saturday night. Fraga called it *The 7pm Show* (which started at 8 p.m.), and it allowed the children and young people to practice all week and perform theater, music, comedy, and dance on the weekend. The theater was located at the bottom of the hill, and neighbors would pack the small theater each week. It was a huge success, and many leaders would continue with this project indefinitely. Many of the active members of *The 7pm Show* continue today as prominent professional actors and performers.[22]

For Fraga, however, each generation of young people needed their own projects and challenges. After a decade of *The 7pm Show*, Fraga decided to take culture to the top of the hill, and the *Campinho Show* was born. *Campinho Show* is a variety show presented every other Wednesday night in an outdoor space that accommodates 1,000 spectators. Crowds of families attend the show that is emceed by Fraga and includes every imaginable performance art and performers of all ages (figure 7.5). Fraga believes that the act of performing on stage in front of a large audience is a formative experience for young people in the favelas. "There is nothing more beautiful than a child, or a maid, or a student, often living in difficult situations, performing before their community, receiving applause! This is addictive and builds self-esteem and commitment."[23]

Fraga expanded the horizons of the participants with joint programs with the Royal Shakespeare Company and other companies throughout Europe.[24] The opportunity to travel and perform is life-changing, whether it be a fifty-year old maid performing in England,

Figure 7.5 Guti Fraga at *Campinho Show*

a teenage female musical trio touring Europe, or a group performing theater in São Paulo.

"Since its inauguration, Nós do Morro has transformed something rotten and dirty into a colorful place. We find the poetic amongst the garbage."[25] Nós do Morro has served 12,374 individuals over three decades with free courses on theater, music, dance, and other performance activities. All participants must be enrolled in and attending school, with 72 percent of the members graduating high school and 25 percent entering the university.

Fraga's passion and talent in acting and performance produced a lasting legacy. As of June 2020, 34 percent of the current or past participants in Nós do Morro work in art and culture; 4,084 people followed their dreams, did lots of hard physical labor, studied, rehearsed and performed, and now work professionally in all aspects of the performing arts.

In 2016, Fraga relaunched yet again, mentoring a new generation of young people to construct an entirely new space and to fill it with poetry and handicrafts. To survive in the favela, one must juggle continuously, constantly finding solutions to the most intractable problems. Fraga, like all the successful leaders we met, wants to show the doubters precisely what the people of the hill are capable of. They are highly motivated. And as he always reminds us whenever we meet, "Life is only possible if it is reinvented."

Rise Up & Care was delighted to receive a proposal from Fraga. He asked for money to professionalize *Campinho Show* and offer some benefits to the local performers. Campinho Show is the heart and soul of this disadvantaged community of 13,000. Fraga has been a stellar grantee, and he received a total of seven grants. It is always a joy to hear from Fraga or Nós do Morro documenting the impact and destination of the money with reports, photos, and video clips.

Due to the crises in contemporary Brazil, this relatively small amount of money kept *Campinho Show* entertaining and training until the coronavirus ended the run. On March 26, 2020, Rise Up & Care wired $2,000 to Nós do Morro without conditions or stipulations. They could have spent that money anyway they wanted. One month later, Nós do Morro sent an email with twenty-two photos documenting the destination of that money. They distributed 182 basic monthly food baskets, 150 hygiene and sanitation kits, 700 kilos of fresh produce, and sixty dozen eggs (figure 7.6).

Not all of the beneficiaries of Nós do Morro are young, some are merely youthful. Marília Furacão (*furacão* means "hurricane" in Portuguese) is a maid. She began training with Fraga years ago and has performed as a singer and actor not only at *Campinho Show* (figure 7.7) but as far away as Lisbon and London. She also composes viral songs about local social issues, such as eliminating dengue and encouraging condom use. Today, Marília and Nós do Morro produce music videos on social distancing and wearing masks. For Marília, "Art nourishes people. With theater, old people can be young again."[26]

Figure 7.6 The actors of Nós do Morro preparing food baskets

Figure 7.7 Marília Furacão performing at *Campinho Show*

CASA DO JONGO DA SERRINHA AND
TIA MARIA DO JONGO

The Serrinha neighborhood in Rio's northern zone pulsates with music, dance, and the rhythm of drums. Settled by newly freed slaves at the end of the nineteenth century, Serrinha is the birthplace of the Império Serrinha Samba School and is the cradle of Jongo music and dance. Jongo is a cultural inheritance from West Africa that arrived with the slaves to the coffee plantations in the Paraíba Valley in southeastern Brazil. Jongo is the African musical root of the beat of samba music and includes Afro-Brazilian religious elements.

Tia Maria do Jongo and other female leaders founded Jongo da Serrinha in 2000. In 2005, Jongo da Serrinha was registered as an Immaterial Heritage of the South-East of Brazil at the National Historic Heritage Institute (IPHAN). Jongo da Serrinha had an essential role in this milestone and developed innovative practices to preserve this cultural treasure. The association belongs to an eighteen-member network of *Jongueiras* communities of Rio de Janeiro to create public policies for education, culture, work, and the environment. Jongo music and dance are the principal tools for social development.

To nurture this cultural heritage, the Casa do Jongo da Serrinha trains children and teens in the percussion, singing, and dances of this beautiful expression (figure 7.8). For an introduction to Jongo rhythm, you can watch the short trailer and the award-winning documentary about it and the incredible women behind it at www.jongofevermovie. com. Jongo flourished under Tia Maria's extraordinary leadership. Tia Maria do Jongo passed in 2018, at the age of ninety-eight.

Life in the favela of Serrinha is very difficult, with violent drug gangs and corrupt police. In addition, the booming evangelical Christian movement in Brazil and in Serrinha announced war on anything associated with African religions, condemning it as sinful and devilish.

I used to work teaching music at a private school, and I introduced Jongo music there. They had a small drum, and I played caxambu

Figure 7.8 Tia María, Lazir Sinval, and Jongo da Serrinha dancing in the streets

(rhythm) there. The director heard the music and said, "Stop this, it's ungodly." So I told her, "Did you know that in Jesus Christ's days there was no piano, guitar, or ukulele; just drums. Before you were even born, you already heard a drum in your mother's heartbeat. . . . There was rhythm all the time." We're in the 21st century, and black culture is still trampled upon and humiliated.[27]

In 2014, police destroyed the Jongo da Serrinha center, and the organization was under threat. Rather than hunker down or consolidate in that time of crisis, the Jongo women leaders decided to be bold and secured the use and remodeling of a 17,000-square-feet community center located next to the area's main highway. This allowed the organization to emerge as the principal center of community activity in Serrinha and provided space for a number of new activities such as the martial arts dance of capoeira, professional training, education, child care, and more.

The innovation in Serrinha actually began decades ago when a survey revealed that nearly all of the Jongo dancers and musicians

Figure 7.9 Teaching Jongo to the next generation

had died. Jongo had two sacred traditions that were leading the cultural jewel to extinction:, the rule that dancers had to be elderly, with completely white hair and not even a single streak of dark hair, and the norm that only men could play the various drums. Women took charge and energized Jongo, first by learning and excelling at playing the drums and then by teaching Jongo dancing, singing, and drumming to children and young people (figure 7.9).[28] The first female master drummer and inspirational community leader, Luiza Marmello, passed in 2019.

Rise Up & Care is proud to partner with Casa do Jongo da Serrinha, and the organization uses donations to enhance youth programming. The women of Jongo have been conscientious stewards of this money, and the grants have been impactful and efficient.

Rise Up arrived at a very important moment for Jongo da Serrinha, in which we were making a great expansion: leaving our small headquarters in Morro da Serrinha still trying to understand what life would be like in this new headquarters and to deal with all the demands that this would bring. Rise Up funded so many activities in the new cultural center, it was a miracle.[29]

Imagine that, instead of giving additional funds to Jongo da Serrinha, we raised funds to start our own music and dance program in the Serrinha favela.

Jongo is an African cultural expression and therefore is opposed by a lot of people. Also, the fact that we are an organization coordinated exclusively by women makes the work very challenging and satisfying. Rise Up believed in us and our work in passing the Jongo music and dance to a new generation and invigorating this cultural jewel.

Other local leaders took charge with the deaths of vital community leaders Tia Maria do Jongo, Grandma Maria Joana, and Luiza Marmello. Damiana Alves, Dyonne Boy, Andreia Caetano, Valeria Marchón, Deli Monteiro, Lazir Sinval, and others are moving the Casa do Jongo da Serrinha forward. Rise Up & Care is particularly pleased to provide funds for the celebration of the one hundredth anniversary of do Jongo's birth, the twentieth-year commemoration of the founding of the nonprofit organization, and the sixtieth anniversary of the Jongo da Serrinha community organization, all taking place in 2021.[30]

In March 2020, Rise Up & Care sent $2,000 to Casa do Jongo da Serrinha. The *jongeiras* used these funds in campaigns for masks and for broadcasting Jongo concerts to nourish the souls of the community in the time of the pandemic. Casa do Jongo da Serrinha has received four grants to date. These powerful women maximize and leverage these funds to maintain the vitality of their organization, transform the youth of Serrinha, and preserve a precious cultural expression. The act of passing on Jongo to future generations is a form of resistance against violence and discrimination.

A DIFFERENT TEST: ZEFA DA GUIA AND
THE MIDWIVES OF NORTHEASTERN BRAZIL

When we describe the demonstration project with various groups in Rio de Janeiro, people sometimes ask if the model would work in other sectors and in other environments. They wonder if perhaps there is something singular and nongeneralizable about the favelas of Rio de Janeiro. Maybe Rio is a black swan or magic unicorn. We decided to add a small additional demonstration project. We were interested in the power of the community bank model (CBM) in small towns and rural communities. We were also curious about trying the model in a sector that is very different from the youth performance organizations in Rio de Janeiro. How would we identify superstar local leaders in rural and small-town Brazil? We would, once again, think like community bankers. Community bankers nurture a core client base of high-character individuals, people with whom they have established confidence; then they go to these trusted individuals for referrals of other high-character potential customers.

We developed a strong working relationship with two young women in São Paulo who were making a documentary film on traditional midwives. Mayara Boaretto and Isadora Carneiro spent nearly a decade traveling Brazil and the world interviewing midwives and developing powerful relationships with many of them. Among the hundreds of midwives that Mayara and Isadora encountered, three midwives stood out as dedicated, long-term superheroes who were improving the lives of their communities in the impoverished areas of northeastern Brazil. Based on our relationship and trust with Mayara and Isadora and their long-term relationships with the midwives, Rise Up & Care provided small one-time grants of US$5,000 to three midwives. This is a relatively small amount of money, but all three women had been working in their communities for decades, and they could do a lot with a modest amount of money. To learn more about these powerful women, go to www.womenofearthfilm.com. We briefly examine the life of one of these extraordinary women, Zefa da Guia, next (figure 7.10).

Figure 7.10 Zefa da Guia
Source: Photo by Isadora Carneiro

Zefa da Guia was born in 1944 in the Quilombo Serra da Guia in the arid northeastern state of Sergipe. The word *quilombo* refers to a runaway slave community, and the Quilombo Serra da Guia took form in the mid-1800s with runaway slaves from Pernambuco.[31] Zefa da Guia is an illiterate seventy-seven-year-old black descendent of runaway slaves in an impoverished, arid hinterland town of 200 families. Zefa da Guia is also one of the most powerful and important leaders we ever met. She began preaching at the age of nine and working as a midwife at the age of eleven. She has eight children of her own and has adopted eighteen more. Zefa da Guia has delivered well over 5,000 babies and is the undisputed leader of her community.[32]

Mayara and Isadora spoke in the most glowing of terms about their long relationship with Zefa da Guia and with two other mentors: the indigenous midwife and community leader D'Ajuda, and the midwife Zezé. We met these noble women once and provided a one-time grant of $5,000 to each midwife. There were no conditions; the women could do anything they wanted with the money. Zezé used the money to renovate her home and birthing center, which receives 5,000 patients per year. D'Ajuda constructed a new birthing center. And Zefa da Guia purchased a new statue of a saint for her community and refurbished a community center. Relatively small amounts of money can have a huge impact. Again, the midwives were proud to share videos and photos of the impact of the donations.

In May 2020 and to celebrate International Midwives Day, Rise Up & Care joined forces with Mayara, Isadora, and Women of Earth to raise $33,000. These funds are to empower Zefa da Guia, d'Ajuda, and Zezé to provide food and hygienic supplies to hundreds of families during the pandemic that is devastating northeastern Brazil.

This demonstration project with various projects in Brazil illustrates the payoff of CBM. The findings are even more compelling for three reasons. First, this demonstration project took place during the 2014–2020 period, when Brazil's economy crashed; the political system crumbled; crime rates soared; and institutions such as law enforcement, health, and education buckled. Then came COVID-19. This was a stress test of the highest order. Many local organizations in Rio de Janeiro have conserved energy by downsizing to endure the crisis. Our four principal partner organizations all suffered heavy losses of funding from Brazilian institutions, the ire of the ascendant drug traffickers, extortion from the *milícias*, and deteriorating conditions in the households of the youth that they serve. Nevertheless, they adjusted, innovated, reduced and refocused activities, worked harder and smarter, and continued to deliver vital services and hope to their communities thanks to the incredible character and integrity of the leaders, the support of parents and volunteers, the capacity of the organizations, and the goodwill of their communities. It is difficult to imagine that foreign start-ups could have survived these unprecedented bleak conditions.

Second, all the organizations are in a constant state of innovation and reinvention. The leaders are continuously evaluating shifting conditions, threats, and opportunities, and creating new methodologies and strategies to survive and succeed. With the boom-and-bust economy of Brazil, this also includes contracting and expanding. This differs significantly from similar organizations in the Global North, where detailed, long-term plans are the norm. Time horizons are shorter in the Global South.

Third, they are all motivated by two prime objectives. First, they want to help young people traverse the problematic teenage years through the demands, lessons, discipline, bonds, and experiences of high-level performance. The mission is always more important than the organization. Second, they want to show the asphalt, elite, "legitimate" people of Rio de Janeiro what can be accomplished in the stereotypically invisible, illegitimate, substandard, drug- and gang-ridden favelas. This motivation is enormous and produces long-term drive, ambition, creativity, innovation, and effort. It creates individual and community pride and undercuts implicit bias and discrimination.

This demonstration project also answers the two major critiques of CBM. One of our greatest surprises was to encounter so many organizations in Rio de Janeiro with local leadership and long track records of achievement. One of our greatest regrets is that we were unable to partner formally with all of them. We also visited Colombia in search of similar organizations, those with innovative local leaders who were helping youth with high-performance programs for many years. There were literally hundreds of programs utilizing sports and other hundreds of programs using film or photography. We confidently reject the hypothesis that CBM will not work due to the scarcity of the right types of ongoing local programs with superhero leaders.

We also want to address directly the hypothesis that these organizations and leaders are embedded in a culture of corruption and therefore they would not use the grants for the agreed-to purposes. It is true that corruption is rife in Brazil. It is also true that these leaders and organizations know that they are representing the favelas and the oft-discarded populations in Rio de Janeiro. Their reputation is the most valuable resource that they have, and they protect it at all cost. They have decades of demonstrated love and service to their communities and multiple cohorts of young people. Our experience is that they go above and beyond the requirements for avoiding any connection to corruption.

We were with Oliveira at dinner in Washington, D.C., as part of a presentation to the Inter-American Development Bank. Oliveira looked at us and began to weep. His deep personal pain was evident. Someone at his organization, Miratus Badminton Association, had misused a very small amount of money. The other leaders begged Oliveira to forgive that individual but also to require repayment and a public expression of remorse. Oliveira had no problem forgiving that person but expressed through his tears and great anguish that he and Miratus are under constant observation and judgment. His character and the integrity of Miratus required zero tolerance, and they had to be far cleaner than other organizations in Brazil. And so they are.

What do these organizations have in common besides their long-term success in using high-level performance to transform youth and communities? First, locals lead all of the organizations and develop all of the ideas; they are people who live in the communities, identify with their community, and understand the constantly shifting conditions. Local leadership is an asset to their communities and brings respect and self-esteem to their neighborhoods. They are critical community resources in times of crisis. Children in marginalized communities need dreams and role models who look like them.

Finally, each organization targets a wide age range and builds a step-by-step ladder of success whereby newcomers and younger children can see the progression of other participants to desirable levels of success. The older participants mentor the younger participants. These programs require high levels of commitment, and children are much more likely to stick with the work if they see the tangible payoff of travel, prestige, awards, economic benefits, performance acclaim, status at school and in the community, praise from family, and college education.

Local and international observers and the media portray the favelas of Rio de Janeiro as crime-ridden, violent, and impoverished. This portrayal reinforces inherent biases and misses the reality and the emergence of hundreds of locally led organizations that are transforming individuals and their communities.

TABLE 7.1
Comparison of two approaches

	Community Bank Model—Build on Local Success	Traditional International Philanthropic Start-Up
Time needed to effect positive impact	Immediate because the program has been fully functioning for many years and can utilize new funds quickly.	Years to build infrastructure and start program.
What can be accomplished with only $1,300 to $25,000	This amount of money can have a huge impact because all fixed costs are already covered, and the money goes only to variable costs such as enhanced programs for youth.	This amount of money covers very little given the high fixed and start-up costs needed for this type of program.
Cost efficiency	All of the money goes to the program, with an immediate effect.	Traditional expected cost efficiency is low because of the high failure rate of start-ups and lots of overhead expenses.
Lifting local leaders (subversive)	All ideas, leadership, credit, and acclaim stay local. Local leaders are the superheroes, and the outside partners are the invisible sidekicks. This approach erodes hierarchies and enhances incredible local role models of innovative and courageous Afro-Brazilians in their communities.	The outside partners would be the senior partners and would get the credit and the acclaim. The local leaders would be the sidekicks or junior partners. This approach reinforces hierarchies and does not empower local role models.
Innovation	Knowledge of the community leads to incredible innovation in each organization.	Without knowledge of the community, we would likely blame the culture of the locals for any failure instead of innovating to meet their needs.

Final result	Everyone is thrilled and grateful.	Hard feelings, unfulfilled promises, abandoned projects.
Acclaim and fame	Always for the local leaders, volunteers, and participants.	Often for the senior partner from the United States or Europe.
Impact assessment	Cooperative division of labor that is harmonious and collaborative. Leaders are good stewards and accountable. They document with photos, video clips, and reports. Assessment inspires local leaders and donors.	Make-work imposed assessment with very low value and high opportunity costs, which creates an antagonistic and demoralizing atmosphere. Leaders are frustrated. They shrug, wink, and plug in numbers the best that they can.

From 2015 to June 2020, Rise Up & Care provided $546,871 in thirty-two total grants. The partners in Brazil accounted for every dollar with detailed reports and verifying images. We are consistently overjoyed and energized with how much they achieve.

8

A CALL TO ACTION

Our work in the favela is resistance. Small gestures
produce great outcomes.

—GUTI FRAGA

As we write this conclusion in early 2021, the world faces two
important issues: COVID-19 and the heightened struggle for
racial justice and equality. These two firestorms magnify this book's
lessons and ramifications. More than ever, the global philanthropic
sector must be far more efficient and considerably more subversive of existing power structures by empowering leaders, mentors,
changemakers, and advocates in the local communities of Africa,
Latin America, and Asia.

COVID-19 AND EFFICIENCY

Resources for global philanthropy are always scarce. Current practice produces far too little return on investment, and start-up
projects fail far too often. There are economic, ethical, and logical
reasons why we must strive to maximize impact and cost efficiency.
The community bank model (CBM) multiplies the expected return
on investment for international giving.

In the post-COVID-19 world, the need for assistance will be far
greater just as the supply of philanthropic dollars decreases. The
Chronicle of Philanthropy is but one source with headlines warn-
ing of an impending tsunami of nonprofit closures when greater

numbers of people need nonprofit services.[1] The World Bank predicts that an additional 50 million people will plunge into poverty in Latin America alone.[2]

It was never wise to spend meager resources on questionable activities such as orphanage voluntourism or on start-up projects in far-off lands with low likelihoods of success. After the end of the coronavirus pandemic, an even greater share of the limited resources should go to locally led initiatives with long track records of success. These leaders and organizations can deliver quickly, efficiently, and flexibly. For example, partner organizations in Brazil responded rapidly and effectively to the COVID-19 emergency in their communities.

Now is not the time for Hail Mary passes; long-shot start-ups; and interventions that will take years, if ever, to bear fruit. While it is never the best return on investment to spend thousands of dollars on a charity trip that includes a couple of days of painting a building or laying bricks, we must also seriously consider if these activities are ethical as the coronavirus produces a swathe of unemployment, hunger, and disease that will linger for years. If there was ever a time to adopt CBM, this is it.

RACIAL STEREOTYPES AND SUBVERSION

We are writing this conclusion from Atlanta, Georgia, and Los Angeles, California. Our cities recently experienced one of the largest protest movements in recent decades. The senseless deaths of George Floyd and so many others unleashed pent-up anger and demands. This movement is about far more than merely reforming the police. Black Lives Matter (BLM) groups and other protagonists demand nothing less than an awakening and recognition of the inherent biases against people of color that result in discrimination, inequality, injustice, violence, and death.

Many around the globe are considering their own implicit biases. Corporations, sports leagues, the fashion industry, the media, politicians, universities, churches, and individuals are recognizing, often publicly, their implicit biases and pledging to correct those prejudices and the resulting discrimination. Time will tell if this moment is ephemeral and will produce limited progress or if it is sustainable and will produce enduring change.

The international compassion sector also suffers from extensive implicit bias; it is time to recognize that bias and its deleterious consequences. Table 8.1 presents the evolution of the explicit racism found in Kipling's poem "The White Man's Burden" into the implicit bias of contemporary global philanthropy. Implicit bias results from patterns, images, and associations in our brains that lead us to reproduce stereotypes and categorizations that, in turn, reinforce implicit bias in the future. It is a vicious cycle. These patterns and the resulting implicit bias result in a development practice whereby Global North participants are the leaders, innovators,

Table 8.1

The explicit racism of colonialism and the implicit bias of global philanthropy

Kipling's Characteristics of the White Man's Burden Associated With:		Characteristics of the Philanthropist's Burden Associated With:	
Colonizers	Colonized	Global North	Global South
white	dark	superhero	sidekick
best ye breed	half child	innovator	heavy lifter
patient	half devil	leader	follower
toil	wild	disciplined	lethargic
reward	sullen	senior partner	junior partner
kings	savages	trustworthy	corrupt
praiseworthy	sloth	policymaker	stakeholder
adulthood	folly	charitable	grateful
wisdom	foolishness	brilliant	uneducated
judgment	threat of terror	praiseworthy	admirer
selfless	silent	administrator	assistant
peacemakers	heathens	take charge	subordinate
enlightening	hateful	efficient	inefficient
logical	bondage	culture of success	culture of failure

superheroes, senior partners, and so on, while practitioners in the Global South are followers, stakeholders, junior partners, and subordinates.

Implicit bias is like an infection, and we can eradicate it only with extensive, deliberate action. Seminars and workshops on stereotypes and bias are probably insufficient. CBM inverts the traditional functions and stereotypes of Global North and Global South team members. Most important, the model shines a spotlight on local female and male role models for the children in marginalized communities. Children of color in the favelas of Rio de Janeiro have their implicit biases too. They need to grow up with the norm, image, and pattern that men and women of color from their communities are innovators; praiseworthy, trustworthy leaders; and superheroes, not merely junior partners and subordinates.

We admit that we are products of our environments and have our own deep-seated implicit biases and stubborn stereotypes. The practice of consciously adopting the role of heavy-lifting sidekick to assist innovative high-character leaders in the favelas helps us erase those biases. We still have a long way to go.

During the 2016 Summer Olympics in Rio de Janeiro, we worked with a talented and committed group of local activists and community cultural leaders to present the Reimagine Rio Film Festival (figure 8.1). Ten activists with a passion for film organized free screenings of five documentary movies, those featuring the Casa do Jongo da Serrinha, Cinema Nosso, Crescer e Viver circus, Miratus Badminton Association, and Nós do Morro. These ten managers had considerable freedom in determining the format and venues for the screenings. They hosted screenings in schools, soccer courts, libraries, theaters, amphitheaters, and plazas and at slumber parties. In the end, the five films screened in seventy-four locations. The smallest screenings had an audience of a couple of dozen; the largest had over 1,000. Many parents brought their families to watch all five films. Popcorn and Guaraná drinks were served.

Many warned us that children would not sit through fifty- to sixty-five-minute documentary films. We were pleasantly surprised.

Figure 8.1 Poster for the Reimagine Rio Film Festival

The children loved the films! Someone posted a photo on social media showing four young boys sitting on a blanket and transfixed watching a documentary movie on a makeshift outdoor screen. The caption of the social media post simply said, "After Reimagine Rio, it is forever prohibited to say that children do not like documentary films." In total, there were 455 free screenings. Schoolteachers

Figure 8.2 "After Reimagine Rio, it is forever prohibited to say that children do not like documentary films"

requested DVDs for schools, and Rise Up & Care provided the films and a supplemental teacher's manual to hundreds of schools.

We asked several people why young children, often as young as four to ten years old, would have the attention and interest to watch five one-hour documentary films (figures 8.2 and 8.3). The answer was always the same. This was the first time that these young people saw media portrayals where the protagonists looked like them and were leaders, superheroes, and role models, and not criminals or drug dealers. Their implicit biases are eroding. This is subversive.

You can further explore how to embolden local leaders at www.sidekickmanifesto.org. You might even sign the manifesto, which includes the following:

- I will ride in the sidecar.
- I will question the utility of technical gadgets and my utility belt.
- I will ignore the siren singing songs of scale.
- I will step out of the spotlight.

Figure 8.3 Reimagine Rio Film Festival viewers at badminton center

- I will read "To hell with good intentions" again and again.
- I will hang up my cape.

WHAT CAN YOU DO?

It is difficult to describe the joy and personal satisfaction that comes from using CBM. We have grown to love our senior partners in Brazil, to celebrate their successes, and to feel their disappointments and sorrows. We follow the young beneficiaries of the projects as they grow and achieve. As a sidekick, you make friends for life, your cynicism melts away, and you feel unprecedented fulfillment. When we started this journey, we planned on a four-year demonstration project before moving on to the next project somewhere else. That original goal became impossible, even as we continue to update and replicate the demonstration project in new countries. Sebastião, Guti, Junior, Vinicius, Dyonne, Lazir, and many others are now family.

You can easily leverage your passion about almost anything—for example, the environment, gender issues, health, youth, literacy, education—with networking to identify local superheroes who have a track record of success and a neighborhood focus. If you travel internationally, ask people you meet about the organizations and leaders who make a difference in their community. Communicate with journalists, bloggers, consular officials, and tour guides and identify innovative, successful organizations. Visit them and observe. Follow their social media and do some research on the Internet. When you find an organization and leaders that you admire, become a sidekick. Donate money. Even small amounts can make a difference; small gestures produce great outcomes. If you feel comfortable doing so, ask them what they would do with a $100, $500, or $5,000 donation. Perhaps you can help them with their social media or their webpage. Make the connection a long-term commitment, and you will receive more than you give.

Even if you do not spend any time in the Global South, you can easily do research and network to identify outstanding organizations working in arenas and countries that match your interests and passions. The search itself is a very rewarding process. Talk to friends and relatives who travel regularly or talk to connections who have family in targeted countries. We may all be six degrees from Kevin Bacon; we assure you that you are fewer degrees of separation from a superstar in the Global South who works in an area that excites you.

One of the great surprises in our journey was discovering the degree to which many already practice CBM. Many, from individuals to student groups, to foundations, act as anonymous supporters. We applaud celebrities, such as Lin-Manuel Miranda, who are generous and largely anonymous sidekicks. Miranda became a global superstar after his Broadway hit *Hamilton*. After the devastation of Hurricane Maria, Miranda wanted to help his beloved Puerto Rico. With his money and fame, he could have easily opted to create a vanity project from scratch. Instead, he chose to be efficient and subversive by providing resources to existing successful organizations focused on the performing arts.

Miranda's Flamboyán Foundation provides funds to twelve existing organizations with long-term records of success and inspired local leaders. One is the contemporary dance organization Andanza. Andanza has been providing high-performance dance training to youth in San Juan for twenty years, often struggling to generate sufficient funds. Miranda's grant was a miracle for them: "It's the first time that we have funds guaranteed for the beginning of the year so it's been very important," notes Andanza executive director Lolita Villanúa. Flamboyán also supports the theater company Y No Había Luz, which uses art experiences to foster creativity, social justice, and solidarity since 2005. Flamboyán provides resources to Y No Había Luz for activities and outreach that would not be possible otherwise.[3]

Many have the urge to travel to another country, create personal connections with people, and join a voluntourism project or other short-term experience. We understand this feeling. Voluntourism, study abroad, and other activities can be significantly improved by providing services that you are highly qualified to do and by relentlessly empowering local leaders. Here is a tangible example. Spending tens of thousands of dollars to paint a school or lay some bricks is incredibly inefficient because of the simple law of comparative advantage. Most communities of the Global South include highly qualified and underemployed painters and bricklayers. Students from Atlanta, Georgia, have other comparative advantages. Georgia Tech students excel in webpage design, branding, fundraising, and speaking native English. English language skills provide a significant career and life advantage to individuals around the world.[4] Travel to Honduras. Fall in love with the community. Work as an assistant to a local teacher and provide English tutoring to young people. Coronavirus popularized teaching via Skype and Zoom. Don't just helicopter into a community for a week. Tutor remotely once a week for an hour or two. Return every year or two. Give praise and credit to the local teacher.

Suffolk University students traveled from Boston (where the university is located) to Brazil every year before the COVID-19 pandemic as part of a study abroad. They explore cultural, economic, and business topics. The students always spend a full day at Miratus Badminton Association, learning samba dancing from the children, playing badminton, and hearing about Sebastião Oliveira's inspiring life story. After they return to Boston, the students raise several thousand dollars for Miratus, which boosts Oliveira's spirits and provides for critical activities.

A second option is to volunteer for organizations in your community. Organizations almost everywhere have impressive track records of neighborhood impact. One benefit of staying local with your service is the opportunity for regular acts of in-person volunteering.

What if you feel a personal calling to start an organization or a development project in the Global South? You have fallen in love with a community, and you have a great idea. We strongly urge you to become a local by moving there. The world is full of expatriates (expats) who were captivated by a region, a country, or a community, and moved there. We have met many individuals who spend their lives improving a community to which they have relocated. These individuals are often former Peace Corps volunteers, missionaries, or scholars who spent years in a new country, learned the language, gained an appreciation for the culture, made friends, and decided to stay.

One example is Victor Bonito. Bonito studied marine biology at the University of North Carolina, Chapel Hill, and subsequently served in Fiji as a Peace Corps volunteer. He fell for Fiji and the Fijians. He later earned his master's degree in biology at the University of Guam Marine Laboratory. He moved to the coastal village of Korolevu, Fiji, in 2005 and founded Reef Explorer Fiji, which he directs to this day. Reef Explorer Fiji works with stakeholders and international partners to improve local knowledge about marine ecology and conservation, conduct research for management planning and evaluation, and assist in the development of sustainable livelihood opportunities for local communities based on conservation actions and management strategies. Bonito's work includes coral restoration projects with significant local participation, youth and adult capacitation in marine management, village infrastructure, and more.

Another example is Maryam Montague, an American who spent twenty-five years working as a humanitarian aid worker. She eventually developed a kinship with Morocco and its people and settled permanently in Marrakesh. Montague wanted to help the young women of Morocco because many drop out of school at the onset of puberty. She founded Project Soar in 2013, which offers empowerment coaching, health education, sports, and arts to 475 girls in twenty-one neighborhoods.[5]

Theresa Williamson earned her PhD in city and regional planning at the University of Pennsylvania. She moved to Rio de Janeiro and founded Catalytic Communities in 2000. Catalytic Communities is a nongovernmental organization (NGO) working to support Rio de Janeiro's favelas through asset-based community development. Williamson and her team produce *RioOnWatch*, an indispensable favela news platform. If you are interested in journalism or community planning, support her exceptional work.

The most effective expats may be those who serve as anonymous sidekicks, like Gwenaelle (Gwen) Maitre (figure 8.4). Maitre is from Lyon, France, but spent seven years in her youth in Brazil. She earned her master's degree in accounting sciences at Lille and began a career working for the French multinational sports retail firm DECATHLON in Brazil. Maitre is active in sports and deeply committed to harnessing high-performance sports to change individuals and communities. Maitre has directed Nissan Olympic sponsorships for Brazil since 2014, and her work includes managing twelve Brazilian athletes. Maitre met Oliveira in 2007 and dedicated thousands of hours volunteering with accounting, programming, organizing dozens of international trips for the athletes, and securing institutional grants for Miratus Badminton Association. She currently manages the careers of Ygor Coelho (age twenty-three, with a Badminton Federation World ranking of 48) and Jonathan Matias (age twenty, with a Badminton Federation World Ranking of 334). Maitre possesses exceptional talents and works tirelessly because she loves the kids of Chacrinha

Figure 8.4 Gwen Maitre at Miratus Badminton Association in 2008

and knows the power of sports to transform youth. Yes, the world needs more innovative social entrepreneurs like Sebastião Oliveira. The world also needs many more heavy-lifting supporters like Gwen Maitre.

You do not need to provide personal funds. You can do a fundraiser on your own campus, help improve a webpage, or start a crowdfunding campaign. If you are entrepreneurial, try your hand at social enterprise to generate resources for a program you support. Social enterprise uses business tools for social needs, and such enterprises often earn money through products or services to support social projects. Rise Up & Care practices social enterprise with a CBM twist. With students at Georgia Tech and the Rio street artist Cazé, Rise Up & Care works in a vertically integrated project (VIP) on global social entrepreneurship[6] to produce a children's book series.[7] The books in the series follow the adventures of a curious kid from Atlanta named Scout, whose mother is a pilot and

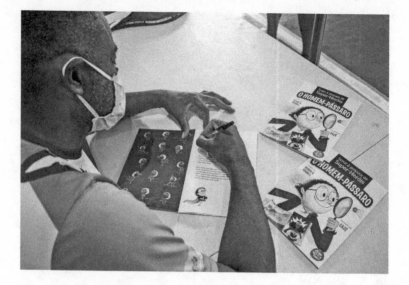

Figure 8.5 Sebastião Oliveira autographing 800 free children's books for the Chacrinha community in October 2020

takes the family on lots of international vacations. Scout has a special gift of finding real-life superheroes. The books detail Scout's discovery of superheroes; the parents' doubt and pushback; and the real-life story of incredible local leaders in unexpected locations, like favelas, for superheroes. The first book, *Scout's Superhero Search: The Birdieman of Rio de Janeiro* (www.scoutheroes.com), features Sebastião Oliveira (figures 8.5 and 8.6). For every book sold in the United States, two are distributed to families in favelas in Brazil. The books also include both English and Portuguese language sections, family activities, digital games that counter stereotypes and implicit bias, and access to the matching documentary films. Any additional money earned is split evenly between all the partner organizations in Rio de Janeiro.

The *Scout's Superhero Search* follows the basic principles of CBM. The purpose is not to earn money; the purpose is to celebrate local superheroes and their youth participants in their communities,

Figure 8.6 English language version of the book about Sebastião Oliveira, *Scout's Superhero Search: The Birdieman of Rio de Janeiro*

in their cities, and abroad. All of the elements of the series—books, games, supplemental materials, documentary films, digital enhancements—are designed to battle implicit bias and build up local role models. The product must be worthwhile and have a strong positive impact, even if no profits result. Selling lots of books and generating lots of money for social programs in Rio de Janeiro would be fantastic, but it is the icing on the cake.

One of the easiest ways to follow CBM is to donate through entities that act as clearinghouses for local projects. These organizations do the vetting, aggregate donations, and provide additional resources: You merely need to zero in on your preferred type of organization and the location. We already introduced one example: GiveDirectly. Another impressive organization is GlobalGiving (globalgiving.org). Mari Kuraishi and Dennis Whittle were two World Bank employees concerned with the large number of exemplary small social entrepreneurs with limited opportunities for grants and institutional funding. To solve that problem, they launched the crowdfunding nonprofit GlobalGiving in 2002. To date, the GlobalGiving community has raised more than $450 million—from more than 1 million people—for nearly 26,000 projects in 170 countries. GlobalGiving's purpose is to shift the focus of funders and nonprofits toward communities. Their vision is that, when nonprofits listen to the people they intend to help, act on what they hear, and continuously learn from the results, a virtuous cycle is created, and social progress is possible.

One of the potential benefits of smaller clearinghouse organizations such as Rise Up & Care is that sponsors pay 100 percent of the nonprofit administrative costs so that 100 percent of your donations go to organizations like those described in this book. That is efficiency.

KEEPING IT SIMPLE

At its core, the highest quality philanthropy is both highly efficient and subversive. Before you provide resources to an organization or activity or travel as a participant in a philanthropic endeavor, ask yourself, "Can I make this more efficient and more subversive?" (See table 8.2.) When you travel with your friends, university, church, or family, do not think that you love the peoples of Guatemala or The Gambia; resist the urge to start a new NGO and transform youth.

If you want to give back and make a tangible difference, give up the Philanthropist's Burden and international start-ups. Instead, adopt the framework used by community banks. Identify successful local organizations with a long track record of success and leaders with high character. Invest in those organizations as a sidekick and empower locals as leaders and role models. Tell the world about those organizations and local heroes through word of mouth and public relations.

You will make lifetime friends with incredible people. Your optimism will increase. Your travel will be purposeful and enriched. You will learn that the keys to real happiness are gratitude, service,

TABLE 8.2

Questions about maximizing the efficiency and subversion of philanthropic organizations

Efficient: Greatest Cost Efficiency	Subversive: Empower Local Leaders
What percentage of money actually goes to project activities?	Whose idea is it? Who innovates?
How much money do directors make?	Who is the leader and who is the junior partner?
Is there a more cost-effective way to deliver the same services?	Is my participation taking employment away from locals (painters, bricklayers, shoemakers, etc.)?
Is the organization an outright scam? Are the orphans really orphans who need hugs? Does the school really need painting?	Whose photos are on the webpage and other materials? Who gets the praise and applause?
Can my contribution make a difference?	Is the activity exacerbating divisions in the community?
What is the real likelihood of the partial or full failure of the project?	What is my long-term commitment to this community, or will I just helicopter in and out?
What is the time lag from my participation to the delivery of real benefits for the community?	Who is learning from whom?
Is the unit of social change appropriate?	Does the impact assessment inspire or demoralize local leaders?
Does the impact assessment maximize impact?	

connection, and passion. Your contributions of time and money will have the maximum possible impact. Unleash your inner sidekick and help change the world!

NOTES

PREFACE

1. Through the Swiss sport and development activist Pascal Wattiaux, whom we have never met, but to whom we are grateful.

2. This is a social and professional circus in Rio de Janeiro that we will revisit in chapter 7.

3. Albert O. Hirschman, "A Dissenter's Confession: 'The Strategy of Economic' Revisited," in *Pioneers in Development*, ed. Gerald Meier and Dudley Seers (London: Oxford University Press, 1984), 88. See also Albert O. Hirschman, *The Strategy of Economic Development* (New Haven, Conn.: Yale University Press, 1958), 1:230.

1. REASSESSING THE PHILANTHROPIST'S BURDEN

1. The *New York Times*, the *Washington Post*, the *Christian Science Monitor*, and dozens of other global media are equally impressed with Miratus and Sebastião: Dado Galdieri, "An Unlikely Olympic Story," *New York Times*, July 31, 2016, https://www.nytimes.com/slideshow/2016/07/31/sports/an-unlikely-olympic -story.html; David Segal, "In Rio Slum, a Gleaming Hotbed of . . . Badminton?" *New York Times*, July 26, 2016, https://www.nytimes.com/2016/07/31/sports/olympics /badminton-rio-de-janeiro-ygor-coelho-de-oliveira.html; Whitney Eulich, "How a Favela Kid Became Brazil's Top Badminton Player," *Christian Science Monitor*, August 13, 2016, https://www.csmonitor.com/World/Olympics/2016/0813 /How-a-favela-kid-became-Brazil-s-top-badminton-player.

2. The following sources all featured our work: Jane Sanders, "Scientists Help Fijian Villagers Conserve Coral Reef While Earning a Living from It," *EurekAlert!* July 19, 2005, http://www.eurekalert.org/pub_releases/2005-07/giot -shf071905.php; Nancy Bazilchuk, "Live Rock," University of Washington— Conservation, July 29, 2008, https://www.conservationmagazine.org/2008/07 /live-rock/; Jane Sanders, "Reefing the Benefits," *Research Horizons* 23 (Fall 2005): 6–11.

3. A zombie project is common in international philanthropic projects, where a project remains an enduring nongovernmental organization (NGO) even though nothing or precious little is happening.

4. These works include the following: Peter Frumkin, *Strategic Giving: The Art and Science of Philanthropy* (Chicago: University of Chicago Press, 2006), 458; Charles Bronfman and Jeffrey Solomon, *The Art of Doing Good: Where Passion Meets Action* (San Francisco: Jossey-Bass, 2012), 276; Eric Friedman, *Reinventing Philanthropy: A Framework for More Effective Giving* (Washington D.C.: Potomac, 2013), 205; Matthew Bishop and Michael Green, *Philanthro-Capitalism: How the Rich Can Save the World* (New York: Bloomsbury, 2008), 298; Rob Reich, *Just Giving: Why Philanthropy Is Failing Democracy and How It Can Do Better* (Princeton, N.J.: Princeton University Press, 2018), 252; Lester M. Salamon, ed. *New Frontiers of Philanthropy: A Guide to the New Tools and Actors Reshaping Global Philanthropy and Social Investing* (New York: Oxford University Press, 2014), 726; Anand Giridharadas, *Winners Take All: The Elite Charade of Changing the World* (New York: Vintage, 2018), 304.

5. Dinyar Godrej, "NGOs—Do They Help?," *New Internationalist*, December 1, 2014, https://newint.org/features/2014/12/01/ngos-keynote.

6. The terms *Global South* and *Global North* have replaced terminology such as *developed world*, *undeveloped world*, and *third world*. Most countries of the world, including those in Africa, Latin America, and much of Asia, comprise the Global South. Countries of the Global South share a common history of colonialism and neocolonialism.

7. Charity and philanthropy have a long tradition outside the Global North as well. There is a particularly rich history in the Islamic world. See: Amy Singer, *Charity in Islamic Societies* (Cambridge: Cambridge University Press, 2008), 260.

8. There is considerable debate about the number of waves of globalization and the time periods. We contend that the first great wave of globalization (1870–1913) resulted from advances in transportation and led to massive migration and colonization. The second great wave of globalization (1944–1971) witnessed the widespread use of jet airplanes and an ease of travel. The third wave of globalization (1980s to present) resulted from advances in communication and other technology that flowed from the invention and subsequent use of the microprocessor.

9. Patrick Brantlinger, "Kipling's 'The White Man's Burden' and Its Afterlives," *English Literature in Transition, 1880–1920*, 50, no. 2 (2007): 172–191.

10. Brantlinger, "Kipling's 'The White Man's Burden,'" 179.

11. Henry Labouchére, "The Brown Man's Burden," *Literary Digest* 18, no. 8 (1899): 219.

12. In recent years, neoconservatives such as Max Boot and others have rediscovered the white man's burden, claiming that the United States did a great service to the Philippines. See: Max Boot, *The Savage Wars of Peace: Small Wars and the Rise of American Power* (New York: Basic Books, 2002), 456.

13. We have taken the liberty of updating the language for the contemporary Philanthropist's Burden. If Theodore Roosevelt found Kipling's work "poor poetry," we are sure he would find our poem to be dreadful, but we believe, unfortunately, that he would similarly conclude that it made "good sense."

> TAKE up the Philanthropist's burden—
> Send forth your daughters and sons—
> To fly across the oceans
> To serve the poorest ones;
> To trudge into the jungles,
> Encounter those in need—
> Your new friends cannot flourish,
> Without your awesome deeds.
> Take up the Philanthropist's burden—
> Avoiding all the crooks,
> To pose with poor dark children
> On Snapchat and Facebook;
> By work and innovation,
> And leadership galore,
> To transform entire peoples,
> With web pages that soar.
> Take up the Humanitarian's burden—
> So they can live like you—
> Technology solves all problems
> If they just follow through.
> And when success is nearest,
> True sustainability.
> Their super backward culture
> Stops viability.

14. Rudyard Kipling, with his colonizing project, and present-day helpers, with their development projects, are most gifted in blaming the victims. It is their sloth and backwardness that forestalls success. Later in the original poem, Kipling notes:

Take up the White man's burden—
And reap his old reward:
The blame of those ye better,
The hate of those ye guard.

15. You can test your implicit biases at https://implicit.harvard.edu/implicit/.

16. For lessons from Argentina and other Latin American countries, see Felipe Arocena and Kirk S. Bowman, *Lessons from Latin America: Innovations in Politics, Culture, and Development* (Toronto: University of Toronto Press, 2014), 204.

17. We invite you to read the entire speech: Ivan Illich, Speech, Presented at the Conference of InterAmerican Student Projects, Mexico, April 20, 1968, http://www.ciasp.ca/CIASPhistory/IllichCIASPspeech.htm#_ftn2.

18. Examples of Arturo Escobar's work include the following: "Reflections on 'Development': Grassroots Approaches and Alternative Politics in the Third World," *Futures* 24, no. 5 (June 1992): 411–43; *Encountering Development: The Making and Unmaking of the Third World* (Princeton N.J.: Princeton University Press, 1995), 312; "Planning," in *The Development Dictionary*, ed. Wolfgang Sachs (London: Zed, 1992), 132–145; "Imagining a Post-Development Era" in *Power of Development*, ed. Jonathan Crush (London: Routledge, 1995), 211–227.

19. See the following for an excellent review of this movement: Andrew McGregor, "New Possibilities?: Shifts in Post-Development Theory and Practice," *Geography Compass* 3, no. 5 (September 2009): 1688–1702; Serge Latouche, *In the Wake of the Affluent Society: An Exploration of Post-Development*, translated by Martin O'Connor and Rosemary Arnoux (London: Zed Books, 1993), 268; Aram Ziai, *Development Discourse and Global History: From Colonialism to the Sustainable Development Goals* (London: Routledge, 2015), 252.

20. Anand Giridharadas, *Winners Take All: The Elite Charade of Changing the World* (New York: Vintage, 2018), 304. See also: Donald Fisher, "The Role of Philanthropic Foundations in the Reproduction and Production of Hegemony: Rockefeller Foundations and the Social Sciences," *Sociology* 17, no. 2 (May 1983): 206–33; Rob Reich, Chiara Cordelli, and Lucy Bernholz, eds, *Philanthropy in Democratic Societies: History, Institutions, Values* (Chicago: University of Chicago Press, 2016), 344.

21. Rob Reich, *Just Giving: Why Philanthropy Is Failing Democracy and How It Can Do Better* (Princeton, N.J.: Princeton University Press, 2018), 252. Reich develops a political theory of philanthropy where it is both a form of power and deeply entwined in government policy. Policy and philanthropy are mutually reinforcing forces with a plutocratic bias and upside-down incentives.

22. Niall McCarthy, "America's Most and Least Trusted Professions [Infographic]," *Forbes*, January 4, 2018, https://www.forbes.com/sites/niallmccarthy/2018/01/04/americas-most-and-least-trusted-professions-infographic/.

23. "Sidekick," *Merriam-Webster.com*, accessed May 12, 2020, https://www.merriam-webster.com/dictionary/sidekick.

24. Teman Cooke, "Sidekicks Are the Real Heroes," A Study in Contradictions, June 21, 2013, http://thcooke.com/2013/06/sidekicks-are-the-real-heroes/.

25. James Mittelman and Mustapha Pasha, *Out from Underdevelopment Revisited: Changing Global Structures and the Remaking of the Third World*, 2nd ed. (London: MacMillan, 1997), 24.

26. Research shows that the neighborhood is the most effective unit of social change. For long-term impact, it is far better to transform five hundred young people in a single neighborhood than a thousand individuals scattered around the planet. See: David Brooks, "The Neighborhood Is the Unit of Change," *New York Times*, October 18, 2018, https://www.nytimes.com/2018/10/18/opinion/neighborhood-social-infrastructure-community.html.

27. We want to emphasize what this book is about and what it is not about. We are most interested in the enormous number of discrete international development projects initiated and voluntarily led by elites from the Global North. We are not concerned with foreign aid or international financial institutions such as the World Bank and the International Monetary Fund. The debate on foreign aid is particularly active: Dambisa Moyo, *Dead Aid: Why Aid Is Not Working and How There Is a Better Way for Africa* (New York: Farrar, Straus and Giroux, 2010), 208; Haley J. Swedlund, *The Development Dance: How Donors and Recipients Negotiate the Delivery of Foreign Aid* (Ithaca, N.Y.: Cornell University Press, 2017), 188; Inder Sud, *Reforming Foreign Aid: Reinvent the World Bank: Lessons in Global Poverty Alleviation from 40 Years of Adventures (and Misadventures) in International Development* (CreateSpace Independent Publishing Platform, 2017), 240. See also the many lectures and articles by Bill and Melinda Gates: "Bill and Melinda Gates: Let's Keep Investing in the World's Poor," *Wall Street Journal*, September 13, 2017, https://www.wsj.com/articles/bill-and-melinda-gates-lets-keep-investing-in-the-worlds-poor-1505300401; Bill Gates' most persuasive writing on foreign aid is found at https://www.gatesfoundation.org/es/Who-We-Are/Resources-and-Media/Annual-Letters-List/Annual-Letter-2014. The most sustained critic of the World Bank and International Monetary Fund is William Easterly: William Easterly, *The White Man's Burden: Why the West's Efforts to Aid the Rest Have Done So Much Ill and So Little Good* (New York: Penguin, 2006), 436. See also Catherine Caufield, *Masters of Illusion: The World Bank and the Poverty of Nations* (New York: Henry Holt, 1996), 432; Dani Rodrik, "Goodbye Washington Consensus, Hello Washington Confusion?: A Review of the World Bank's Economic Growth in the 1990s: Learning from a Decade of Reform," *Journal of Economic Literature* 44, no. 4 (December 2006): 973–987. For an excellent read on international monetary institutions in Argentina, see Paul Blustein, *And the Money Kept Rolling in (and out) Wall Street, the IMF, and the Bankrupting of Argentina* (New York: PublicAffairs, 2006), 304. Considerable research and debate exist on those activities. Health programs and agriculture

projects may be scalable and of a technical nature that is outside the scope of this work. Finally, our research has little to say directly to those organizations and individuals doing disaster relief, refugee work, or hunger relief.

28. Harry Eckstein, "Case Study and Theory in Political Science," in *Handbook of Political Science. Political Science: Scope and Theory*, by Fred I. Greenstein and Nelson W. Polsby (Reading, Mass.: Addison-Wesley Press, 1975), 94–137.

29. See: https://www.gatesfoundation.org/es/Who-We-Are/Resources-and -Media/Annual-Letters-List/Annual-Letter-2014.

2. EVERYBODY WANTS TO CHANGE THE WORLD: THE BOOM IN INTERNATIONAL PHILANTHROPY

1. Our category of philanthropists is broad; it includes those activities and individual expenditures of resources (time or money) to uplift the human conditions of individuals that one does not know. Some activities include both personal effort and government programs, such as the Peace Corps. We include the Peace Corps, nonprofits, religious organizations, members of religious organizations helping individuals or communities outside their church, college professors, university groups such as Engineers Without Borders, families, and individuals.

2. Robert D. Lupton, *Toxic Charity: How Churches and Charities Hurt Those They Help (and How to Reverse It)* (New York: HarperOne, 2012), 2.

3. For more on the history of philanthropy, see William L. Jackson, *The Wisdom of Generosity: A Reader in American Philanthropy* (Waco, Tex.: Baylor University Press, 2008), 427; Lawrence J. Friedman and Mark D. McGarvie, *Charity, Philanthropy, and Civility in American History* (Cambridge: Cambridge University Press, 2004), 467; Olivier Zunz, *Philanthropy in America: A History*, Politics and Society in Modern America 80 (Princeton, N.J.: Princeton University Press, 2011), 381; Rob Reich, Lucy Bernholz, and Chiara Cordelli, eds., *Philanthropy in Democratic Societies: History, Institutions, Values* (Chicago: University of Chicago Press, 2016), 344. There is a vigorous debate on the benefits of the billionaire philanthropists; see Anand Giridharadas, *Winners Take All: The Elite Charade of Changing the World* (New York: Vintage Books, 2018), 304; Rob Reich, *Just Giving: Why Philanthropy Is Failing Democracy and How It Can Do Better* (Princeton, N.J.: Princeton University Press, 2018), 252; Mark Warren, *Democracy and Association* (Princeton, N.J.: Princeton University Press, 2001), 280.

4. Peace Corps volunteers occupy a middle ground, but we consider the volunteers as philanthropists who give their time to elevate the human condition.

5. An example that uses charity and philanthropy as coterminous: Reich, *Just Giving*, 19–20.

6. Wealthy benefactors also found universities outside the United States. Supermarket mogul Juan Roig transformed the port of Valencia, Spain, with his Edem business university in an attempt to enhance the culture of entrepreneurship and start-ups in the region.

7. Peter Dobkin Hall, "A Historical Overview of Philanthropy, Voluntary Associations, and Nonprofit Organizations in the United States, 1600–2000," in *The Nonprofit Sector: A Research Handbook*, ed. Walter W. Powell and Richard Steinberg, 2nd ed. (New Haven, Conn.: Yale University Press, 2006), 32–65.

8. For more on social entrepreneurship and enterprise, see David Bornstein and Susan Davis, *Social Entrepreneurship: What Everyone Needs to Know* (New York: Oxford University Press, 2010), 147; Jean Block, *The Nonprofit Guide to Social Enterprise: Show Me the (Unrestricted) Money!* (Rancho Santa Margarita, Calif.: Charity Channel Press, 2013), 146; Robert D. Putnam, *Bowling Alone: The Collapse and Revival of American Community* (New York: Touchstone, 2001), 541.

9. There were also political and security considerations because the missions served as frontier forts. The Tupi and others were actually more widespread.

10. Olga Merino and Linda A. Newson, "Jesuit Missions in Spanish America: The Aftermath of the Expulsion," *Revista de Historia de América*, no. 118 (1994): 7–32.

11. Adlaberto Lopez, "The Economics of Yerba Mate in the Seventeenth-Century in South America," *Agricultural History* 48, no. 4 (1974): 493.

12. Roland Joffé, *The Mission*, Historical drama, Warner Bros., 1986.

13. See Greg Grandin, *Fordlandia: The Rise and Fall of Henry Ford's Forgotten Jungle City* (New York: Metropolitan, 2009), 416; Drew Reed, "Lost Cities #10: Fordlandia—the Failure of Henry Ford's Utopian City in the Amazon," *Guardian*, August 19, 2016, https://www.theguardian.com/cities/2016/aug/19/lost-cities-10-fordlandia-failure-henry-ford-amazon.

14. Another example of a rubber city is Harbel, Liberia. Named after Firestone Tire & Rubber founder Harvey Firestone and his wife Idabelle, the Firestone experiment began in 1926 and manages 8 million rubber trees on 200 square miles. Firestone's workers live in shanty towns and earn US$4 per day. Firestone's Liberia operations aroused controversy with the discovery that the company paid tens of millions to convicted war-crimes perpetrator Charles Taylor. See Tarnue Johnson, *Critical Examination of Firestones Operations in Liberia: A Case Study Approach* (Bloomington, Ind.: Authorhouse, 2010), 160.

15. Adam Hochschild, *King Leopold's Ghost: A Story of Greed, Terror, and Heroism in Colonial Africa* (Boston: Mariner, 1998), 44.

16. Hochschild, *King Leopold's Ghost*, 111–112.

17. Stephen Bates, "The Hidden Holocaust," *Guardian*, May 13, 1999, https://www.theguardian.com/theguardian/1999/may/13/features11.g22.

18. Hochschild, *King Leopold's Ghost*, 134.

19. Hochschild, *King Leopold's Ghost*, 135.

20. Kate Hodal, "JK Rowling Urges Students Not to Volunteer at Orphanages," *Guardian*, October 24, 2019, https://www.theguardian.com/global-development /2019/oct/24/jk-rowling-urges-students-not-to-volunteer-at-orphanages.

21. Hodal, "JK Rowling Urges Students Not to Volunteer at Orphanages."

22. Jimmy Stamp, "Fact of Fiction? The Legend of the QWERTY Keyboard," *Smithsonian Magazine*, May 3, 2003, https://www.smithsonianmag.com /arts-culture/fact-of-fiction-the-legend-of-the-qwerty-keyboard-49863249/.

23. For more on critical junctures and path dependency, see Giovanni Capoccia, "Critical Junctures," in *The Oxford Handbook of Historical Institutionalism*, ed. Karl Orfeo Fioretos, Tulia Gabriela Falleti, and Adam D. Sheingate (Oxford: Oxford University Press, 2016), 95–108; James Mahoney, "Path Dependence in Historical Sociology," *Theory and Society* 29, no. 4 (2000): 507–548.

24. David Collier and Gerardo Munck, "Building Blocks and Methodological Challenges: A Framework for Studying Critical Junctures," *Qualitative & Multi-Method Research* 15, no. 1 (Spring 2017): 2–9.

25. David Wilsford, "Path Dependency, or Why History Makes It Difficult but Not Impossible to Reform Health Care Systems in a Big Way," *Journal of Public Policy* 14, no. 3 (July 1994): 251–283; Robin Cowan and Philip Gunby. "Sprayed to Death: Path Dependence, Lock-in and Pest Control Strategies," *The Economic Journal* 106, no. 436 (1996): 521–542; Amy L. Stein, "Breaking Energy Path Dependencies," *Brook Law Review* 82, no. 2 (2017): 559–604.

26. There are path dependence studies for the nonprofit sector specifically for East Asia, for example, Japan, South Korea, and Taiwan: Helmut K. Anheier and Lester M. Salamon, "The Nonprofit Sector in Comparative Perspective," in *The Nonprofit Sector: A Research Handbook*, ed. Walter W. Powell and Richard Steinberg, 2nd ed. (New Haven, Conn.: Yale University Press, 2006), 89–116. See also Chang Bum Ju and Shui-Yan Tang, "Path Dependence, Critical Junctures, and Political Contestation: The Developmental Trajectories of Environmental NGOs in South Korea," *Nonprofit and Voluntary Sector Quarterly* 40, no. 6 (2011): 1048–1072; Sunhyuk Kim, "Democratization and Environmentalism: South Korea and Taiwan in Comparative Perspective," *Journal of Asian and African Studies* 35, no. 3 (January 1, 2000): 287–302.

27. K. Sabeel Rahman, "Democracy and Productivity: The Glass-Steagall Act and the Shifting Discourse of Financial Regulation," *Journal of Policy History* 24, no. 4 (2012): 612–643. Glass-Steagall also created deposit insurance and the Federal Deposit Insurance Corporation (FDIC) to oversee it, and expanded the powers of the Federal Reserve.

28. Charity and alms have a very long tradition and rich history, particularly within religious organizations. See Gary A. Anderson, *Charity: The Place of the Poor in the Biblical Tradition* (New Haven, Conn.: Yale University Press, 2013), 222; Amy Singer, *Charity in Islamic Societies* (Cambridge: Cambridge University Press, 2008), 260.

29. See Seymour Martin Lipset, *American Exceptionalism: A Double-Edged Sword* (New York: Norton, 1997), 352; Abram C. Van Engen, *City on a Hill: A History of American Exceptionalism* (New Haven, Conn.: Yale University Press, 2020), 379.

30. Alexis de Tocqueville, "On the Use That the Americans Make of Association in Civil Life," in *Democracy in America*, ed. Harvey C. Mansfield and Delba Winthrop (Chicago: University of Chicago, 2002), 489–492, http://www.press.uchicago.edu/Misc/Chicago/805328.html.

31. See also Joshua Cohen and Joel Rogers, eds., *Associations and Democracy*, The Real Utopias Project 1 (London: Verso, 1995), 167.

32. Peter Dobkin Hall, "A Historical Overview of Philanthropy, Voluntary Associations, and Nonprofit Organizations in the United States, 1600–2000," in *The Nonprofit Sector: A Research Handbook*, ed. Walter W. Powell and Richard Steinberg, 2nd ed. (New Haven, Conn.: Yale University Press, 2006), 32–65.

33. Rockefeller made a fortune in the oil industry and lived by his purpose of "to work, to save, and to give." By the time of his death in 1937 at age ninety-seven, he had given away $540 million (unadjusted for inflation).

34. Paul Arnsberger, Melissa Ludlum, Margaret Riley, and Mark Stanton, "A History of the Tax-Exempt Sector: An SOI Perspective," *Statistics of Income Bulletin* (2008), 105–135, https://www.irs.gov/pub/irs-soi/tehistory.pdf.

35. "The Charitable Sector," Independent Sector, accessed May 22, 2020, https://independentsector.org/about/the-charitable-sector/.

36. Datasets for 2020 tax rates in all states are downloadable at Katherine Loughead, "State Individual Income Tax Rates and Brackets for 2020," Tax Foundation, February 4, 2020, https://taxfoundation.org/state-individual-income-tax-rates-and-brackets-for-2020/.

37. Ken Stern, "Why the Rich Don't Give to Charity," *Atlantic*, April 2013, https://www.theatlantic.com/magazine/archive/2013/04/why-the-rich-dont-give/309254/.

38. The 2017 federal tax legislation raised the standard deduction for individuals ($12,400) and joint filers ($24,800). Only taxpayers with itemized deduction greater than those amounts continue to benefit from charitable contributions, raising fears of a decline in charitable giving in the United States. *Giving USA 2019: The Annual Report on Philanthropy for the Year 2018* reported that individual giving fell by 1.1 percent in the first year after the Tax Cuts and Jobs Act of 2017. IUPUI Lilly Family School of Philanthropy, "Giving USA 2019: The Annual Report on Philanthropy for the Year 2018," (Chicago: Giving USA Foundation, 2019).

39. This idea that tax-deductible giving can replace the role of government is not supported by the data. In 2012, not a single one of the largest individual gifts to public charities went to a social service organization or to a charity that principally serves the poor and the dispossessed. Thirty-four of the fifty went to educational institutions, including one to an elite prep school. Stern, "Why the Rich Don't Give to Charity."

40. Cheyenne Macdonald, "What Travel Looked Like 100 Years Ago," *Daily Mail Online*, November 30, 2015, https://www.dailymail.co.uk/sciencetech/article -3339902/What-travel-looked-like-100-years-ago-Map-shows-DAYS-took -travel-abroad-1900s.html.

41. Kirk S. Bowman, *Peddling Paradise: The Politics of Tourism in Latin America* (Boulder, Colo.: Lynne Rienner, 2013), 186.

42. World Tourism Organization, *Yearbook of Tourism Statistics, 1990*, Vol. 2 (University Park, Penn.: Pennsylvania State University Press, 1991), 4–21.

43. Bowman, *Peddling Paradise*, 186.

44. "U.S. Study Abroad Destinations," Institute of International Education, 2019, https://www.iie.org:443/en/Research-and-Insights/Open-Doors/Data/US -Study-Abroad/Destinations.

45. Maya Wesby, "The Exploitative Selfishness of Volunteering Abroad," *Newsweek* (August 18, 2015), https://www.newsweek.com/exploitative-selfishness -volunteering-abroad-363768.

46. Mike Slack, "Volunteer Work Tax Deductions," H&R Block, February 2, 2018, https://www.hrblock.com/tax-center/filing/adjustments-and-deductions /volunteer-work-tax-deductions/.

47. "Publication 526 (2019), Charitable Contributions," Internal Revenue Service, 2019, https://www.irs.gov/publications/p526.

48. See Jonathan Haidt, *The Righteous Mind: Why Good People Are Divided by Politics and Religion* (New York: Pantheon, 2012), 528.

49. Cold warrior and social scientist W. W. Rostow published *The Stages of Economic Growth: A Non-Communist Manifesto* in 1960, one of the principal academic explanations of the theory: W. W. Rostow, *The Stages of Economic Growth: A Non-Communist Manifesto* (New York: Cambridge University Press, 1960), 178.

50. Tom Lamont, "Blinded by Technology: Has Our Belief in Silicon Valley Led the World Astray?," *Guardian*, August 30, 2015, http://www.theguardian .com/technology/2015/aug/30/kentaro-toyama-geek-heresy-interview-technology. See also Kentaro Toyama, *Geek Heresy: Rescuing Social Change from the Cult of Technology* (New York: PublicAffairs, 2015), 334.

51. Toyama, *Geek Heresy*, 17–56.

52. Kirk Bowman, "Should the Kuznets Effect Be Relied on to Induce Equalizing Growth," *World Development* 25, no. 1 (1997): 127–143.

53. Chad Stone, Danilo Trisi, Arloc Sherman, and Jennifer Beltrán, "A Guide to Statistics on Historical Trends in Income Inequality" (Washington, D.C.: Center on Budget and Policy Priorities, January 13, 2020), https://www .cbpp.org/research/poverty-and-inequality/a-guide-to-statistics-on-historical -trends-in-income-inequality.

54. Forbes Staff, "Forbes' 31st Annual World's Billionaires Issue," *Forbes*, March 20, 2017, https://www.forbes.com/sites/forbespr/2017/03/20/forbes-31st -annual-worlds-billionaires-issue/.

55. See Davey Alba, "Zuckerberg Sold His Facebook Shares for Charity—But He's No Hero Yet," *Wired*, August 23, 2016, https://www.wired.com/2016/08/zuckerberg-sold-facebook-shares-charity-hes-no-hero-yet/; Mathew Ingram, "Mark Zuckerberg Is Giving Away His Money, but with a Silicon Valley Twist," *Fortune*, December 2, 2015.

56. Elizabeth Segran, "Use These Two Words on Your College Essay to Get into Harvard," *Fast Company*, August 3, 2015, https://www.fastcompany.com/3049289/use-these-two-words-on-your-college-essay-to-get-into-harvard.

57. Elizabeth Currid-Halkett, *The Sum of Small Things: A Theory of the Aspirational Class* (Princeton, N.J.: Princeton University Press, 2017), 254.

58. Andrea van Niekerk, "Stop Writing the Same Four Cliched College Essays," Quartz, May 2, 2013, https://qz.com/80136/heres-the-secret-to-cracking-the-college-essay/.

59. Dozens of students in personal conversations with the authors have confirmed this observation.

3. LESSONS FROM THE CONTEMPORARY GLOBAL PHILANTHROPY PRACTICE

1. David Fitzpatrick and Drew Griffin, "Government Says Four Cancer Charities Are Shams," CNN, May 19, 2015, https://www.cnn.com/2015/05/19/us/scam-charity-investigation/index.html.

2. "CharityWatch Hall of Shame: The Personalities Behind Charity Scandals," CharityWatch, August 24, 2018, https://www.charitywatch.org/charity-donating-articles/charitywatch-hall-of-shame; Jeneva Rose, "10 of the Biggest Celebrity Charity Scandals," The Richest, July 24, 2014, https://www.therichest.com/money/10-of-the-biggest-celebrity-charity-scandals/.

3. Adam Nagourney, "Madonna's Charity Fails in Bid to Finance School," *New York Times*, March 24, 2011, https://www.nytimes.com/2011/03/25/us/25madonna.html; Godfrey Mapondera and David Smith, "Malawi Accuses Madonna of Exaggerating Humanitarian Efforts," *Guardian*, April 11, 2013, https://www.theguardian.com/world/2013/apr/11/malawi-madonna-exaggerating-humanitarian-efforts.

4. Tracy McVeigh, "Forget Madonna—Malawi's Parents Find Their Own Way of Keeping Girls in School," *Guardian*, February 28, 2015, https://www.theguardian.com/world/2015/mar/01/malawi-forget-madonna-parents-keep-girls-at-school.

5. Deborah Sontag, "In Haiti, Little Can Be Found of a Hip-Hop Artist's Charity," *New York Times*, October 11, 2012, https://www.nytimes.com/2012/10/12/world/americas/quake-hit-haiti-gains-little-as-wyclef-jean-charity-spends-much.html.

6. Sontag, "In Haiti, Little Can Be Found of a Hip-Hop Artist's Charity."

7. Greg Mortenson and David Oliver Relin, *Three Cups of Tea: One Man's Extraordinary Journey to Promote Peace—One School at a Time* (London: Penguin Books, 2007), 349.

8. Peter Hessler, "What Mortenson Got Wrong," *New Yorker*, April 21, 2011, https://www. newyorker.com/news/news-desk/what-mortenson-got-wrong.

9. Jon Krakauer, "Greg Mortenson, Disgraced Author of 'Three Cups of Tea,' Believes He Will Have the Last Laugh. He Might Be Right," Medium, July 20, 2014, https://medium.com/galleys/greg-mortenson-disgraced-author-of-three -cups-of-tea-believes-he-will-have-the-last-laugh-760949b1f964.

10. Hessler, "What Mortenson Got Wrong."

11. Mortenson, *Three Cups of Tea*, 22.

12. Ian Bogost, "Mini Object Lesson: No, There Are Not 100 Eskimo Words for 'Snow,'" *Atlantic*, January 23, 2016, https://www.theatlantic.com /notes/2016/01/mini-object-lesson-no-there-are-not-a-hundred-eskimo-words -for-snow/426651/.

13. Harry Eckstein, "Case Study and Theory in Political Science," in *Handbook of Political Science. Political Science: Scope and Theory*, by Fred I. Greenstein and Nelson W. Polsby (Reading, Mass.: Addison-Wesley Press, 1975), 94–137.

14. Maïa Gedde, *Working in International Development and Humanitarian Assistance: A Career Guide* (New York: Routledge, 2015), 13.

15. Nina Munk, *The Idealist: Jeffrey Sachs and the Quest to End Poverty* (New York: Anchor Books, 2013), 87.

16. Bill Gates, "The Bono of Economics—Jeffrey Sachs—Commentary," CNBC, May 22, 2014, https://www.cnbc.com/2014/05/22/the-bono-of-economicsjeffrey -sachscommentary.html.

17. W. W. Rostow, *The Stages of Economic Growth: A Non-Communist Manifesto* (New York: Cambridge University Press, 1960).

18. Munk, *The Idealist*, 159.

19. Munk, *The idealist*, 159.

20. Munk, *The Idealist*, 53.

21. Munk, *The Idealist*, 181.

22. Munk, *The Idealist*, 28.

23. Munk, *The Idealist*, 47–48.

24. Munk, *The Idealist*, 209.

25. Munk, *The Idealist*, 113.

26. Daniel Stellar, "The PlayPump: What Went Wrong?" State of the Planet—Columbia University, July 1, 2010, https://blogs.ei.columbia.edu/2010/07/01/the -playpump-what-went-wrong/; Michael Hobbes, "Stop Trying to Save the World," *New Republic*, November 17, 2014, https://newrepublic.com/article/120178/problem -international-development-and-plan-fix-it.

27. Andrew Chambers, "Africa's Not-so-Magic Roundabout," *Guardian*, November 24, 2009, https://www.theguardian.com/commentisfree/2009/nov/24 /africa-charity-water-pumps-roundabouts.

28. Amy Costello, "Frontline: Southern Africa: Troubled Water," PBS, 2010, http://www.pbs.org/frontlineworld/stories/southernafrica904/video_index.html.

29. See Tom Murphy, "How PlayPumps Are an Example of Learning from Failure," Humanosphere, July 2, 2013, http://www.humanosphere.org/basics /2013/07/how-playpumps-are-an-example-of-learning-from-failure/.

30. Scaling up might work in some health-care and agricultural domains; evidence is very hard to come by. Indeed, there is a vigorous debate in the development field about scientific experimentation in development. Led by Esther Duflo and her colleagues at MIT, many microdevelopment scholars believe in experimentation of development policy with a control community and a treatment community. Other scholars, such as Dani Rodrik, claim that, with only two communities as cases and lots of potential variables, these randomized evaluation experiments have no external validity. Dani Rodrik, "The New Development Economics: We Shall Experiment, but How Shall We Learn?," in *What Works in Development? Thinking Big and Thinking Small*, ed. Jessica Cohen and William Easterly (Washington D.C: Brookings Institution Press, 2009), 24–48. As Cohen and Easterly note, we "wonder whether the particular outcome of a particular program carried out on a particular population in a particular country by a particular organization would be found in other circumstances." Jessica Cohen and William Easterly, eds. *What Works in Development? Thinking Big and Thinking Small* (Washington D.C: Brookings Institution Press, 2009), 9.

31. Wayan Vota, "Goodbye One Laptop per Child," OLPC News, March 11, 2014, http://www.olpcnews.com/about_olpc_news/goodbye_one_laptop_per_child .html; Dan Nosowitz, "Has One Laptop per Child Totally Lost Its Way?," *Popular Science*, July 18, 2013, https://www.popsci.com/gadgets/article/2013-07/one -laptop-childs-de-evolution/; Audrey Watters, "The Failure of One Laptop per Child," Hack Education, April 9, 2012, http://hackeducation.com/2012/04/09 /the-failure-of-olpc; Namank Shah, "A Blurry Vision: Reconsidering the Failure of the One Laptop per Child Initiative," *Boston University: Journal of the Arts & Sciences Writing Program*, no. 3 (2011): 89–98, http://www.bu.edu/writingprogram /journal/past-issues/issue-3/shah/; Joshua Keating, "Why Did One Laptop per Child Fail?," *Foreign Policy*, September 9, 2009, https://foreignpolicy.com /2009/09/09/why-did-one-laptop-per-child-fail/.

32. Alanna Shaikh, "One Laptop Per Child: The Dream is Over," UN Dispatch, September 9, 2009, https://www.undispatch.com/one-laptop-per-child -the-dream-is-over/.

33. "The Founding Moment," Peace Corps, https://www.peacecorps.gov /about/history/founding-moment/.

34. For critiques of the Peace Corps, see Jonathan D. Trobe, "Peace Corps in Brazil: Lesson from Failure," *Harvard Crimson*, October 23, 1963, https:// www.thecrimson.com/article/1963/10/23/peace-corps-in-brazil-lesson-from/; Sheryl Gay Stolberg, "Peace Corps Volunteers Speak Out on Rape," *New York Times*, May 10, 2011, https://www.nytimes.com/2011/05/11/us/11corps.html;

Ryan Rommann, "The Peace Corps: Out-Dated and Out-Performed?," *Guardian*, November 21, 2013, https://www.theguardian.com/global-development-professionals -network/2013/nov/21/peace-corps-us-development-policy.

For works with a positive view of the Peace Corps, see Stanley Meisler, *When the World Calls: The Inside Story of the Peace Corps and Its First Fifty Years* (Boston: Beacon Press, 2011), 272; Pat Alter and Bernie Alter, eds. *Gather the Fruit One by One*, 50 Years of Amazing Peace Corps Stories, vol. 2, The Americas (Palo Alto, Calif.: Travelers Tales, 2011), 315.

35. "Peace Corps in Fiji," Peace Corps, https://www.peacecorps.gov/fiji/.

36. Victor Bonito, Fiji Peace Corps, interview by Kirk Bowman, 2015.

37. E-mail correspondence with Victor Bonito in 2019.

38. Engineers Without Borders, "Failure Report," 2016, http://reports.ewb.ca/; Engineers Without Borders, "Admitting Failure," https://www.admittingfailure.org/.

39. See Denise Deby, "How Engineers Without Borders Learned to Embrace Failure (and Learn from It, Too)," *This Magazine*, December 1, 2011, https://this .org/2011/12/01/admitting-failure/; David Damberger, "What Happens When an NGO Admits Failure," TED Talks presented at the TEDxYYC, April 2011, https://www.ted.com/talks/david_damberger_what_happens_when_an_ngo _admits_failure/transcript.

40. Robert D. Lupton, *Toxic Charity: How Churches and Charities Hurt Those They Help (and How to Reverse It)* (New York: HarperOne, 2012), 2.

41. Lupton, *Toxic Charity*, 208.

42. See Alexandra Coghlan and Steve Noakes, "Towards an Understanding of the Drivers of Commercialization in the Volunteer Tourism Sector," *Tourism Recreation Research* 37, no. 2 (2015): 123–31; Maya Wesby, "The Exploitative Selfishness of Volunteering Abroad," *Newsweek* (August 18, 2015), https://www .newsweek.com/exploitative-selfishness-volunteering-abroad-363768.

43. Lupton, *Toxic Charity*, 14.

44. Lupton, *Toxic Charity*, 18.

45. Lupton, *Toxic Charity*, 15.

46. Lupton, *Toxic Charity*, 21.

47. Lupton, *Toxic Charity*, 16.

48. P. Biddle, "The Problem with Little White Girls, Boys, and Voluntourism," *Huffington Post*, August 5, 2014. See also Carrie Kahn, "As 'Voluntourism' Explodes in Popularity, Who's It Helping Most?," *NPR—Morning Edition*, July 31, 2014, https:// www.npr.org/sections/goatsandsoda/2014/07/31/336600290/as-volunteerism -explodes-in-popularity-whos-it-helping-most; Rachel Banning-Lover, "The Seven Sins of Humanitarian Douchery," *Guardian*, April 16, 2015, https://www .theguardian.com/global-development-professionals-network/2015/apr/16 /humanitarian-douchery-volunteering-voluntourism-endhumanitariandouchery.

49. Ian Birrell, "Before You Pay to Volunteer Abroad, Think of the Harm You Might Do," *Guardian*, November 14, 2010, https://www.theguardian.com /commentisfree/2010/nov/14/orphans-cambodia-aids-holidays-madonna.

50. Nalini Visvanathan and Karla Yoder, "Women and Microcredit: A Critical Introduction," in *The Women, Gender and Development Reader*, 2nd ed., edited by Nalini Visvanathan, Lynn Duggan, Nan Wiegersma, and Laurie Nisonoff (London: Zed Books, 2011), 47.

51. Abdul Latif Jameel Poverty Action Lab, "Measuring the Impact of Microfinance in Hyderabad, India," n.d., https://www.povertyactionlab.org/evaluation/measuring-impact-microfinance-hyderabad-india.

52. Interest rates of Kiva retrieved from Kiva "Funded Loans" and available at https://en.wikipedia.org/wiki/Kiva_(organization).

53. Karl Laemmermann, *Crowdfunding: Raising Capital Online* (Scotts Valley, Calif.: CreateSpace Independent Publishing Platform, 2012), 232.

54. Visvanathan and Yoder, "Women and Microcredit: A Critical Introduction," 53.

55. As is the case of Banco Compartamos: Jason Hickel, "The Microfinance Delusion: Who Really Wins?," *Guardian*, June 10, 2015, https://www.theguardian.com/global-development-professionals-network/2015/jun/10/the-microfinance-delusion-who-really-wins.

56. Hickel, "The Microfinance Delusion: Who Really Wins?"

57. Banerjee and colleagues examined six randomized evaluations of microcredit from six countries and four continents. The mean average interest rate in the six programs was 34.9 percent. The authors found very modest signs of positive outcomes but nothing remotely transformative. Abhijit Banerjee, Dean Karlan, and Jonathan Zinman, "Six Randomized Evaluations of Microcredit: Introduction and Further Steps," *American Economic Journal: Applied Economics* 7, no. 1 (2015): 1–21.

58. Joseph Hanlon, Armando Barrientos, and David Hulme, *Just Give Money to the Poor: The Development Revolution from the Global South* (West Hartford, Conn.: Kumarian Press, 2010), 216.

59. Felipe Arocena and Kirk S. Bowman, *Lessons from Latin America: Innovations in Politics, Culture, and Development* (Toronto: University of Toronto Press, 2014), 123–138.

60. A list of thirty-one peer-reviewed articles on the benefits of unconditional cash transfers in the Global South can be found at "Research on Cash Transfers," GiveDirectly, https://www.givedirectly.org/research-on-cash-transfers/.

4. THE COMMUNITY BANK MODEL OF INTERNATIONAL PHILANTHROPY

1. See S. J Grove and R. A Dodder, "Construction Measures to Assess Perceptions of Sport Functions," *International Journal of Sports Psychology* 13 (1982): 96–106; Elmer Spreitzer and Eldon E. Snyder, "The Psychosocial Functions of Sport as Perceived by the General Population," *International Review of*

Sport Sociology 10, no. 3–4 (September 1, 1975): 87–95; Jessica L. Fraser-Thomas, Jean Côté, and Janice Deakin, "Youth Sport Programs: An Avenue to Foster Positive Youth Development," *Physical Education & Sport Pedagogy* 10, no. 1 (2005): 19–40; Nicholas L. Holt, ed., *Positive Youth Development Through Sport*, International Studies in Physical Education and Youth Sport (Abingdon, UK: Routledge, 2008), 152.

2. Hernando de Soto, *The Other Path: The Economic Answer to Terrorism* (New York: Harper and Row, 1989), 273.

3. One of the reasons for this is the large numbers of zombie projects—those that still appear on the books as legitimate NGOs, but where nothing is happening.

4. H. G. Parsa, John T. Self, David Njite, and Tiffany King, "Why Restaurants Fail," *Cornell Hotel and Restaurant Administration Quarterly* 46, no. 3 (August 1, 2005): 304–322.

5. Some may argue that if you are replicating an existing surfing program, then establishing a program in Colombia is more like a franchise and the failure rate is much lower. The Cornell study found that franchises have almost the same failure rate as nonfranchise restaurant start-ups.

6. Max Marmer, Bjoern Herrmann, Ertan Dogrultan, and Ron Burman, "Startup Genome Report Extra on Premature Scaling," Startup Genome, August 29, 2011, http://innovationfootprints.com/wp-content/uploads/2015/07/startup-genome-report-extra-on-premature-scaling.pdf; Sohaib Shahid Bajwa, Xiaofeng Wang, Anh Nguyen Duc, and Pekka Abrahamsson, "'Failures' to Be Celebrated: An Analysis of Major Pivots of Software Startups," *Empirical Software Engineering* 22, no. 5 (2016): 2373–2408.

7. Carmen Nobel, "Why Companies Fail—and How Their Founders Can Bounce Back," Harvard Business School: Working Knowledge, March 7, 2011, http://hbswk.hbs.edu/item/why-companies-failand-how-their-founders-can-bounce-back.

8. Nobel, "Why Companies Fail."

9. Greg A. Stevens and James Burley, "3,000 Raw Ideas = 1 Commercial Success!," *Research-Technology Management* 40, no. 3 (May 1, 1997): 16–27.

10. The rate is greater than zero, and there are lots of projects and launches. While the failure rate is high, there are successes.

11. These are the two regions with the highest levels of bureaucratic hurdles and corruption.

12. Luciani Gomes, "Brazil's Business Labyrinth of Bureaucracy," *BBC News*, May 17, 2012, https://www.bbc.com/news/business-18020623.

13. World Bank Group, "Doing Business 2018 to Create Jobs," Washington, D.C.: World Bank, 2018, https://www.doingbusiness.org/content/dam/doingBusiness/media/Annual-Reports/English/DB2018-Full-Report.pdf.

14. Eric Klinenberg, *Heat Wave: A Social Autopsy of Disaster in Chicago*, 2nd ed. (Chicago: University of Chicago Press, 2015), 328.

15. David Brooks, "The Neighborhood Is the Unit of Change," *New York Times*, October 18, 2018, https://www.nytimes.com/2018/10/18/opinion/neighborhood -social-infrastructure-community.html.

16. William MacAskill, *Doing Good Better: How Effective Altruism Can Help You Help Others, Do Work That Matters, and Make Smarter Choices About Giving Back* (New York: Penguin Random House, 2015), 32.

17. Parsa, "Why Restaurants Fail," 309.

18. Unless the failure was hidden behind widespread fraud, as in the case of Theranos.

19. *It's a Wonderful Life*, directed by Frank Capra (1946; California: Liberty Films).

20. Or gross margin comparing to other industries.

21. For charge-offs and delinquency, see "Charge-Off Rates on Loans and Leases at Commercial Banks," Board of Governors of the Federal Reserve System, February 18, 2020, https://www.federalreserve.gov/releases/chargeoff /chgallnsa.htm; "Delinquency Rates on Loans and Leases at Commercial Banks," Board of Governors of the Federal Reserve System, February 18, 2020, https:// www.federalreserve.gov/releases/chargeoff/delallnsa.htm.

For a comprehensive account of community bank performance over thirty years, see "FDIC Quarterly: Core Profitability of Community Banks: 1985 to 2015" (Arlington, VA: Division of Insurance and Research of the Federal Deposit Insurance Corporation, 2016), 37–46, https://www.fdic.gov/bank /analytical/quarterly/2016-vol10-4/fdic-v10n4-3q16-quarterly.pdf.

22. We eliminated *collateral* from our philanthropic model because it is typically considered a second source for repayment and a way to minimize a bank's loss in the event of default. Because we are not expecting our donations to be repaid, it is not a useful tool for our philanthropic model and investing in social organizations.

23. Contracts and loan agreements are all about defining what happens if the borrower cannot pay back a loan.

24. It is important to match short-term liabilities with short-term assets and to match long-term debt with longer-term assets such as equipment and buildings. The business can be measured on an annual, quarter, or even a daily basis, depending on the balance sheet leverage and the reliance on the assets to create availability under a line of credit to finance working capital.

25. There is considerable literature on global power hierarchies, their establishment, and the difficulty of changing those relations. For a much-criticized version of dependency theory with a zero-sum exploitation of the Global South by the Global North, see Andre Gunder Frank, "The Development of Underdevelopment," *Monthly Review* 18, no. 4 (September 2, 1966): 17–31; Eduardo Galeano, *Open Veins of Latin America: Five Centuries of the Pillage of a Continent*, 25th anniversary ed. (New York: Monthly Review Press, 1997), 317.

For a more sophisticated version of dependency theory, see Fernando Henrique Cardoso and Enzo Faletto, *Dependency and Development in Latin America* (Berkeley: University of California Press, 1979), 227; Johan Galtung, "A Structural Theory of Imperialism," *Journal of Peace Research* 8, no. 2 (June 1, 1971): 81–117. Galtung models a global system of imperialism with a harmony of interest between elites of the Global North and Global South and a disharmony of interests between nonelites. In that model, both the elites of the United States and Brazil can benefit from activities, while the nonelites of Brazil would be exploited. In Latin America, racial norms and laws enhanced the disharmony of interests between elites and nonelites. The colonial Catholic Church employed a caste system where the caste of a baby resulted from the caste of the parents. If one parent was Spanish and the other parent was indigenous, the caste of the baby was mestizo. The church assigned the caste on the birth certificate. There were sixteen castes, including "lobo" (wolf). Sadly, some elites in Latin America continue to see some castes as subhuman. Brazilian President Jair Bolsonaro stated in January 2020, "Indians are undoubtedly changing. . . . They are increasingly becoming human beings just like us." Tom Phillips, "Jair Bolsonaro's Racist Comment Sparks Outrage from Indigenous Groups," *Guardian*, January 24, 2020, https://www.theguardian.com/world/2020/jan/24/jair-bolsonaro-racist-comment-sparks-outrage-indigenous-groups.

5. RISE UP & CARE: THE DEMONSTRATION PROJECT

1. Those are Cape Verde (48), Chile (26), Costa Rica (38), Rwanda (48), and Uruguay (23). See "Corruption Perceptions Index 2017," Transparency.org, February 21, 2018, https://www.transparency.org/en/news/corruption-perceptions-index-2017.

2. Conditional on satisfactory annual performance reviews.

3. Jack W. Berryman, "Motion and Rest: Galen on Exercise and Health," *The Lancet* 380, no. 9838 (2012): 210–211.

4. S. J. Grove and R. A. Dodder, "Construction Measures to Assess Perceptions of Sport Functions," *International Journal of Sports Psychology* 13 (1982): 96–106; Elmer Spreitzer and Eldon E. Snyder, "The Psychosocial Functions of Sport As Perceived by the General Population," *International Review of Sport Sociology* 10, no. 3–4 (September 1, 1975): 87–95; Christine Green, "Chapter 6—Sport as an Agent for Social and Personal Change," in *Management of Sports Development*, ed. Vassil Girginov (Oxford: Butterworth-Heinemann, 2008), 129–145; Fred Coalter, *Sport for Development: What Game Are We Playing?* (New York: Routledge, 2013); Nicholas L. Holt, ed., *Positive Youth Development Through Sport*, International Studies in Physical Education and Youth Sport (Abingdon: Routledge, 2008), 1–152.

5. Neurologist Frances Jensen confirms that teenage brains are prone to addiction in her book *The Teenage Brain: A Neuroscientist's Survival Guide to Raising Adolescents and Young Adults* (New York: Harper, 2016).

6. Emma Young, "How Iceland Got Teens to Say No to Drugs," *Atlantic*, January 19, 2017, https://www.theatlantic.com/health/archive/2017/01/teens -drugs-iceland/513668/.

7. See I. D. Sigfusdottir, T. Thorlindsson, A. L. Kristjansson, K. M. Roe, and J. P. Allegrante, "Substance Use Prevention for Adolescents: The Icelandic Model," *Health Promotion International* 24, no. 1 (2008): 16–25; Alfgeir L. Kristjansson, Michael J. Mann, Jon Sigfusson, Ingibjorg E. Thorisdottir, John P. Allegrante, and Inga Dora Sigfusdottir, "Development and Guiding Principles of the Icelandic Model for Preventing Adolescent Substance Use," *Health Promotion Practice* 21, no. 1 (2020): 62–69.

8. "Why Has Icelandic Football Been So Successful Recently?," Football Association of Iceland, 2019; https://www.ksi.is/library/contentfiles/Why%20is%20 Icelandic%20football%20so%20successful%20recently%202018%20upd.pdf.

9. William MacAskill, *Doing Good Better: How Effective Altruism Can Help You Help Others, Do Work That Matters, and Make Smarter Choices about Giving Back* (New York: Penguin Random House, 2015), 34–38.

10. Harry Eckstein, "Case Study and Theory in Political Science," in *Handbook of Political Science. Political Science: Scope and Theory*, ed. Fred I. Greenstein and Nelson W. Polsby (Reading: MA: Addison-Wesley Press, 1975), 94–137.

11. Felipe Arocena and Kirk S. Bowman, *Lessons from Latin America: Innovations in Politics, Culture, and Development* (Toronto: University of Toronto Press, 2014), 128–130.

12. "Brazil Takes Off," *Economist*, November 14, 2009, https://www.economist .com/weeklyedition/2009-11-14.

13. As of September 6, 2019. These are Cabral, Garotinho husband, Garotinho wife, and Pezão.

14. "Brazil's Temer Approval Rating in a New Record: 4 percent," *MercoPress*, June 30, 2018, https://en.mercopress.com/2018/06/30/brazil-s-temer-approval -rating-in-a-new-record-4.

15. Vanessa Barbara, "The Rise of the Milícia State," *New York Times*, April 10, 2019, https://www.nytimes.com/2019/04/10/opinion/brazil-bolsonaro-militias.html.

16. According to the outstanding work of Rio on Watch: "Why We Should Call Them Favelas," Rio On Watch, August 13, 2012, https://www.rioonwatch .org/?page_id=15162.

17. There are many excellent published works on the favelas, the two classics are Janice E. Perlman, *Favela: Four Decades of Living on the Edge in Rio de Janeiro* (New York: Oxford University Press, 2010); and Janice E. Perlman, *The Myth of Marginality: Urban Poverty and Politics in Rio de Janeiro* (Berkeley: University of California Press, 1979).

18. Henry Louis Gates, Jr., "How Many Slaves Landed in the US?," The Root, January 6, 2014, https://www.theroot.com/how-many-slaves-landed-in-the-us -1790873989.

19. Robert M. Levine, *Vale of Tears: Revisiting the Canudos Massacre in Northeastern Brazil, 1893–1897* (Berkeley: University of California Press, 2006,) 353; Mario Vargas Llosa, *The War of the End of the World* (New York: Picador, 2008).

20. Christopher Gaffney, "Securing the Olympic City," *Georgetown Journal of International Affairs*, no. 13 (Summer/Fall 2012): 75–82.

21. Max Opray, "How Google Is Putting Rio's Invisible Favelas Back on the Map," *Guardian*, October 9, 2016, https://www.theguardian.com/sustainable -business/2016/oct/09/invisible-favelas-brazil-rio-maps-erasing-poorer-parts -city; Natalie Southwick, "The Importance and Challenges of Putting Favelas on the Map," Rio On Watch, October 11, 2016, https://www.rioonwatch .org/?p=32519.

22. Clare Huggins, "Olympics Poverty Torch Arrives in Vila Autódromo at First 'Run for Vila,'" Rio On Watch, March 29, 2016, https://www.rioonwatch .org/?p=27714; "In Rio, Poor Families Are Pushed Out of Their Neighborhoods to Make Way for the Olympics," *Los Angeles Times*, August 4, 2016, https://www .latimes.com/world/mexico-americas/la-fg-olympic-land-grab-snap-story.html. The best research on land appropriation in the buildup to the 2016 Olympic Games is Lucas Faulhaber and Lena Azevedo, *Remoções No Rio de Janeiro Olímpico* (Rio de Janeiro: Mórula Editorial, 2015).

23. The driving question for the conservative banker is this: Is the organization sufficiently impressive in its results and likely to continue for a large donation or loan?

24. Sebastião Oliveira, personal correspondence, 2019. Unless otherwise indicated, subsequent quotes from Oliveira are from this correspondence.

25. Miratus badminton coaches Aleksander Silva and Marcos Conceição confirmed that their greatest joy is hearing from parents of the young players about their improvement in school grades and behavior.

26. The documentary film *Bad & the Birdieman* was the official selection in festivals such as the Atlanta International Film Festival, and it was the winner in the documentary category at the 2017 Cine Esporte Film Festival.

27. Fernando Lannes Fernandes, "Youth Gang Members in Rio de Janeiro: The Face of a 'Lost Generation' in an Age of Fear and Mistrust," *Bulletin of Latin American Research* 32, no. 2 (2013): 210–223.

28. Alba Zaluar, "Youth, Drug Traffic and Hypermasculinity in Rio de Janeiro," *Vibrant Virtual Brazilian Anthropology* 7, no. 2 (December 2010): 7–27, https://www.redalyc.org/pdf/4069/406941910001.pdf.

29. Alba Zaluar, "Crimes and Violence Trends in Rio de Janeiro, Brazil," Case Study Prepared for Enhancing Urban Safety and Security: Global Report on Human Settlements 2007, United Nations, 2007, http://citeseerx.ist.psu.edu /viewdoc/download?doi=10.1.1.580.220&rep=rep1&type=pdf.

30. Jo Griffin, "Is Brutal Treatment of Young Offenders Fuelling Crime Rates in Brazil?," *Guardian*, March 3, 2017, https://www.theguardian.com/global-development/2017/mar/03/brazil-crime-rates-brutal-treatment-young-offenders.

31. All of our partners have confirmed a dramatic rise in violence since 2018. See: Nadine Terasa and Pauline Beaumont, "2019 Report Shows Rising Armed Violence in Complexo Da Maré, Continued State Impunity," Rio on Watch, February 19, 2020, https://www.rioonwatch.org/?p=57860.

32. The history and innovation of Oliveira and Miratus are now told in the award-winning, one-hour documentary film *Bad & the Birdieman*, directed by Lili Fialho and Kátia Lund (2016, Vimeo), www.badbirdiemanmovie.com.

33. For information on a film about Sebastião Oliveira and Miratus and to watch the trailer, see www.badbirdiemanmovie.com.

34. Sebastião Oliveira, personal correspondence, 2018.

35. Sebastião Oliveira, personal correspondence, 2020.

36. See Dimitrius Dantas, "Herdeiro Da Família Imperial, Dom Antônio Está Hospitalizado Com Coronavirus," *O Globo Newspaper*, March 19, 2020; Eliane Trindade, "Os Circuitos Dos Ricos e Famosos Que Disseminaram Coronavírus No Brasil," *Folha de São Paulo*, March 29, 2020; Tom Phillips and Caio Barretto Briso, "Brazil's Super-Rich and the Exclusive Club at the Heart of a Coronavirus Hotspot," *Guardian*, April 4, 2020, https://www.theguardian.com/world/2020/apr/04/brazils-super-rich-and-the-exclusive-club-at-the-heart-of-a-coronavirus-hotspot.

37. Tom Phillips, "Jair Bolsonaro Claims Brazilians 'Never Catch Anything' As Covid-19 Cases Rise," *Guardian*, March 27, 2020, https://www.theguardian.com/global-development/2020/mar/27/jair-bolsonaro-claims-brazilians-never-catch-anything-as-covid-19-cases-rise.

38. "Brazil Coronavirus: 1,073,376 Cases and 50,182 Deaths," Worldometer, 2020, https://www.worldometers.info/coronavirus/country/brazil/.

6. REIMAGINING IMPACT ASSESSMENT

1. Jaco Renken and Richard Heeks, "Conceptualising ICT4D Project Champions," ICTD '13: *Proceedings of the Sixth International Conference on Information and Communications Technologies and Development* (December 2013): 128–131.

2. For example: Marc J. Epstein and Kristi Yuthas, *Measuring and Improving Social Impacts: A Guide for Nonprofits, Companies, and Impact Investors* (San Francisco: Berrett-Koehler, 2014), 54; Morgan Simon, *Real Impact: The New Economics of Social Change* (New York: Nation, 2017), 246.

3. Measuring impact is a large and growing industry in many sectors, including academia and the nonprofit world. Armies of consultants, administrators,

and experts oversee this current boom in assessment. In the modern university, it is the "drive to measure *learning outcomes*." Molly Worthen, "The Misguided Drive to Measure 'Learning Outcomes,' " *New York Times*, February 23, 2018, https://www.nytimes.com/2018/02/23/opinion/sunday/colleges-measure-learning-outcomes.html. See also Martin G. Erikson and Malgorzata Erikson, "Learning Outcomes and Critical Thinking—Good Intentions in Conflict," *Studies in Higher Education* 44, no. 12 (December 2, 2019): 2293–2303.

There is scant evidence of any tangible benefit from the huge drain of time and money on assessing learning outcomes in college courses. Many faculty members believe that assessment efforts are meaningless work done for the sake of accreditors, politicians, and/or administrators and do not serve the interests of the students. See Doug Lederman, "Conflicted Views of Technology: A Survey of Faculty Attitudes." Inside Higher Ed, October 31, 2018, https://www.insidehighered.com/news/survey/conflicted-views-technology-survey-faculty-attitudes.

After a few iterations, professors merely pretend to take them seriously, and administrators in expanding assessment offices pretend that the mountains of data hold some answers to the mysteries of higher education. They could learn just as much by interpreting Turkish coffee grounds.

4. Mary Kay Gugerty and Dean Karlan, "Ten Reasons Not to Measure Impact—and What to Do Instead," *Stanford Social Innovation Review* (Summer 2018): 41–47, https://ssir.org/articles/entry/ten_reasons_not_to_measure_impact_and_what_to_do_instead.

5. Esther Duflo and Michael Kremer, "Use of Randomization in the Evaluation of Development Effectiveness," (Washington, D.C.: World Bank, 2003): 4, https://economics.mit.edu/files/765.

6. Abhijit Banerjee and Esther Duflo, eds., *Handbook of Economic Field Experiments*, Vol.1 Handbooks in Economics (Amsterdam: North-Holland, 2017), 528.

7. These are for evaluations "on a budget." See "Rigorous Program on a Budget: How Low-Cost Randomized Trials Are Possible in Many Areas of Social Policy," Coalition for Evidence Based Policy, March 2012, https://www.thirdsectorcap.org/wp-content/uploads/2015/02/Rigorous-Program-Evaluations-on-a-Budget-March-2012.pdf.

8. Some of this research appears in Abhijit V. Banerjee and Esther Duflo, *Poor Economics: A Radical Rethinking of the Way to Fight Global Poverty* (New York: PublicAffairs, 2012), 320.

9. Duflo and Kremer, "Use of Randomization in the Evaluation of Development Effectiveness", 2. The best volume on debates about randomized evaluation is Jessica Cohen and William Easterly, eds. *What Works in Development? Thinking Big and Thinking Small* (Washington, D.C: Brookings Institution Press, 2009), 245.

10. Dani Rodrik, "The New Development Economics: We Shall Experiment but How Shall We Learn?," in *What Works in Development? Thinking Big and*

Thinking Small, edited by Jessica Cohen and William Easterly (Washington, D.C: Brookings Institution Press, 2009), 24–54.

11. Cohen and Easterly, *What Works in Development?*, 23.

12. Abhijit Banerjee, Dean Karlan, and Jonathan Zinman, "Six Randomized Evaluations of Microcredit: Introduction and Further Steps," *American Economic Journal: Applied Economics* 7, no. 1 (2015): 1–21.

13. "Opportunities for Impact Evaluation," USAID, June 12, 2019, https://www.usaid.gov/project-starter/program-cycle/cdcs/anticipating-evaluation-needs/opportunities-for-impact-evaluation.

14. Including NGO staff members with whom we have spoken.

15. Just as many college professors with learning outcomes do.

16. Cyril Northcote Parkinson, "Parkinson's Law," *Economist*, November 19, 1955, https://www.economist.com/news/1955/11/19/parkinsons-law.

17. Parkinson's Law helps explain why the British colonial administration and naval administration grew even as the British Empire shrank.

18. Jerry Pournelle, "Current Chaos Manor Mail," JerryPournelle.com, accessed June 28, 2020, https://www.jerrypournelle.com/mail/2011/Q3/mail680.html.

19. Sarah Cooper went viral with her post on the ten tricks people used to look smart in Google meetings. Two of our favorites are "Ask the Presenter to Go Back a Slide" and always ask "Will This Scale?" See Sarah Cooper, "10 Tricks to Appear Smart in Meetings," The Cooper Review, January 30, 2015, https://thecooperreview.com/10-tricks-appear-smart-meetings/.

20. David Graeber, *Bullshit Jobs* (New York: Simon & Schuster, 2018), 368.

21. David Graeber, *Bullshit Jobs* (New York: Simon & Schuster, 2018), 17.

22. Kim Christensen, "Is UC Spending Too Little on Teaching, Too Much on Administration?," *Los Angeles Times*, October 17, 2015, https://www.latimes.com/local/education/la-me-uc-spending-20151011-story.html.

23. Kim Christensen, "Is UC Spending Too Little on Teaching, Too Much on Administration?," *Los Angeles Times*, October 17, 2015, https://www.latimes.com/local/education/la-me-uc-spending-20151011-story.html.

24. David Wertheimer, deputy director for the Pacific Northwest Initiative at the Bill and Melinda Gates Foundation. Quoted in Paul Klein, "Are Nonprofits Getting in the Way of Social Change?," *Stanford Social Innovation Review*, May 15, 2015, https://ssir.org/articles/entry/are_nonprofits_getting_in_the_way_of_social_change.

25. Vinicius Daumas, personal correspondence, 2020.

26. William MacAskill, *Doing Good Better: How Effective Altruism Can Help You Help Others, Do Work That Matters, and Make Smarter Choices about Giving Back* (New York: Penguin Random House, 2015), 108.

27. You could also find wonderful mangrove planting organizations and vet them online, without ever leaving your home.

7. ACTORS OF RESISTANCE

1. "A New Census Shows How a Brazilian Favela Really Works," *Economist*, May 30, 2019, https://www.economist.com/the-americas/2019/05/30/a-new-census -shows-how-a-brazilian-favela-really-works.

2. Isaías Dalle and Thainã de Medeiros, "Militias Are Involved in Drug Traf- ficking and Operate in Rio's Wealthy Districts," Rio On Watch, March 19, 2019, https://www.rioonwatch.org/?p=51875.

3. Since 1998, there is a national test, known as the ENEM, but universities and departments can still have their own custom tests, and expensive *cursinhos* are still prevalent for the middle and upper class.

4. "Who We Are—Our History," Redes da Maré, accessed June 29, 2020, https://www.redesdamare.org.br/en/quemsomos/historia.

5. Sérgio Ramalho, "Who Killed Marielle Franco? An Ex-Rio de Janeiro Cop with Ties to Organized Crime, Say Six Witnesses in Police Report," *Intercept*, January 18, 2019, https://theintercept.com/2019/01/17/marielle-franco-brazil -assassination-suspect/.

6. David Brennan, "Police Are Killing More and More People in Brazil's Favelas—and Community Leaders Say Bolsonaro and His Allies Are to Blame," *Newsweek*, October 30, 2019, https://www.newsweek.com/police-killings-brazil -favelas-jair-bolsonaro-marielle-franco-wilson-witzel-1468428.

7. See "Lia Rodrigues Companhia de Danças," Lia Rodrigues, 2019, http:// www.liarodrigues.com/index.php.

8. See "Program Integração Pela Música," Mapa de Cultura RJ, accessed June 30, 2020, http://mapadecultura.rj.gov.br/headline/program-integracao-pela -musica; PIM—Programa Integração pela Música, "PIM Posts," PIM-org.com, 2017, http://www.pim-org.com/.

9. For the trailer, see Vice, "Dancing Through Gunshots in Brazil's Favelas," YouTube, October 25, 2018, https://youtu.be/tooevRbb9lY.

10. For a film trailer about Alan Duarte, see Beija Films, "The Good Fight (a Vida é Uma Luta)—Trailer," Vimeo, March 1, 2017, https://vimeo.com/206223039.

11. See the trailer for the film and full documentary about Cinema Nosso at www.moviemagicmotion.com.

12. See the "Favela Rising Trailer," YouTube, June 1, 2006, https://youtu.be /B5_DnxeEkts.

13. These principles embody much of the ideas of the famous Brazilian soci- ologist Paulo Friere and his empowering handbook *Pedagogy of the Oppressed* (New York: Continuum, 2000).

14. From the one-hour documentary film *Gira and the Circus of Life*, directed by Lili Fialho and Kátia Lund, 2016; you can watch the trailer and full docu- mentary at www.giracircusmovie.com.

15. The story of Junior Perim, Vinicius Daumus, D'Jeferson, and the Crescer e Viver circus are told in *Gira and the Circus of Life*.

16. Alex Robinson and Gardênia Robinson, *Rio de Janeiro Focus Guide*, 2nd ed., Footprint Focus (Bath, UK: Footprint, 2014), 44.

17. Vinicius Daumus, personal correspondence, 2019.

18. Vinicius Daumus, personal correspondence, 2019.

19. We of the Hill: Most of the favelas of Rio are on hills, and *morro* is another word for "favela."

20. Guti Fraga, personal correspondence, 2016.

21. From the film *Guti and the Theater of Dreams*, directed by Lili Fialho and Kátia Lund, 2016.

22. The list of professional actors, musicians, and artists launched by Guti Fraga is impressive. The list of actors includes Jonathan Haagensen, Micael Borges, Thiago Martins, Roberta Rodrigues, Marcelo Melo Jr., Sabrina Rosa, Cintia Rosa, Mary Sheila, and Roberta Santiago.

23. Guti Fraga, personal correspondence, 2017.

24. The Guti Fraga story is told in the one-hour documentary film *Guti and the Theater of Dreams*. You can watch the trailer and the full documentary film at www.gutidreamsmovie.com.

25. Vanessa Suares, personal correspondence, 2019.

26. *Guti and the Theater of Dreams*.

27. Rise Up & Care, the one-hour documentary film *Jongo Fever*, directed by Lili Fialho and Kátia Lund, 2016.

28. The history and innovation of Casa do Jongo da Serrinha are told in *Jongo Fever*. You can watch the trailer and the full documentary film at www .jongofevermovie.com.

29. Dyonne Boy, personal correspondence, 2018.

30. Or when safe after the taming of the coronavirus pandemic.

31. Frizero Mariana Gonçalves, "Comunidade Quilombola Serra Da Guia," Terras de Quilombos Coleção (Belo Horizonte: FAFISH—Federal University of Minas Gerais, 2016), http://www.incra.gov.br/sites/default/files/terras_de _quilombos_serra_da_guia-se.pdf.

32. Zefa Da Guia, "Parteira & Rezadeira Do Sertão," ZefaDaGuia Blogspot, May 4, 2011, http://zefadaguia.blogspot.com/2011/05/quilombola-serra-da-guia -em-poco.html.

8. A CALL TO ACTION

1. Dan Parks, "Wave of Nonprofit Closures Likely on the Way Soon, Nonprofit Leaders Forecast," *Chronicle of Philanthropy*, June 4, 2020, https://www .philanthropy.com/article/Wave-of-Nonprofit-Closures/248924.

2. Michael Scott, "Latin America 'to Lose 20 Years of Progress' in Poverty Reduction," *Financial Times*, June 29, 2020, https://www.ft.com/content /9be51e4f-e89f-4ffc-a6a7-1313240e0624.

3. Jessica Flores and Melisa Bivian, "Lin-Manuel Miranda's 'Hamilton' Funds Give Puerto Rican Art Groups a Second Chance," NBC News, September 6, 2019, https://www.nbcnews.com/news/latino/lin-manuel-miranda-s-hamilton -funds-give-puerto-rican-art-n1040891.

4. Max de Lotbinière, "Research Backs English as Key to Development," *Guardian*, July 5, 2011, https://www.theguardian.com/education/2011/jul/05 /research-backs-english-language-delotbiniere.

5. Marjorie Olster, "Empowering Teenage Girls in a Traditional Village and Across Morocco," *New York Times*, August 17, 2018, https://www.nytimes .com/2018/08/17/world/africa/morocco-maryam-montague.html.

6. See https://www.vip.gatech.edu/teams/global-social-entrepreneurship.

7. The author, George P. Burdell, was a fictional student officially enrolled at Georgia Tech in 1927 as a practical joke, and is the pen name for the collective of students that participated in the writing of the book (see https:// en.wikipedia.org/wiki/George_P._Burdell).

BIBLIOGRAPHY

Abdul Latif Jameel Poverty Action Lab. "Measuring the Impact of Microfinance in Hyderabad, India." Accessed May 30, 2020. https://www.povertyactionlab .org/evaluation/measuring-impact-microfinance-hyderabad-india.

Ackerman, Andy. "The Strike." *Seinfeld.* NBC, December 18, 1997. http://www .seinfeldscripts.com/TheStrike.htm.

Alba, Davey. "Zuckerberg Sold His Facebook Shares for Charity—but He's No Hero Yet." *Wired*, August 23, 2016. https://www.wired.com/2016/08 /zuckerberg-sold-facebook-shares-charity-hes-no-hero-yet/.

Alter, Pat, and Bernie Alter, eds. *Gather the Fruit One by One.* 50 Years of Amazing Peace Corps Stories, vol. 2, The Americas. Palo Alto: Travelers Tales, 2011.

Anderson, Gary A. *Charity: The Place of the Poor in the Biblical Tradition.* New Haven, CT: Yale University Press, 2013.

Anheier, Helmut K., and Lester M. Salamon. "The Nonprofit Sector in Comparative Perspective." In *The Nonprofit Sector: A Research Handbook*, ed. Walter W. Powell and Richard Steinberg, 2nd ed., 89–116. New Haven, CT: Yale University Press, 2006.

Arnsberger, Paul, Melissa Ludlum, Margaret Riley, and Mark Stanton. "A History of the Tax-Exempt Sector: An SOI Perspective." *Statistics of Income Bulletin* (2008): 105–135.

Arocena, Felipe, and Kirk S. Bowman. *Lessons from Latin America: Innovations in Politics, Culture, and Development.* Toronto: University of Toronto Press, 2014.

Bajwa, Sohaib Shahid, Xiaofeng Wang, Anh Nguyen Duc, and Pekka Abrahamsson. "'Failures' to Be Celebrated: An Analysis of Major Pivots of Software

Startups." *Empirical Software Engineering* 22, no. 5 (2016): 2373–2408. https://doi.org/10.1007/s10664-016-9458-0.

Banerjee, Abhijit, and Esther Duflo, eds. *Handbook of Economic Field Experiments*. Vol. 1. Handbooks in Economics. Amsterdam: North-Holland, 2017.

Banerjee, Abhijit V., and Esther Duflo. *Poor Economics: A Radical Rethinking of the Way to Fight Global Poverty*. New York: PublicAffairs, 2012.

Banerjee, Abhijit, Dean Karlan, and Jonathan Zinman. "Six Randomized Evaluations of Microcredit: Introduction and Further Steps." *American Economic Journal: Applied Economics* 7, no. 1 (January 2015): 1–21. https://doi.org/10.1257/app.20140287.

Banning-Lover, Rachel. "The Seven Sins of Humanitarian Douchery." *Guardian*, April 16, 2015, sec. Working in development. https://www.theguardian.com/global-development-professionals-network/2015/apr/16/humanitarian-douchery-volunteering-voluntourism-endhumanitariandouchery.

Barbara, Vanessa. "The Rise of the Milícia State." *New York Times*, April 10, 2019. https://www.nytimes.com/2019/04/10/opinion/brazil-bolsonaro-militias.html.

Bates, Stephen. "The Hidden Holocaust." *Guardian*, May 13, 1999, sec. World news. https://www.theguardian.com/theguardian/1999/may/13/features11.g22.

Bazilchuk, Nancy. "Live Rock." *University of Washington—Conservation* (blog), July 29, 2008. https://www.conservationmagazine.org/2008/07/live-rock/.

Beija Films. "The Good Fight (a Vida é Uma Luta)—Trailer." *Vimeo* (blog), March 1, 2017. https://vimeo.com/206223039.

Berryman, Jack W. "Motion and Rest: Galen on Exercise and Health." *Lancet* 380, no. 9838 (July 2012): 210–211. https://doi.org/10.1016/S0140-6736(12)61205-7.

Biddle, Pippa. "The Problem with Little White Girls (and Boys): Why I Stopped Being a Voluntourist." October 28, 2014. https://pippabiddle.com/2014/02/18/the-problem-with-little-white-girls-and-boys/.

Birrell, Ian. "Before You Pay to Volunteer Abroad, Think of the Harm You Might Do." *Guardian*, November 14, 2010. https://www.theguardian.com/commentisfree/2010/nov/14/orphans-cambodia-aids-holidays-madonna.

Bishop, Matthew, and Michael Green. *Philanthro-Capitalism: How the Rich Can Save the World*. New York: Bloomsbury Press, 2008.

Block, Jean. *The Nonprofit Guide to Social Enterprise: Show Me the (Unrestricted) Money!* Rancho Santa Margarita, CA: CharityChannel Press, 2013.

Blustein, Paul. *And the Money Kept Rolling in (and out): Wall Street, the IMF, and the Bankrupting of Argentina*. New York: PublicAffairs, 2006.

Board of Governors of the Federal Reserve System. "Charge-Off Rates on Loans and Leases at Commercial Banks," February 18, 2020. https://www.federalreserve.gov/releases/chargeoff/chgallnsa.htm.

Board of Governors of the Federal Reserve System. "Delinquency Rates on Loans and Leases at Commercial Banks," February 18, 2020. https://www.federalreserve.gov/releases/chargeoff/delallnsa.htm.

Boaretto, Mayara, Isadora Carneiro, and Kátia Lund. dir. *Women of Earth*. Documentary, 2019. www.womenofearthfilm.com.

Bogost, Ian. "Mini Object Lesson: No, There Are Not 100 Eskimo Words for 'Snow.'" *Atlantic*, January 23, 2016. https://www.theatlantic.com/notes/2016/01/mini-object-lesson-no-there-are-not-a-hundred-eskimo-words-for-snow/426651/.

Bonito, Victor. Fiji Peace Corps. Interview by Kirk Bowman, 2015.

——. "Fiji Peace Corps," 2019.

Boot, Max. *The Savage Wars of Peace: Small Wars and the Rise of American Power*. New York: Basic Books, 2002.

Bornstein, David, and Susan Davis. *Social Entrepreneurship: What Everyone Needs to Know*. New York: Oxford University Press, 2010.

Bowman, Kirk S. *Peddling Paradise: The Politics of Tourism in Latin America*. Boulder, CO: Lynne Rienner, 2013.

Bowman, Kirk. "Should the Kuznets Effect Be Relied on to Induce Equalizing Growth." *World Development* 25, no. 1 (1997): 127–43.

Brantlinger, Patrick. "Kipling's 'The White Man's Burden' and Its Afterlives." *English Literature in Transition, 1880–1920* 50, no. 2 (2007): 172–91.

"Brazil Takes Off." *The Economist*, November 14, 2009. https://www.economist.com/weeklyedition/2009-11-14.

"Brazil's Temer Approval Rating in a New Record: 4 Percent." *MercoPress*. June 30, 2018. https://en.mercopress.com/2018/06/30/brazil-s-temer-approval-rating-in-a-new-record-4.

Brennan, David. "Police Are Killing More and More People in Brazil's Favelas—and Community Leaders Say Bolsonaro and His Allies Are to Blame." *Newsweek*, October 30, 2019. https://www.newsweek.com/police-killings-brazil-favelas-jair-bolsonaro-marielle-franco-wilson-witzel-1468428.

Bronfman, Charles, and Jeffrey Solomon. *The Art of Doing Good: Where Passion Meets Action*. San Francisco: Jossey-Bass, 2012.

Brooks, David. "The Neighborhood Is the Unit of Change." *New York Times*, October 18, 2018. https://www.nytimes.com/2018/10/18/opinion/neighborhood-social-infrastructure-community.html.

Capoccia, Giovanni. "Critical Junctures." In *The Oxford Handbook of Historical Institutionalism*, ed. Karl Orfeo Fioretos, Tulia Gabriela Falleti, and Adam D. Sheingate, 95–108. Oxford: Oxford University Press, 2016.

Capra, Frank, dir. *It's a Wonderful Life*. Liberty Films, 1946.

Cardoso, Fernando Henrique, and Enzo Faletto. *Dependency and Development in Latin America*. Berkeley: University of California Press, 1979.

Caufield, Catherine. *Masters of Illusion: The World Bank and the Poverty of Nations*. New York: Henry Holt, 1996.

Chambers, Andrew. "Africa's Not-so-Magic Roundabout." *Guardian*, November 24, 2009. https://www.theguardian.com/commentisfree/2009/nov/24/africa-charity-water-pumps-roundabouts.

Charity Watch. "CharityWatch Hall of Shame: The Personalities Behind Charity Scandals," August 24, 2018. https://www.charitywatch.org/charity -donating-articles/charitywatch-hall-of-shame.

Christensen, Kim. "Is UC Spending Too Little on Teaching, Too Much on Administration?" *Los Angeles Times*, October 17, 2015. https://www.latimes .com/local/education/la-me-uc-spending-20151011-story.html.

Coalter, Fred. *Sport for Development: What Game Are We Playing?* New York: Routledge, 2013.

Coghlan, Alexandra, and Steve Noakes. "Towards an Understanding of the Drivers of Commercialization in the Volunteer Tourism Sector." *Tourism Recreation Research* 37, no. 2 (January 12, 2015): 123–131.

Cohen, Jessica, and William Easterly, eds. *What Works in Development? Thinking Big and Thinking Small*. Washington, DC Brookings Institution Press, 2009.

Cohen, Joshua, and Joel Rogers, eds. *Associations and Democracy*. The Real Utopias Project 1. London: Verso, 1995.

Collier, David, and Gerardo Munck. "Building Blocks and Methodological Challenges: A Framework for Studying Critical Junctures." *Qualitative & Multi-Method Research* 15, no. 1 (Spring 2017): 2–9.

Cooke, Teman. "Sidekicks Are the Real Heroes." *A Study in Contradictions* (blog), June 21, 2013. http://thcooke.com/2013/06/sidekicks-are-the-real-heroes/.

Cooper, Sarah. "10 Tricks to Appear Smart in Meetings." *The Cooper Review* (blog), January 30, 2015. https://thecooperreview.com/10-tricks-appear-smart-meetings/.

Costello, Amy. "Southern Africa: Troubled Water." PBS, 2010. http://www.pbs .org/frontlineworld/stories/southernafrica904/video_index.html.

Cowan, Robin, and Philip Gunby. "Sprayed to Death: Path Dependence, Lock-in and Pest Control Strategies." *The Economic Journal* 106, no. 436 (May 1996): 521–542.

Currid-Halkett, Elizabeth. *The Sum of Small Things: A Theory of the Aspirational Class*. Princeton, NJ: Princeton University Press, 2017.

Dalle, Isaías, and Thainã de Medeiros. "Militias Are Involved in Drug Trafficking and Operate in Rio's Wealthy Districts." Rio On Watch, March 19, 2019. https://www.rioonwatch.org/?p=51875.

Damberger, David. "What Happens When an NGO Admits Failure." TED Talks presented at the TEDxYYC, April 2011. https://www.ted.com/talks /david_damberger_what_happens_when_an_ngo_admits_failure/transcript.

Dantas, Dimitrius. "Herdeiro Da Família Imperial, Dom Antônio Está Hospitalizado Com Coronavirus." *O Globo Newspaper*, March 19, 2020.

Deby, Denise. "How Engineers Without Borders Learned to Embrace Failure (and Learn from It, Too)." *This Magazine*, December 1, 2011. https://this .org/2011/12/01/admitting-failure/.

Duflo, Esther, and Michael Kremer. "Use of Randomization in the Evaluation of Development Effectiveness," 37. Washington, DC, 2003. https://economics .mit.edu/files/765.

Easterly, William. *The White Man's Burden: Why the West's Efforts to Aid the Rest Have Done So Much Ill and So Little Good*. New York: Penguin Press, 2006.

Eckstein, Harry. "Case Study and Theory in Political Science." In *Handbook of Political Science. Political Science: Scope and Theory*, ed. Fred I. Greenstein and Nelson W. Polsby, 94–137. Reading: MA: Addison-Wesley Press, 1975.

Engineers Without Borders. "Admitting Failure." Accessed May 29, 2020. https://www.admittingfailure.org/.

Epstein, Marc J., and Kristi Yuthas. *Measuring and Improving Social Impacts: A Guide for Nonprofits, Companies, and Impact Investors*. San Francisco: Berrett-Koehler, 2014.

Erikson, Martin G., and Malgorzata Erikson. "Learning Outcomes and Critical Thinking—Good Intentions in Conflict." *Studies in Higher Education* 44, no. 12 (December 2, 2019): 2293–2303. https://doi.org/10.1080/03075079.2018.1486813.

Escobar, Arturo. *Encountering Development: The Making and Unmaking of the Third World*. Princeton, NJ: Princeton University Press, 1995.

——. "Imagining a Post-Development Era." In *Power of Development*, ed. Jonathan Crush, 211–227. London: Routledge, 1995.

——. "Planning." In *The Development Dictionary*, ed. Wolfgang Sachs, 132–145. London: Zed Books, 1992.

——. "Reflections on 'Development': Grassroots Approaches and Alternative Politics in the Third World." *Futures* 24, no. 5 (June 1992): 411–436.

Eulich, Whitney. "How a Favela Kid Became Brazil's Top Badminton Player." *Christian Science Monitor*, August 13, 2016. https://www.csmonitor.com/World/Olympics/2016/0813/How-a-favela-kid-became-Brazil-s-top-badminton-player.

"Failure Report." Canada: Engineers Without Borders, 2016. http://reports.ewb.ca/.

Faulhaber, Lucas, and Lena Azevedo. *Remoções No Rio de Janeiro Olímpico*. Rio de Janeiro: Mórula Editorial, 2015.

"FDIC Quarterly: Core Profitability of Community Banks: 1985 to 2015." Arlington, VA: Division of Insurance and Research of the Federal Deposit Insurance Corporation, 2016. https://www.fdic.gov/bank/analytical/quarterly/2016-vol10-4/fdic-v10n4-3q16-quarterly.pdf.

Fernandes, Fernando Lannes. "Youth Gang Members in Rio de Janeiro: The Face of a 'Lost Generation' in an Age of Fear and Mistrust." *Bulletin of Latin American Research* 32, no. 2 (2013): 210–223. https://doi.org/10.1111/blar.12030.

Fialho, Lili, and Kátia Lund. dir. *Bad & the Birdieman*. Documentary, 2016. www.badbirdiemanmovie.com.

——. *Gira & the Circus of Dreams*. Documentary, 2016. www.giracircusmovie.com.

——. *Guti & the Theater of Dreams*. Documentary, 2016. www.gutidreamsmovie.com.

——. *Jongo Fever*. Documentary, 2016. www.jongofevermovie.com.

——. *Movie Magic Motion*. Documentary, 2016. www.moviemagicmotion.com.

Fisher, Donald. "The Role of Philanthropic Foundations in the Reproduction and Production of Hegemony: Rockefeller Foundations and the Social Sciences." *Sociology* 17, no. 2 (May 1983): 206–233.

Fitzpatrick, David, and Drew Griffin. "Government Says Four Cancer Charities Are Shams." CNN, May 19, 2015. https://www.cnn.com/2015/05/19/us/scam-charity-investigation/index.html.

Flores, Jessica, and Melisa Bivian. "Lin-Manuel Miranda's 'Hamilton' Funds Give Puerto Rican Art Groups a Second Chance." NBC News, September 6, 2019. https://www.nbcnews.com/news/latino/lin-manuel-miranda-s-hamilton-funds-give-puerto-rican-art-n1040891.

Forbes Staff. "Forbes' 31st Annual World's Billionaires Issue." *Forbes*, March 20, 2017. https://www.forbes.com/sites/forbespr/2017/03/20/forbes-31st-annual-worlds-billionaires-issue/.

Frank, Andre Gunder. "The Development of Underdevelopment." *Monthly Review* 18, no. 4 (September 2, 1966): 17–31. https://doi.org/10.14452/MR-018-04-1966-08_3.

Fraser-Thomas, Jessica L., Jean Côté, and Janice Deakin. "Youth Sport Programs: An Avenue to Foster Positive Youth Development." *Physical Education & Sport Pedagogy* 10, no. 1 (February 2005): 19–40. https://doi.org/10.1080/17408980420003348900.

Friedman, Eric. *Reinventing Philanthropy: A Framework for More Effective Giving*. Washington DC: Potomac, 2013.

Friedman, Lawrence J., and Mark D. McGarvie. *Charity, Philanthropy, and Civility in American History*. Cambridge: Cambridge University Press, 2004.

Frumkin, Peter. *Strategic Giving: The Art and Science of Philanthropy*. Chicago: University of Chicago Press, 2006.

Gaffney, Christopher. "Securing the Olympic City." *Georgetown Journal of International Affairs* no. 13 (Summer/Fall 2012): 75–82.

Galdieri, Dado. "An Unlikely Olympic Story." *New York Times*, July 31, 2016, sec. Sports. https://www.nytimes.com/slideshow/2016/07/31/sports/an-unlikely-olympic-story.html.

Galeano, Eduardo. *Open Veins of Latin America: Five Centuries of the Pillage of a Continent*. 25th anniversary ed. New York: Monthly Review Press, 1997.

Galtung, Johan. "A Structural Theory of Imperialism." *Journal of Peace Research* 8, no. 2 (June 1, 1971): 81–117. https://doi.org/10.1177/002234337100800201.

Gates, Bill. "The Bono of Economics—Jeffrey Sachs—Commentary." CNBC, May 22, 2014. https://www.cnbc.com/2014/05/22/the-bono-of-economicsjeffrey-sachscommentary.html.

Gates, Bill, and Melinda Gates. "Bill and Melinda Gates: Let's Keep Investing in the World's Poor." *Wall Street Journal*, September 13, 2017, sec.

Life & Arts. https://www.wsj.com/articles/bill-and-melinda-gates-lets-keep
-investing-in-the-worlds-poor-1505300401.

Gates, Henry Louis, Jr. "How Many Slaves Landed in the US?" *The Root*, January 6, 2014. https://www.theroot.com/how-many-slaves-landed-in-the-us
-1790873989.

Gedde, Maïa. *Working in International Development and Humanitarian Assistance: A Career Guide.* New York: Routledge, 2015.

Giridharadas, Anand. *Winners Take All: The Elite Charade of Changing the World.* New York: Vintage Books, 2018.

GiveDirectly. "Research on Cash Transfers." https://www.givedirectly.org
/research-at-give-directly/. Accessed May 31, 2020.

Godrej, Dinyar. "NGOs—Do They Help?" *New Internationalist*, December 1, 2014. https://newint.org/features/2014/12/01/ngos-keynote.

Gomes, Luciani. "Brazil's Business Labyrinth of Bureaucracy." *BBC News*, May 17, 2012. https://www.bbc.com/news/business-18020623.

Gonçalves, Frizero Mariana. "Comunidade Quilombola Serra Da Guia." Terras de Quilombos Coleção. Belo Horizonte: FAFISH—Federal University of Minas Gerais, 2016. http://www.incra.gov.br/sites/default/files/terras_de
_quilombos_serra_da_guia-se.pdf.

Graeber, David. *Bullshit Jobs.* New York: Simon & Schuster, 2018.

Grandin, Greg. *Fordlandia: The Rise and Fall of Henry Ford's Forgotten Jungle City.* New York: Metropolitan Books, 2009.

Green, Christine. "Chapter 6—Sport as an Agent for Social and Personal Change." In *Management of Sports Development*, ed. Vassil Girginov, 129–145. Oxford: Butterworth-Heinemann, 2008.

Griffin, Jo. "Is Brutal Treatment of Young Offenders Fuelling Crime Rates in Brazil?" *Guardian*, March 3, 2017. https://www.theguardian.com/global
-development/2017/mar/03/brazil-crime-rates-brutal-treatment-young
-offenders.

Grove, S. J., and R. A. Dodder. "Construction Measures to Assess Perceptions of Sport Functions." *International Journal of Sports Psychology* 13 (1982): 96–106.

Gugerty, Mary Kay, and Dean Karlan. "Ten Reasons Not to Measure Impact—and What to Do Instead." *Stanford Social Innovation Review*, Summer 2018. https://
ssir.org/articles/entry/ten_reasons_not_to_measure_impact_and_what_to
_do_instead.

Guia, Zefa Da. "Parteira & Rezadeira Do Sertão." *ZefaDaGuia Blogspot* (blog), May 4, 2011. http://zefadaguia.blogspot.com/2011/05/quilombola-serra-da-guia
-em-poco.html.

Haidt, Jonathan. *The Righteous Mind: Why Good People Are Divided by Politics and Religion.* New York: Pantheon, 2012.

Hall, Gareth, and Arianne Reis. "A Case Study of a Sport-for-Development Programme in Brazil: Sport for Development in Brazil." *Bulletin of Latin*

American Research 38, no. 3 (July 2019): 317–332. https://doi.org/10.1111/blar.12921.

Hall, Peter Dobkin. "A Historical Overview of Philanthropy, Voluntary Associations, and Nonprofit Organizations in the United States, 1600–2000." In *The Nonprofit Sector: A Research Handbook*, ed. Walter W. Powell and Richard Steinberg, 2nd ed., 32–65. New Haven, CT: Yale University Press, 2006.

Hanlon, Joseph, Armando Barrientos, and David Hulme. *Just Give Money to the Poor: The Development Revolution from the Global South*. Sterling, VA: Kumarian, 2010.

Hessler, Peter. "What Mortenson Got Wrong." *New Yorker*, April 21, 2011. https://www.newyorker.com/news/news-desk/what-mortenson-got-wrong.

Hickel, Jason. "The Microfinance Delusion: Who Really Wins?" *Guardian*, June 10, 2015. https://www.theguardian.com/global-development-professionals-network/2015/jun/10/the-microfinance-delusion-who-really-wins.

Hirschman, Albert. "A Dissenter's Confession: 'The Strategy of Economic Development' Revisited." In *Pioneers in Development*, ed. Gerald Meier and Dudley Seers, 88. London: Oxford University Press, 1984.

——. *The Strategy of Economic Development*. New Haven, CT: Yale University Press, 1958.

Hobbes, Michael. "Stop Trying to Save the World." *New Republic*, November 17, 2014. https://newrepublic.com/article/120178/problem-international-development-and-plan-fix-it.

Hochschild, Adam. *King Leopold's Ghost: A Story of Greed, Terror, and Heroism in Colonial Africa*. Boston: Mariner Books, 1998.

Hodal, Kate. "JK Rowling Urges Students Not to Volunteer at Orphanages." *Guardian*, October 24, 2019, sec. Global development. https://www.theguardian.com/global-development/2019/oct/24/jk-rowling-urges-students-not-to-volunteer-at-orphanages.

Holt, Nicholas L., ed. *Positive Youth Development Through Sport*. International Studies in Physical Education and Youth Sport. Abingdon: Routledge, 2008.

Huggins, Clare. "Olympics Poverty Torch Arrives in Vila Autódromo at First 'Run for Vila.'" Rio On Watch, March 29, 2016. https://www.rioonwatch.org/?p=27714.

Illich, Ivan. Untitled speech presented at the Conference of InterAmerican Student Projects, Mexico, April 20, 1968. http://www.ciasp.ca/CIASPhistory/IllichCIASPspeech.htm#_ftn2.

Independent Sector. "The Charitable Sector." Accessed May 22, 2020. https://independentsector.org/about/the-charitable-sector/.

Ingram, Mathew. "Mark Zuckerberg Is Giving Away His Money, but With a Silicon Valley Twist." *Fortune*, December 2, 2015. https://fortune.com/2015/12/02/zuckerberg-charity/.

"In Rio, Poor Families Are Pushed out of Their Neighborhoods to Make Way for the Olympics." *Los Angeles Times*, August 4, 2016. https://www.latimes.com/world/mexico-americas/la-fg-olympic-land-grab-snap-story.html.

Institute of International Education. "U.S. Study Abroad Destinations," 2019. https://www.iie.org:443/en/Research-and-Insights/Open-Doors/Data/US-Study-Abroad/Destinations.

Internal Revenue Service. "Publication 526 (2019), Charitable Contributions," 2019. https://www.irs.gov/publications/p526.

IUPUI Lilly Family School of Philanthropy. "Giving USA 2019: The Annual Report on Philanthropy for the Year 2018." Chicago: Giving USA Foundation, 2019.

Jackson, William L. *The Wisdom of Generosity: A Reader in American Philanthropy*. Waco, TX: Baylor University Press, 2008.

Jensen, Frances E. *The Teenage Brain: A Neuroscientist's Survival Guide to Raising Adolescents and Young Adults*. New York: Harper, 2016.

Joffé, Roland, dir. *The Mission*. London: Goldcrest Films, 1986.

Johnson, John J. *Latin America in Caricature*. Texas Pan American Series. Austin: University of Texas Press, 1993.

Johnson, Tarnue. *Critical Examination of Firestones Operations in Liberia: A Case Study Approach*. Bloomington, IN: AuthorHouse, 2010.

Ju, Chang Bum, and Shui-Yan Tang. "Path Dependence, Critical Junctures, and Political Contestation: The Developmental Trajectories of Environmental NGOs in South Korea." *Nonprofit and Voluntary Sector Quarterly* 40, no. 6 (December 2011): 1048–1072.

Kahn, Carrie. "As 'Voluntourism' Explodes in Popularity, Who's It Helping Most?" *NPR—Morning Edition*, July 31, 2014. https://www.npr.org/sections/goatsandsoda/2014/07/31/336600290/as-volunteerism-explodes-in-popularity-whos-it-helping-most.

Keating, Joshua. "Why Did One Laptop per Child Fail?" *Foreign Policy*, September 9, 2009. https://foreignpolicy.com/2009/09/09/why-did-one-laptop-per-child-fail/.

Kim, Sunhyuk. "Democratization and Environmentalism: South Korea and Taiwan in Comparative Perspective." *Journal of Asian and African Studies* 35, no. 3 (January 1, 2000): 287–302.

Klein, Paul. "Are Nonprofits Getting in the Way of Social Change?" *Stanford Social Innovation Review*, May 15, 2015. https://ssir.org/articles/entry/are_nonprofits_getting_in_the_way_of_social_change.

Klinenberg, Eric. *Heat Wave: A Social Autopsy of Disaster in Chicago*. 2nd ed. Chicago: University of Chicago Press, 2015.

Krakauer, Jon. "Greg Mortenson, Disgraced Author of 'Three Cups of Tea,' Believes He Will Have the Last Laugh. He Might Be Right." Medium, July 20, 2014. https://medium.com/galleys/greg-mortenson-disgraced-author-of-three-cups-of-tea-believes-he-will-have-the-last-laugh-760949b1f964.

Kristjansson, Alfgeir L., Michael J. Mann, Jon Sigfusson, Ingibjorg E. Thorisdottir, John P. Allegrante, and Inga Dora Sigfusdottir. "Development and Guiding Principles of the Icelandic Model for Preventing Adolescent Substance

Use." *Health Promotion Practice* 21, no. 1 (June 4, 2019): 62–69. https://doi
.org/10.1177/1524839919849032.

Labouchére, Henry. "The Brown Man's Burden." *Literary Digest* 18, February 25, 1899.

Laemmermann, Karl. *Crowd Funding: Raising Capital Online.* Scotts Valley, CA: CreateSpace, 2012.

Lamont, Tom. "Blinded by Technology: Has Our Belief in Silicon Valley Led the World Astray?" *Guardian*, August 30, 2015. http://www.theguardian.com /technology/2015/aug/30/kentaro-toyama-geek-heresy-interview-technology.

Latouche, Serge. *In the Wake of the Affluent Society: An Exploration of Post-Development.* Trans. Martin O'Connor and Rosemary Arnoux. London: Zed Books, 1993.

Lederman, Doug. "Conflicted Views of Technology: A Survey of Faculty Attitudes." *Inside Higher Ed*, October 31, 2018. https://www.insidehighered.com /news/survey/conflicted-views-technology-survey-faculty-attitudes.

Levine, Robert M. *Vale of Tears: Revisiting the Canudos Massacre in Northeastern Brazil, 1893–1897.* Berkeley: University of California Press, 2006.

Lipset, Seymour Martin. *American Exceptionalism: A Double-Edged Sword.* New York: W. W. Norton, 1997.

Lopez, Adlaberto. "The Economics of Yerba Mate in the Seventeenth-Century in South America." *Agricultural History* 48, no. 4 (1974): 493.

Lotbinière, Max de. "Research Backs English as Key to Development." *Guardian*, July 5, 2011. https://www.theguardian.com/education/2011/jul/05/research -backs-english-language-delotbiniere.

Loughead, Katherine. "State Individual Income Tax Rates and Brackets for 2020." *Tax Foundation* (blog), February 4, 2020. https://taxfoundation.org /state-individual-income-tax-rates-and-brackets-for-2020/.

Lupton, Robert D. *Toxic Charity: How Churches and Charities Hurt Those They Help (and How to Reverse It).* New York: HarperOne, 2012.

MacAskill, William. *Doing Good Better: How Effective Altruism Can Help You Help Others, Do Work That Matters, and Make Smarter Choices about Giving Back.* New York: Penguin Random House, 2015.

Macdonald, Cheyenne. "What Travel Looked like 100 Years Ago." *Daily Mail Online.* November 30, 2015. https://www.dailymail.co.uk/sciencetech/article -3339902/What-travel-looked-like-100-years-ago-Map-shows-DAYS-took -travel-abroad-1900s.html.

Mahoney, James. "Path Dependence in Historical Sociology." *Theory and Society* 29, no. 4 (August 2000): 507–548.

Mapa de Cultura RJ. "Program Integração Pela Música." Accessed June 29, 2020. http://mapadecultura.rj.gov.br/headline/program-integracao-pela-musica.

Mapondera, Godfrey, and David Smith. "Malawi Accuses Madonna of Exaggerating Humanitarian Efforts." *Guardian*, April 11, 2013, sec. World news.

https://www.theguardian.com/world/2013/apr/11/malawi-madonna-exaggerating-humanitarian-efforts.

Marmer, Max, Bjoern Herrmann, Ertan Dogrultan, and Ron Burman. "Startup Genome Report Extra on Premature Scaling." Startup Genome, August 29, 2011. http://innovationfootprints.com/wp-content/uploads/2015/07/startup-genome-report-extra-on-premature-scaling.pdf.

McCarthy, Niall. "America's Most and Least Trusted Professions [Infographic]." *Forbes*, January 4, 2018. https://www.forbes.com/sites/niallmccarthy/2018/01/04/americas-most-and-least-trusted-professions-infographic/.

McGregor, Andrew. "New Possibilities? Shifts in Post-Development Theory and Practice." *Geography Compass* 3, no. 5 (September 2009): 1688–1702.

McVeigh, Tracy. "Forget Madonna—Malawi's Parents Find Their Own Way of Keeping Girls in School." *Guardian*, February 28, 2015. https://www.theguardian.com/world/2015/mar/01/malawi-forget-madonna-parents-keep-girls-at-school.

Meisler, Stanley. *When the World Calls: The Inside Story of the Peace Corps and Its First Fifty Years*. Boston: Beacon, 2011.

Merino, Olga, and Linda A. Newson. "Jesuit Missions in Spanish America: The Aftermath of the Expulsion." *Revista de Historia de América* no. 118 (1994): 7–32.

Mittelman, James, and Mustapha Pasha. *Out from Underdevelopment Revisited: Changing Global Structures and the Remaking of the Third World*. 2nd ed. London: MacMillan, 1997.

Mochary, Matt, and Jeff Zimbalist. dir. "Favela Rising Trailer." YouTube (blog), June 1, 2006. https://www.youtube.com/watch?v=B5_DnxeEkts&feature=youtu.be.

Mortenson, Greg, and David Oliver Relin. *Three Cups of Tea: One Man's Extraordinary Journey to Promote Peace—One School at a Time*. London: Penguin, 2007.

Moyo, Dambisa. *Dead Aid: Why Aid Is Not Working and How There Is a Better Way for Africa*. New York: Farrar, Straus and Giroux, 2010.

Munk, Nina. *The Idealist: Jeffrey Sachs and the Quest to End Poverty*. New York: Anchor, 2013.

Murphy, Tom. "How PlayPumps Are an Example of Learning from Failure." Humanosphere, July 2, 2013. http://www.humanosphere.org/basics/2013/07/how-playpumps-are-an-example-of-learning-from-failure/.

Nagourney, Adam. "Madonna's Charity Fails in Bid to Finance School." *New York Times*, March 24, 2011. https://www.nytimes.com/2011/03/25/us/25madonna.html.

"A New Census Shows How a Brazilian Favela Really Works." *Economist*, May 30, 2019. https://www.economist.com/the-americas/2019/05/30/a-new-census-shows-how-a-brazilian-favela-really-works.

Niekerk, Andrea van. "Stop Writing the Same Four Cliched College Essays." *Quartz*, May 2, 2013. https://qz.com/80136/heres-the-secret-to-cracking-the -college-essay/.

Nobel, Carmen. "Why Companies Fail—and How Their Founders Can Bounce Back." Harvard Business School: Working Knowledge, March 7, 2011. http:// hbswk.hbs.edu/item/why-companies-failand-how-their-founders-can -bounce-back.

Nosowitz, Dan. "Has One Laptop per Child Totally Lost Its Way?" *Popular Science*, July 18, 2013. https://www.popsci.com/gadgets/article/2013-07/one-laptop-childs -de-evolution/.

Olster, Marjorie. "Empowering Teenage Girls in a Traditional Village and Across Morocco." *New York Times*, August 17, 2018. https://www.nytimes .com/2018/08/17/world/africa/morocco-maryam-montague.html.

Opray, Max. "How Google Is Putting Rio's Invisible Favelas Back on the Map." *Guardian*, October 9, 2016. https://www.theguardian.com/sustainable-business /2016/oct/09/invisible-favelas-brazil-rio-maps-erasing-poorer-parts-city.

Parkinson, Cyril Northcote. "Parkinson's Law." *Economist*, November 19, 1955. https://www.economist.com/news/1955/11/19/parkinsons-law.

Parks, Dan. "Wave of Nonprofit Closures Likely on the Way Soon, Nonprofit Leaders Forecast." *Chronicle of Philanthropy*, June 4, 2020. https://www.philanthropy .com/article/Wave-of-Nonprofit-Closures/248924.

Parsa, H. G., John T. Self, David Njite, and Tiffany King. "Why Restaurants Fail." *Cornell Hotel and Restaurant Administration Quarterly* 46, no. 3 (August 1, 2005): 304–322. https://doi.org/10.1177/0010880405275598.

Patel, Neil. "90 percent of Startups Fail: Here's What You Need to Know About the 10 Percent." *Forbes*, January 16, 2015. https://www.forbes.com/sites /neilpatel/2015/01/16/90-of-startups-will-fail-heres-what-you-need-to-know -about-the-10/.

Peace Corps. "The Founding Moment." Accessed May 29, 2020. https://www .peacecorps.gov/about/history/founding-moment/.

Peace Corps. "Peace Corps in Fiji." Accessed May 29, 2020. https://www .peacecorps.gov/fiji/.

Perlman, Janice E. *Favela: Four Decades of Living on the Edge in Rio de Janeiro*. New York: Oxford University Press, 2010.

——. *The Myth of Marginality: Urban Poverty and Politics in Rio de Janeiro*. Berke- ley: University of California Press, 1979.

Phillips, Tom. "Jair Bolsonaro Claims Brazilians 'Never Catch Anything' as Covid-19 Cases Rise." *Guardian*, March 27, 2020. https://www.theguardian .com/global-development/2020/mar/27/jair-bolsonaro-claims-brazilians -never-catch-anything-as-covid-19-cases-rise.

——. "Jair Bolsonaro's Racist Comment Sparks Outrage from Indigenous Groups." *Guardian*, January 24, 2020. https://www.theguardian.com/world/2020/ jan/24/jair-bolsonaro-racist-comment-sparks-outrage-indigenous-groups.

Phillips, Tom, and Caio Barretto Briso. "Brazil's Super-Rich and the Exclusive Club at the Heart of a Coronavirus Hotspot." *Guardian*, April 4, 2020. https://www.theguardian.com/world/2020/apr/04/brazils-super-rich-and -the-exclusive-club-at-the-heart-of-a-coronavirus-hotspot.

PIM—Programa Integração pela Música. "PIM Posts." PIM, 2017. http://www .pim-org.com./.

Pournelle, Jerry. "Current Chaos Manor Mail." Accessed June 28, 2020. https:// www.jerrypournelle.com/mail/2011/Q3/mail680.html.

Putnam, Robert D. *Bowling Alone: The Collapse and Revival of American Community*. New York: Touchstone, 2001.

Rahman, K. Sabeel. "Democracy and Productivity: The Glass-Steagall Act and the Shifting Discourse of Financial Regulation." *Journal of Policy History* 24, no. 4 (2012): 612–643.

Ramalho, Sérgio. "Who Killed Marielle Franco? An Ex-Rio de Janeiro Cop with Ties to Organized Crime, Say Six Witnesses in Police Report." *Intercept*, January 18, 2019. https://theintercept.com/2019/01/17/marielle-franco -brazil-assassination-suspect/.

Redes da Maré. "Who We Are—Our History." Accessed June 29, 2020. https:// www.redesdamare.org.br/en/quemsomos/historia.

Reed, Drew. "Lost Cities #10: Fordlandia—the Failure of Henry Ford's Utopian City in the Amazon." *Guardian*, August 19, 2016, sec. Cities. https:// www.theguardian.com/cities/2016/aug/19/lost-cities-10-fordlandia -failure-henry-ford-amazon.

Reich, Rob. *Just Giving: Why Philanthropy Is Failing Democracy and How It Can Do Better*. Princeton, N.J.: Princeton University Press, 2018.

Reich, Rob, Chiara Cordelli, and Lucy Bernholz, eds. *Philanthropy in Democratic Societies: History, Institutions, Values*. Chicago: University of Chicago Press, 2016.

Renken, Jaco, and Richard Heeks. "Conceptualising ICT4D Project Champions." *Proceedings of the Sixth International Conference on Information and Communications Technologies and Development: Notes—Volume 2*, ICTD '13, Vol. 2 (December 7, 2013): 128–131. https://www.givedirectly.org/research-on -cash-transfers/.

"Rigorous Program Evaluations on a Budget: How Low-Cost Randomized Controlled Trials Are Possible in Many Areas of Social Policy." Coalition for Evidence Based Policy, March 2012. https://www.thirdsectorcap.org /wp-content/uploads/2015/02/Rigorous-Program-Evaluations-on-a-Budget -March-2012.pdf.

Rio On Watch. "Why We Should Call Them Favelas," August 13, 2012. https:// www.rioonwatch.org/?page_id=15162.

Robinson, Alex, and Gardênia Robinson. *Rio de Janeiro Focus Guide*. 2nd ed. Footprint Focus. Bath, UK: Footprint Handbooks, 2014.

Rodrigues, Lia. "Lia Rodrigues Companhia de Danças." 2019. http://www .liarodrigues.com/index.php.

Rodrik, Dani. "Goodbye Washington Consensus, Hello Washington Confusion? A Review of the World Bank's Economic Growth in the 1990s: Learning from a Decade of Reform." *Journal of Economic Literature* 44, no. 4 (December 2006): 973–987.

——. "The New Development Economics: We Shall Experiment but How Shall We Learn?" In *What Works in Development? Thinking Big and Thinking Small*, ed. Jessica Cohen and William Easterly, 24–54. Washington, DC: Brookings Institution, 2009.

Rommann, Ryan. "The Peace Corps: Out-Dated and out-Performed?" *Guardian*, November 21, 2013. https://www.theguardian.com/global-development -professionals-network/2013/nov/21/peace-corps-us-development-policy.

Rose, Jeneva. "10 of the Biggest Celebrity Charity Scandals." July 24, 2014. https:// www.therichest.com/money/10-of-the-biggest-celebrity-charity-scandals/.

Rostow, W. W. *The Stages of Economic Growth: A Non-Communist Manifesto*. New York: Cambridge University Press, 1960.

Salamon, Lester M., ed. *New Frontiers of Philanthropy: A Guide to the New Tools and Actors Reshaping Global Philanthropy and Social Investing*. New York: Oxford University Press, 2014.

Sanders, Jane. "Reefing the Benefits." *Research Horizons* 23, no. 1, November 21, 2005.

——. "Scientists Help Fijian Villagers Conserve Coral Reef While Earning a Living from It." *EurekAlert!*, July 19, 2005. http://www.eurekalert.org/pub _releases/2005-07/giot-shf071905.php.

Schoultz, Lars. *Beneath the United States: A History of U.S. Policy Toward Latin America*. Cambridge, MA: Harvard University Press, 1998.

Schwantes, Marcel. "Bill Gates Says This 1 Simple Habit Separates Successful Leaders from Everyone Else." *Inc.* September 23, 2019. https://www.inc .com/marcel-schwantes/bill-gates-says-this-1-simple-habit-separates-successful -leaders-from-everyone-else.html.

Scott, Michael. "Latin America 'to Lose 20 Years of Progress' in Poverty Reduction." *Financial Times*, June 29, 2020. https://www.ft.com/content /9be51e4f-e89f-4ffc-a6a7-1313240e0624.

Segal, David. "In Rio Slum, a Gleaming Hotbed of . . . Badminton?" *New York Times*, July 26, 2016, sec. Sports. https://www.nytimes.com/2016/07/31 /sports/olympics/badminton-rio-de-janeiro-ygor-coelho-de-oliveira.html.

Segran, Elizabeth. "Use These Two Words on Your College Essay to Get into Harvard." *Fast Company*, August 3, 2015. https://www.fastcompany.com/3049289 /use-these-two-words-on-your-college-essay-to-get-into-harvard.

Shah, Namank. "A Blurry Vision: Reconsidering the Failure of the One Laptop per Child Initiative." *Boston University: Journal of the Arts & Sciences Writing Program* no. 3 (2011): 89–98.

"Sidekick." Merriam-Webster. Accessed May 12, 2020. https://www.merriam -webster.com/dictionary/sidekick.

Sigfusdottir, I. D., T. Thorlindsson, A. L. Kristjansson, K. M. Roe, and J. P. Allegrante. "Substance Use Prevention for Adolescents: The Icelandic Model." *Health Promotion International* 24, no. 1 (November 12, 2008): 16–25. https://doi.org/10.1093/heapro/dan038.

Simon, Morgan. *Real Impact: The New Economics of Social Change*. New York: Nation, 2017.

Singer, Amy. *Charity in Islamic Societies*. Cambridge: Cambridge University Press, 2008.

Slack, Mike. "Volunteer Work Tax Deductions." H&R Block, February 2, 2018. https://www.hrblock.com/tax-center/filing/adjustments-and-deductions/volunteer-work-tax-deductions/.

Sontag, Deborah. "In Haiti, Little Can Be Found of a Hip-Hop Artist's Charity." *The New York Times*, October 11, 2012. https://www.nytimes.com/2012/10/12/world/americas/quake-hit-haiti-gains-little-as-wyclef-jean-charity-spends-much.html.

Soto, Hernando de. *The Other Path: The Economic Answer to Terrorism*. New York: Harper and Row, 1989.

Southwick, Natalie. "The Importance and Challenges of Putting Favelas on the Map." Rio On Watch, October 11, 2016. https://www.rioonwatch.org/?p=32519.

Spreitzer, Elmer, and Eldon E. Snyder. "The Psychosocial Functions of Sport as Perceived by the General Population." *International Review of Sport Sociology* 10, no. 3–4 (September 1, 1975): 87–95. https://doi.org/10.1177/101269027501000305.

Stamp, Jimmy. "Fact of Fiction? The Legend of the QWERTY Keyboard." Smithsonian Magazine, May 3, 2003. https://www.smithsonianmag.com/arts-culture/fact-of-fiction-the-legend-of-the-qwerty-keyboard-49863249/.

Stein, Amy L. "Breaking Energy Path Dependencies." *Brook Law Review* 82, no. 2 (2017): 559–604.

Stellar, Daniel. "The PlayPump: What Went Wrong?" *State of the Planet—Columbia University* (blog), July 1, 2010. https://blogs.ei.columbia.edu/2010/07/01/the-playpump-what-went-wrong/.

Stern, Ken. "Why the Rich Don't Give to Charity." *Atlantic*, 2013. https://www.theatlantic.com/magazine/archive/2013/04/why-the-rich-dont-give/309254/.

Stevens, Greg A., and James Burley. "3,000 Raw Ideas = 1 Commercial Success!" *Research-Technology Management* 40, no. 3 (May 1, 1997): 16–27. https://doi.org/10.1080/08956308.1997.11671126.

Stolberg, Sheryl Gay. "Peace Corps Volunteers Speak Out on Rape." *New York Times*, May 10, 2011. https://www.nytimes.com/2011/05/11/us/11corps.html.

Stone, Chad, Danilo Trisi, Arloc Sherman, and Jennifer Beltrán. "A Guide to Statistics on Historical Trends in Income Inequality." Washington, DC: Center on Budget and Policy Priorities, January 13, 2020. https://www.cbpp.org/research/poverty-and-inequality/a-guide-to-statistics-on-historical-trends-in-income-inequality.

Sud, Inder. *Reforming Foreign Aid: Reinvent the World Bank: Lessons in Global Poverty Alleviation from 40 Years of Adventures (and Misadventures) in International Development.* Scotts Valley, CA: CreateSpace, 2017.

Swedlund, Haley J. *The Development Dance: How Donors and Recipients Negotiate the Delivery of Foreign Aid.* Ithaca, NY: Cornell University Press, 2017.

Terasa, Nadine, and Pauline Beaumont. "2019 Report Shows Rising Armed Violence in Complexo Da Maré, Continued State Impunity." Rio on Watch, February 19, 2020. https://www.rioonwatch.org/?p=57860.

Tocqueville, Alexis de. "On the Use That the Americans Make of Association in Civil Life." In *Democracy in America*, ed. Harvey C. Mansfield and Delba Winthrop, 489–492. Chicago: University of Chicago, 2002. https://press.uchicago.edu/Misc/Chicago/805328.html.

Toyama, Kentaro. *Geek Heresy: Rescuing Social Change from the Cult of Technology.* New York: PublicAffairs, 2015.

Transparency.org. "Corruption Perceptions Index 2017," February 21, 2018. https://www.transparency.org/en/news/corruption-perceptions-index-2017.

Trindade, Eliane. "Os Circuitos Dos Ricos e Famosos Que Disseminaram Coronavírus No Brasil." *Folha de São Paulo*, March 29, 2020.

Trobe, Jonathan D. "Peace Corps in Brazil: Lesson from Failure." *Harvard Crimson*, October 23, 1963. https://www.thecrimson.com/article/1963/10/23/peace-corps-in-brazil-lesson-from/.

USAID. "Opportunities for Impact Evaluation," June 12, 2019. https://www.usaid.gov/project-starter/program-cycle/cdcs/anticipating-evaluation-needs/opportunities-for-impact-evaluation.

Van Engen, Abram C. *City on a Hill: A History of American Exceptionalism.* New Haven, CT: Yale University Press, 2020.

Vargas Llosa, Mario. *The War of the End of the World.* New York: Picador, 2008.

Vice. "Dancing Through Gunshots in Brazil's Favelas." *YouTube* (blog), October 25, 2018. https://www.youtube.com/watch?v=tooevRbb9lY.

Visvanathan, Nalini, and Karla Yoder. "Women and Microcredit: A Critical Introduction." In *The Women, Gender and Development Reader*, 2nd ed., ed. Nalini Visvanathan, Lynn Duggan, Nan Wiegersma, and Laurie Nisonoff, 47. London: Zed, 2011.

Vota, Wayan. "Goodbye One Laptop per Child." OLPC News, March 11, 2014. http://www.olpcnews.com/about_olpc_news/goodbye_one_laptop_per_child.html.

Warren, Mark. *Democracy and Association.* Princeton, NJ: Princeton University Press, 2001.

Watters, Audrey. "The Failure of One Laptop per Child." *Hack Education* (blog), April 9, 2012. http://hackeducation.com/2012/04/09/the-failure-of-olpc.

Wesby, Maya. "The Exploitative Selfishness of Volunteering Abroad." *Newsweek* (August 18. 2015. https://www.newsweek.com/exploitative-selfishness-volunteering-abroad-363768.

"Why Has Icelandic Football Been So Successful Recently?" Football Association of Iceland, 2019. https://www.ksi.is/library/contentfiles/Why%20is%20Icelandic%20football%20so%20successful%20recently%202018%20upd.pdf.

Wilsford, David. "Path Dependency, or Why History Makes It Difficult but Not Impossible to Reform Health Care System in a Big Way." *Journal of Public Policy* 14, no. 3 (July 1994): 251–283.

World Bank Group. "Doing Business 2018: Reforming to Create Jobs." Washington, DC: World Bank, 2018. https://www.doingbusiness.org/content/dam/doingBusiness/media/Annual-Reports/English/DB2018-Full-Report.pdf.

Worldometer. "Brazil Coronavirus: 1,073,376 Cases and 50,182 Deaths," 2020. https://www.worldometers.info/coronavirus/country/brazil/.

Worthen, Molly. "The Misguided Drive to Measure 'Learning Outcomes.'" *New York Times*, February 23, 2018. https://www.nytimes.com/2018/02/23/opinion/sunday/colleges-measure-learning-outcomes.html.

Yearbook of Tourism Statistics, 1990. Vol. 2. University Park: Pennsylvania State University, 1991.

Young, Emma. "How Iceland Got Teens to Say No to Drugs." *Atlantic*, January 19, 2017. https://www.theatlantic.com/health/archive/2017/01/teens-drugs-iceland/513668/.

Zaluar, Alba. "Crimes and Violence Trends in Rio de Janeiro, Brazil." Case Study Prepared for Enhancing Urban Safety and Security: Global Report on Human Settlements 2007. United Nations, 2007. http://citeseerx.ist.psu.edu/viewdoc/download?doi=10.1.1.580.220&rep=rep1&type=pdf.

——. "Youth, Drug Traffic and Hypermasculinity in Rio de Janeiro." *Vibrant Virtual Brazilian Anthropology* 7, no. 2 (December 2010): 7–27.

Ziai, Aram. *Development Discourse and Global History: From Colonialism to the Sustainable Development Goals.* London: Routledge, 2015.

Zunz, Olivier. *Philanthropy in America: A History.* Politics and Society in Modern America 80. Princeton, NJ: Princeton University Press, 2011.

INDEX

Page numbers in *italics* indicate figures or tables.

Readers can access five of the documentary films discussed in the book at

www.reimagine.care.

In addition to the films, chapter discussion questions and other supplemental materials are available at the website.